HEALTH, WEALTH, AND POPULATION IN THE EARLY DAYS OF THE INDUSTRIAL REVOLUTION

HEALTH, WEALTH, AND POPULATION IN THE EARLY DAYS OF THE INDUSTRIAL REVOLUTION

BY

M. C. BUER, B.Sc. (Econ.)

Lecturer in Economics in the University of Reading
Author of *Economics for Beginners*

LONDON
GEORGE ROUTLEDGE & SONS, LTD.
BROADWAY HOUSE: 68–74 CARTER LANE, E.C.
1926

301.32941
B928h

BROTHERS COLLEGE

Printed in Great Britain by Stephen Austin & Sons, Ltd., Hertford.

*TO THE MEMORY OF
PROFESSOR LILIAN KNOWLES*

CONTENTS

CHAPTER		PAGE
I.	Introduction	1
II.	Vital Statistics	10
III.	Population Statistics, Birth and Death Rates	22
IV.	Individualism and Laisser Faire	36
V.	The Growth of Commerce	47
VI.	Agriculture	63
VII.	Improvement of Towns	76
VIII.	Water Supply and Drainage	96
IX.	The 18th Century Doctor and the British Pioneers of Public Health	111
X.	The Hospital and Dispensary Movement	126
XI.	General Hygiene and Midwifery	137
XII.	Rickets and Scurvy	151
XIII.	Antiseptics, Segregation, Leprosy and Plague	164
XIV.	Smallpox in the 18th Century	181
XV.	The Anti-Typhus Campaign and the Fever Hospital Movement	193
XVI.	Malaria—General Summary	210
XVII.	The Period 1815–1848	223
XVIII.	Conclusion	236
	Appendix: Notes and References	245
	Statistical Tables	267
	Bibliography	275
	Index	285

PREFACE

THIS book is a small contribution to that new presentation of modern economic and social history towards which much valuable work has been done in recent years. The general effect of this new knowledge is to present the series of events popularly known as the Industrial Revolution as being far more complex and far less dramatic than did earlier accounts. The popular conception is still, perhaps, that the Industrial Revolution destroyed the primitive virtues and idyllic joys of our more remote ancestors and created in their stead every social and economic difficulty with which we have to contend at present. It is, in fact, the villain of the drama of economic history. But, just as nearly all the picturesquely wicked villains whose stories thrilled us in childhood have been proved by biographers and historians to be much maligned and misunderstood persons, so some compensating virtues are being discovered even in the Industrial Revolution. The modification of previous judgments upon individuals has often been unkindly known as whitewashing, but it is, in fact, due not to a covering up but to an uncovering of evidence and to the realization that no historical judgment which wholly praises or wholly condemns can, in the nature of things, be just.

It may be contended by some that more justly balanced views, whether of individuals or of periods, rob history of much of its romantic quality. Instead of the enthralling clash of hero and villain we have presented the drab blunderings of ordinary men and women. But the grey is only grey at a distant and imperfect view, more closely seen it is a queer, jumbled pattern of sharply contrasted colours. Every historical movement has been the result of a medley of motives; self-seeking rubbing shoulders with altruism and the love of a cause intermingling with personal ambition. An appreciation of the complexity of human motives, together with the scientific approach to history with its careful sifting of evidence, tends to make the modern historian loth to make judgments; yet he must not shirk the responsibility of doing so if he is to be more than a mere chronicler.

The main purpose of the research upon which this book is based was to account for the growth of population between 1760 and 1815, a growth which seemed so inexplicable in view of the alleged social deterioration of the period. In the course of this enquiry I have formed the very strong opinion that the period was by no means one of general social retrogression, on the contrary there is evidence of much social progress, both material and moral. It is not of course contended that this progress was either universal or uniform. This opinion accords with the view which has been recently gaining ground among many students, that the evils of the so-called Industrial Revolution were much exaggerated by earlier writers. This exaggeration was partly owing to a failure to allow for the effects and after-effects of the war, but mainly to a totally unjustifiably roseate picture of conditions in earlier periods. Many evils decribed as new were very old, but had been ignored in ages when the social conscience was less awakened.

It is perhaps desirable to say a few words as to the genesis of this book. My original line of research was a study of the general social conditions of the post-war period beginning in 1815. This work was undertaken as a Hutchinson Research Scholar of the London School of Economics. It was, however, hardly begun when it was interrupted by the outbreak of war. One result of the war was that a considerable amount of attention was directed to the period of my special study and, when I was free to return to its consideration, there hardly seemed to be scope for further detailed research upon its general aspects. One important phenomenon, however, still remained in great obscurity, that was the rapid growth of population. Chance having directed my attention to the work of Pringle and Lind I thus found a line of investigation in the pursuit of which my previous work was not altogether wasted.

It is at once my duty and pleasure to acknowledge the valuable help which I have received in the course of preparing this book for publication. I have to thank, first of all, Dr. Charles Singer, whose stimulating encouragement much aided me in

PREFACE

bringing my task to a conclusion. Dr. Singer read through nearly the whole of the medical chapters and gave me much helpful advice and criticism. I owe thanks to Professor Bowley and Professor Cannan for similar help in regard to the statistical chapters and to Colonel James in regard to the section on malaria. I should like to thank my former fellow student, Mrs. George, author of *London Life in the XVIIIth Century*, for many useful references. Mrs. George's work and my own overlapped at certain points and, working quite separately, indeed unaware of each other's activities, we arrived at almost identical conclusions. I have also to thank my friend Mrs. Ormsby for reading a considerable portion of my MS. and for valuable suggestions as to method of presentation.

Finally, I have to record how much I owe to the late Professor Lilian Knowles, under whom I served my apprenticeship in Economic History. She allowed me to draw unreservedly upon her wide knowledge while her trenchant criticism enabled me to purge this book of some of its original imperfections. It is a personal grief to me that she will never see the completed work, in the inception of which she took such a keen and sympathetic interest.

M. C. BUER.

THE UNIVERSITY,
  READING.

7

CHAPTER I

INTRODUCTION

WHEN the historian of two thousand years hence chronicles the history of the world during the two hundred years ending 1900 he will surely find one of its most significant facts to be the increase in numbers and dominance of the European races. Not only did the population of Europe itself increase many fold during that period but European races have also peopled two great continents and one small one ; they have further partly peopled and almost entirely dominated another great continent and partially dominated the remaining one.

Though the peoples of western Europe have spread over many vast waste spaces of the world, yet their civilization has become more and more urban ; for in every community of western European race town dwellers form a large and increasing proportion of the whole. To the political and economic problems of the great nation and the great empire are added the peculiar economic and social difficulties of the great city. To the problems due to absolute size, both of nations and cities, must be added those due to rapidity of growth. Though the classical economists may have been wrong in much of their detailed argument and conclusions their alarm at the rapid growth of population was not nearly so foolish as many lesser minds have thought. It was a new problem, but so short is the memory of mankind that many persons are now terribly alarmed at the idea of a population that is not increasing rapidly.

It is the primary object of this study to endeavour to elucidate the main causes of the rapid growth of population in England in the 18th and early 19th centuries, with special reference to the period 1750–1815. This enquiry is, perhaps, unduly narrow in time and place, but it deals with the time and place in which the rapid growth of population had its origin. The growth of population was European and therefore many of the causes of that growth were also European. But on the Continent of Europe war and civil disorder held back advance in many spheres and changes of many kinds became earlier and more rapidly effective in this country. It seems, then, allowable to study, in the first instance, the rapid increase of population, as other phases of the industrial revolution have so often been studied, in the country of its origin. In pursuit of the main subject of this enquiry certain aspects of the period, previously often ignored, have been brought, it is hoped, into clearer perspective.

The large communities of modern times are at once the effect and the cause of the stupendous changes in technique and industrial organization, the " revolution " by the side of which the great political revolutions are puny and transient affairs. It is of course a commonplace of economic history that the increase of population was a concomitant of the industrial revolution, including in that term the changes in agriculture. The two began together in England in the second half of the 18th century but the exact nature of their connection has never been fully elucidated. It is obvious, of course, that the increased population was dependent upon changes in agriculture and transport, it could not have existed unless it could have been fed. But it is equally obvious that the pressure of population gave the stimulus to those changes and that, in particular, the growth of town population revolutionized agriculture by causing farming for a market to displace subsistence farming. The growth of town population, in view of the recorded sanitary conditions of the towns, was the mysterious fact. The new towns were, of course, largely recruited from the countryside but in the first half of the 19th century there was also a large natural increase of the urban population. As the recorded conditions seemed to preclude any idea of a decreased death rate, historians concluded that the new conditions must have led to an increased birth rate and found possible proximate causes in the lax Poor Law, the break up of apprenticeship and the generally lowered standard of life. The two first seem very local and partial causes to account for such a large movement ; while a lowered standard of life, though it may account for a higher birth rate, will not account for a higher survival rate. As Adam Smith remarked, " a half starved Highland woman frequently bears more than twenty children . . . but poverty though it does not prevent the generation is extremely unfavourable to the rearing of children . . . It is not uncommon . . . in the Highlands of Scotland for a mother who has borne twenty children not to have two alive."

The guesses—for they are little more—as to the cause of the higher birth rate are supported by little evidence. This is not surprising since there is practically no evidence of an increased birth rate during the 18th century, while there is overwhelming evidence of a greatly decreased death rate, especially in the latter part of that century. Exact statements as to birth and death rates are, of course, impossible in the absence of reliable registration of births and deaths and of any census. But though exact statements are impossible, broad tendencies can be deduced from very imperfect records, provided the tendencies are sufficiently marked in character. Contemporary writers found nothing mysterious in the reduction of the death rate, they pointed with pride to the improvements in the quantity and quality of the food supply, to the absence of plague, to the reduction in malaria and dysentery, to the scotching of smallpox and fevers, and to the improved care of infants.

The impression conveyed by many writers on the early 19th century is that the industrial changes and the ineptitude of English local government had worsened health conditions and in particular had led to the prevalence of typhus and cholera. As a matter of fact, typhus had probably always been endemic in English towns, as it was in the rest of Europe, and as it remains in many parts of the world to-day. The difference was that in the 19th century English people had begun to be perturbed about it and to try to fight it. As to cholera, it was a world scourge, the causes of which medical knowledge at the time failed to elucidate and which found a relatively greater number of victims in primitive countries than in England. In fact, the health conditions of a mid 19th century English town, which to us are so appalling, were not caused by the industrial revolution but were a terrible heritage from the past, a heritage moreover which had been considerably reduced.

The ignoring by many social historians of the diminution of the death rate between 1780 and 1815 has mainly arisen from the bad and unscientific habit of writing social history backwards. The comparison of conditions, especially those of the early 19th century, with what came after rather than with what went before, resulted in the production of a picture which was much out of focus. It was a good thing, perhaps, that the reformers of the mid 19th century saw the evils to be overcome with such intensity of horror that they could not imagine worse conditions. They were rightly not concerned with conditions a hundred years before or with contemporary conditions in other countries, but the historian emphatically is concerned with such comparisons. Had the earlier historians of the industrial revolution known a little more about 17th century England, a little more about 18th century conditions on the Continent and a little more about late 19th century conditions in the East they might have been saved many errors. The last is perhaps the most important, for here the living picture can be substituted for the printed word. As a study of the modern Russian village community has thrown a flood of light upon manorial records, so a study of contemporary health conditions in the East will show us what England was like in the 17th century and earlier.

There is a popular idea that the diseases from which, say, India suffers are due partly to climate and partly to a fatalistic and superstitious attitude of mind peculiar to Eastern peoples. Yet three hundred years ago Europe was afflicted with most of the scourges which we now associate with hot countries—plague, smallpox, malaria, acute dysentery—and, in consequence, fatalism and superstition, the result of the general conditions of life, were as characteristic of the bulk of the population as they are in the East to-day. When man stands helpless in the face of nature fatalism is his only refuge and superstition his natural comfort. A modern medical writer has pointed out that plague and other diseases are not in any way dependent upon a hot climate and that many of the diseases which we call " tropical " are in reality diseases of primitive civilization.[1] A writer on present day Persia points out that in that country there are no mining, no shipping, no railways or motors, and no factories, in fact, it is pre-industrial revolution.[2] Persia enjoys a wonderful climate and, normally, a good food supply and yet the health record is very bad. There are no definite statistics but one authority says that in one district 85% of the children die before they are two years old! Another alleges that only 1 in 10 of the children born grow up. The reason for this bad health record is that in Persia there is no good water supply, no sanitation and no knowledge of the simplest hygiene. The predominant diseases are fevers, including relapsing fever, malaria, enteric (which few escape) and typhus. Smallpox, except in a few districts where vaccination is possible, is considered a necessary illness for every child. Oriental sores, scabies and favus are common, so also is tubercular bone trouble, while the ravages of venereal disease are terrible.[3] With a few small emendations this description would stand for that of the health conditions of early 18th century London.

The death rate of India has been estimated at 34 per 1000, the infant mortality at 250 per 1000. The infant mortality in China has been calculated at 500 per 1000. It may appear presumptuous to describe the ancient civilization of China as primitive, but in matters of medicine and hygiene the description is not unjust. Part of the high infant mortality in China is doubtless due to the poverty of large masses of the people, but the mortality is very high even among well-to-do people. A recent writer who describes the losses of a well-to-do and highly educated Chinese family says:

"It is when one actually encounters the losses in Chinese families one knows personally that it is possible to realize the ravages of infant mortality in China. Only then does one grasp something of the anguish and heartbreak this appalling figure means."[4] These families, though living highly civilized lives, suffer from the general unhygienic conditions of society. Ignorant old women are still in charge of child birth and babies are never washed and seldom taken into the fresh air. The women enjoy little or no fresh air or exercise, while young children are given unsuitable food and are over-pampered. These examples could be amplified from many sources.

Instead of asking why population rapidly increased in Europe in the 18th century let us ask why it increased so slowly in previous centuries. The answer is not far to seek. Europe was in a state of primitive civilization. We need not invent a low birth rate, both fiction and biography teach us that very early marriage was customary and that chastity was not a popular virtue, and although, no doubt, abortion was practised among certain sections of the town population, babies came into the world with the frequency to be expected. In fact, quite enough babies were born for the population to have doubled very quickly had the high birth rate not been counterbalanced by the equally high death rate of a primitive civilization. Throughout the Middle Ages famine took a terrible toll of life. The primitive scratching of the soil left the crops open to every vagary of the weather and the lack of transport made each little locality dependent upon its own harvest. In many long settled districts the soil was dangerously exhausted and bad weather conditions easily resulted in widespread harvest failure. The lack of variety of crops, their poor quality and the absence of fresh food in the winter led to much disease. The improvements in agriculture and in transport of the second half of the 18th century led to a food supply more certain in quantity, better in quality and in variety, and this to a degree that is hard to realize. A better food supply not only abolished famine but reduced general malnutrition, as well as such specific diseases as scurvy and rickets.

The almost total absence of all hygienic and medical knowledge had been another factor in the high death rate of the Middle Ages. Here again, in the 18th century knowledge began to replace ignorance. We have been too apt, perhaps, to think of the industrial revolution as a complete social phenomenon, but it was in reality part of a much greater whole, of which whole the advance in agriculture, in science, and in medicine were also parts. To deal with the origins of this great change in every aspect of life, which affected alike the prince and the peasant, and the construction of a philosophy as much as the construction of a pin, would be to write a world history. But it may be ventured that the new world that was evolved was the offspring of the critical, clear cut, reasoned thought of the ancients and of the practical enterprising activities of the trader. Modern science, modern art and literature all had their origin in the eager intense life of the trading cities of Italy and were fostered by the benevolent autocracy of merchant princes. It is no accident that modern banking and modern medicine both had their origins in Italy before the 16th century, were developed in Holland in the 17th century and became effective in France and England in the 18th century. Those who sneer at trade forget that the Greek and the Jew, the two races who have contributed most to the highest thought of the Western world, were essentially traders. Trade breaks down barriers of race and creed and fosters an exchange of ideas as well as of goods. The trader also, like the man of science, is an apostle of freedom. Modern democracy had its origin in free trading communities and modern economic organization in the free markets or fairs of the Middle Ages. As the man of science threw off the trammels with which religion and tradition had bound thought, so the trader threw off the trammels with which the guild and the merchant company had bound industry. The emancipation of the intellect, which began with the Renaissance, in some ways reached its culminating point in the 18th century. In spite of much lumber of obsolete regulation, both the thought and action of the directing classes were extraordinarily free in the 18th century, particularly in England. This freedom had both its good and its bad side. It was undoubtedly used on occasion to oppress the poor and weak, but it was also used to increase production and to advance knowledge in every sphere. As the result man began to have effective control over nature and life became secure to a hitherto unknown degree. Those who have described the change from the medieval to the modern organization of social and economic life, have often pointed out the loss of stability which these changes brought to the worker. From some points of view this is true. Down to the middle of the 18th century the greater part of the population of Europe lived in a social environment that was extraordinarily stable. A man tilled the same land that his father and his grandfather had tilled before him and in the same way. The land might not be his personal property from a legal point of view, though it often was, but in any case his tenure was unlikely to be disturbed. He toiled for hours that to a modern worker would be unthinkable, for miserably meagre return, but his relations to his fellow men were fixed by ancient custom and were unquestioned; and by familiar rights and duties life was bounded from the cradle to the grave. This is true, but from other points of view life was unstable and insecure to a degree that it is almost impossible for a modern man to realize. How anxiously the skies were scanned during the crucial months of harvest, since too much or too little rain might mean acute suffering or death. We are agitated if the price of bread rises by a few pence and argue that it shows great defect in our economic organization that this should happen. It may be so, but with a too wet or too dry summer in the 18th century bread rose in price two or three hundred per cent.; in the Middle Ages a large portion of the population perished from famine, or from disease through eating rotten grain. Those who lived near rivers might see their whole substance washed away in flood time; storms could destroy their fragile dwellings, killing the cattle upon which their livelihood depended. Against disease, no less than against floods and famine, the Middle Ages stood powerless; for a quarter or more of the community to be swept away, for whole families to be wiped out, was part of the ordinary peril of life.

The towns were little more secure than the country. If town granaries did something to avert famine, pestilence was a more frequent danger. Fire also was a deadly enemy when towns were built of wood and insurance was undreamed of. The groups of independent craftsmen were not, it is true, subject to fears of dismissal and unemployment in our modern sense of the term. But famine, pestilence and fire destroyed trade as well as life and how fared the craftsmen when there were none to buy? If modern man has lost one kind of stability he has gained another. In fact, the very changes which brought greater stability in one direction gave less in another. We see the same thing happening in India to-day. Modern conditions are reducing famine and pestilence but they are tending to break up the village community.[5] They are leading too, as they did in Europe, to a rapid growth of population, in itself a source of instability. There is room for difference of opinion as to which kind of stability is the more desirable.

To evaluate human happiness is an impossible sum, there are too many unknowns. Was the 13th century peasant happier than the 19th century factory hand? No one can answer. The eastern European peasant emigrant, the only person who has really tried medieval and modern life, has always been emphatic in his preference for the latter. But he is, perhaps, not a good judge. There is much in modern life which must distress all thinking persons, but perhaps the same might be said of every age in history. When we judge the new social order let us at least judge it as a whole and remember that it brought not only the factory but the laboratory and the hospital ; not only the capitalist but the man of science and the modern doctor. It brought with it many new problems but it solved some terrible old ones. We are not likely to forget the new problems, they are ever with us ; it is well sometimes to remember that for the new social order it can at least be claimed that it has laid those grim spectres of Famine and Pestilence, which were never far distant in that Golden Age to which some thinkers look back with such passionate admiration.

CHAPTER II

VITAL STATISTICS

" I have taken the pains . . . of setting out those Tables, whereby all men may both correct my Positions, and raise others of their own: For herein I have, like a silly Schole-boy, coming to say my Lesson to the World (that Peevish, and Tetchie Master) brought a bundle of Rods wherewith to be whipt, for every mistake I have committed."

GRAUNT.

IN considering the question of population, the first task is to examine such statistical evidence as is available and to make some estimate of its reliability.

Vital statistics is one of the youngest branches of science; for though there were a few enquiries of a statistical nature in Italy and France during the 16th century, it is customary to date the beginning of modern statistics from the publication of Süssmilch's famous work in 1761.[1] The honour of writing the first statistical treatise may however be reasonably claimed for John Graunt whose work was published a century earlier. In 1662 Captain John Graunt presented to the Royal Society his "Natural and Political Observations upon the Bills of Mortality with reference to the Government, Religion, Trade, Growth, Air, Diseases and the several changes in the said City" [London]. Graunt pointed out the constancy of the number of abortions and still births, the constancy of the proportions of deaths from certain diseases to the total number of deaths, the variations of the death rate by seasons, the ratio of male and female births, the ratio of births to deaths in city and country and drew up the rough outline of a table of mortality. His conclusions were faulty, both because of the incompleteness of his data and his ignorance of the law of large numbers, but he sought truth by observation and to draw general conclusions from a confused mass of figures. Upon this basis rests his claim to be the first writer upon vital statistics. Graunt's work is said to have inspired that of Petty, Arbuthnot and King, and, though these writers were primarily concerned with " Political Arithmetic ", their works contained a good deal of material, in particular estimates of the size of the population, which might be classed under the heading vital statistics.[2] Following more directly in Graunt's footsteps Thomas Short, M.D., published in 1750 his " New Observations . . . on the Bills of Mortality ". This work contains a mass of material relating to both London and country parishes, including estimates of death rates in various places with particular reference to the differences due to soil and climate.

In 1761 the Prussian clergyman, J. G. Süssmilch published " Die göttliche Ordnung in den Veränderungen des menschlichen Geschlechts aus der Geburt, dem Tode und der Fortpflanzung desselben, erwiesen ". This famous treatise is said to have been inspired by a passage in a theological work by Sir William Derham published in 1699. The object of Derham's work was to prove design in the universe and one of his arguments was the constancy in the proportion of marriages to births, of births to deaths and of male to female births. Süssmilch's object was to enlarge and substantiate this particular proof of design, and his work was therefore theological in its ultimate aim. Nevertheless its publication was of extreme significance in the history of the science of statistics, for the work not only included a vast number of statistics of the City of Breslau but showed a great advance in method. Süssmilch stressed the importance of the accuracy of data and pointed out the necessity for a large number of observations if reliable conclusions were to be drawn. From this time onward statistical studies of population advanced apace. In England there were several able writers but they were handicapped by the peculiarly unreliable data with which they had to deal and their consequent pre-occupation with the futile controversy as to whether the population was decreasing or increasing. This controversy was started by Dr. Price, who in his Treatise on Annuities (published in 1780) contended that the population of England and Wales had been decreasing progressively since 1688 and that when he wrote it only amounted to 4,763,000. Very able answers to this contention were made by the Rev. John Howlett and by William Wales. The census of 1801 put this particular controversy to rest, but writers on the subject were then plunged into the Malthusian controversy. No doubt these controversies stimulated interest in the subject but, on the other hand, they also led to a great many useless wrangles and prevented a scientific approach. It is possible to claim that a more real advance in the study of vital statistics was made through the practical desire to place Life Annuities upon a sound actuarial basis, than through the various population controversies.

In the 17th century, governments, particularly those of England and France, began to raise money by selling life annuities. A favourite method was that of the tontine, said to be named after its inventor an Italian banker named Tonti. Under a tontine the subscribers were divided into classes, generally according to age; the annuity granted to each class was payable to the surviving members until the death of the last member. The results of this system were not fortunate for the State and it was abolished in France in 1770; in England the last tontine took place in 1789. From the time of William III another favourite form of raising money with the English government was the sale of individual life annuities. In 1692 it undertook the sale of annuities without distinction of age, and the purchasers being shrewd enough to select sound healthy lives, the nation lost heavily. The attention of Edmund Halley, the famous astronomer and mathematician, was called to the matter and he saw at once that the crux of the problem lay in the differing rates of mortality at different ages. There was however no statistical material in England available for his calculations since the Parish Registers did not record age at death. He found, however, that the City of Breslau had kept a register of the age of persons dying from 1687–1691 but unfortunately there was no census of the city and therefore Halley was forced to compute its population. From this imperfect data Halley's Mortality Tables were constructed and the foundation was thereby laid of scientific life insurance. In 1742 a Dutchman,

Kerseboom, published a work on life annuities and in 1746 Deparcieu published a study of the vital statistics of the nominees of two tontines in France between 1695 and 1740 and also those of a number of monks and nuns (Essai sur les probabilités de la durée de la vie humaine). Both these studies were based upon insufficient information but nevertheless certain important observations were made, for instance, Kerseboom remarked the superior expectation of life of the female sex. In this connection it is interesting to find Finlaison's statement that in the annuity loan of the English Government of 1746 " a large proportion of the capital was supplied by Dutchmen who almost universally nominated children and on decided majority girls, whereas the English contributors named people of every age indifferently up to 59 or 60 ".[3] Finlaison points out that Kerseboom's treatise had appeared only four years previously. One wonders if the shrewd purchasers of the 1692 annuities were also Dutch; it is probable, since London was largely financed by Holland at this period. The English Government, however, continued to grant annuities on the old system until Pitt used Dr. Price's table in 1789.

Dr. Price's table was originally drawn up for the use of the Equitable Society which commenced Life Insurance business in 1765, being the first society of its kind. This society was refused a Charter upon the advice of the Law Officers of the Crown on the ground that it was a scheme, "Whereby the chance of Mortality is attempted to be reduced to a certain standard. This is a mere speculation, never tried in practice ".[4] The society found the inconvenience and danger of working without any data as to mortality rates and consulted Dr. Price. The Northampton Table which he compiled in response to this request was based upon the Parish Registers of Northampton. This table over-estimated the death rate. Price's error arose partly because he failed to allow for the large number of unregistered births due to the prevalence of Dissent in Northampton, and, since he calculated the total population from the number of births, this vitiated the calculation of the mortality rate. He calculated the average expectation of life as 24 years whereas it was probably at that time about 30 years. These errors, however, were not generally realized at the time. Price's table was the only one available and it was used, not only by the Equitable, but by other Life Insurance Companies for many years and was adopted by the British Government under Pitt in 1789, to the ultimate loss of the taxpayer. Price has left an unfortunate reputation ; his opinion carried great weight with many of his contemporaries but he is now only remembered by his errors. His absolutely inaccurate views as to a fall in population, at a time when it was rapidly increasing, his misleading and unfortunate scheme for the extinction of the National Debt and, lastly, his inaccurate calculation of the expectation of life form together a not very enviable record. To the writer's knowledge it has never been calculated how much Price's Sinking Fund cost the nation but Finlaison estimated that his erroneous calculation of the expectation of life cost it over £2,000,000 in eleven years. It is fair to state however that Farr asserted that Finlaison himself cost the nation £1,500,000 by his statistical errors.

In 1819 John Finlaison, government actuary and accountant, pointed out to Vansittart the losses which the country was sustaining through the Government granting annuities based upon the Northampton Tables. Later he made further enquiries the results of which were published in a Report on Life Annuities in 1829. Finlaison's calculations were based upon the government records of the tontines and the Life annuity accounts and his results agree substantially with those calculated from the Carlisle Tables, compiled by Dr. Heysham and published in 1815, in his book on Annuities, by Joshua Milne, an actuary employed by the Sun Life Insurance Company. The Carlisle Tables were much superior to anything that had before been available in this country and they continued to be used in Life Insurance calculations until the middle of the 19th century. They were then superseded owing to the mass of data collected by the companies themselves and to the increase both in quantity and quality of the available official statistics.

In the 19th century the study of vital statistics entered on a new phase. For the first time something like adequate material existed and the official figures were illuminated by the comments of those able Civil Servants, John Rickman, who was in charge of the census from 1811 to 1841 inclusive, and his successor William Farr who was Assistant Commissioner for 1851 and 1861 and Commissioner for 1871. Though in the late 18th century and the early 19th century, many medical writers had used such statistical material as was available to illustrate their studies of various diseases, it was William Farr who first showed the importance of vital statistics as an aid in solving the practical problems of public health. The main part of his work lies outside the period covered by this book but there will be frequent occasion to quote such part of it as deals with the earlier period.

Statistical writers in all countries before the 19th century had to work upon extremely unreliable data and thus they occupied a good deal of time in making elaborate estimates and calculations upon matters which are now easily ascertainable by simple arithmetic. In Great Britain in particular the earlier writers were in the position of trying to make bricks without straw. Sweden had led the way in this branch of knowledge by the institution of compulsory parish registration of births, marriages and deaths in 1686, and the first Swedish census took place as early as 1749. Several other countries followed suit but the results were either partial or inaccurate. In Great Britain there was no census until 1801. In 1753 a Census Bill was introduced into the House of Commons by a private member, backed by official support, to provide for the annual compulsory enumeration of the people and of persons in receipt of parochial relief. It was violently opposed as being " subversive of the last remains of English liberty " and as " likely to result in some public misfortune or epidemical disorder ".[5] However, it passed the Commons but was thrown out by the Lords.

A Census Bill introduced by a private member was passed without opposition in 1800. The first Census was held in the following year and a statement as to births, deaths and marriages was also required from the clergy. The work was carried out by the overseers under the Justices and there was no central control. The schedule enquired the number of houses, the numbers of each family, their sex and occupation. The results, owing to the defective organization, were not satisfactory. In 1811 the same set of enquiries (with a slight modification of the occupation query) was repeated. This census was carried out under the direction of Rickman, whose Report which was published with the results is valuable.

Before the first Census the only vital statistics available for the whole country were the Parish Registers which had been kept from the 16th century onwards. These registers suffered from the grave defect of being primarily ecclesiastical and not civil.[6] Births as such were not registered, but baptisms ; similarly it was not deaths that were registered but interments in churchyards belonging to the Established Church. Further, these registers were often very negligently kept, especially in towns.[7] Subsequent to the year 1754 the most reliable register was that of marriages, since Lord Hardwicke's Marriage Act of that year made registration a necessary part of the legalisation of marriage, before that year the marriage registers are believed to have been very unreliable. The deficiencies of the Registers were greater in London than elsewhere owing to the relatively large numbers of Jews and of Roman Catholics who possessed their own burial grounds. The proportionate number of such burials probably increased during the 18th century, partly owing to the acquisition of more burial grounds by these sects. Earlier in the century many Jews, Quakers and Roman Catholics were buried in the churchyards from necessity. With regard to christenings, of course, the children of Quakers and Jews were not christened and christenings in the Roman Catholic church were not registered. Other dissenters who were married and buried in the Established Church were not christened.[8] Private baptisms, which were said to have been fairly general, were sometimes registered and sometimes not ; also we do not know how conscientiously the rite of baptism was observed even among nominal members of the Established Church. What we know of the poorest population of 18th century London does not give the impression of much religious zeal, on the other hand baptism may have had a superstitious vogue and it was certainly important from the point of view of obtaining parish relief, owing to the law of settlement. For this latter reason some of the poorer Dissenters of less strict sects may have conformed. Birch [9] said "Some few dissenters have their children baptized" but that, on the other hand, "perhaps no inconsiderable number among the lowest class of the poeple . . . are never brought to be baptized at all".

The deficiency in the registers was not so great for the whole country as for London. In many places there were few or no dissenters and smaller registers were likely to be more accurately kept. After the periodic census was established the deficiency in the recorded excess of births over deaths was established and estimates were made as to the extent of the deficiency in the two registers. Rickman estimated the deficiency of registration of births to be 19% (some authorities thought 21% nearer) and of deaths about half this; [10] these estimates were made in connection with the census of 1831. It is generally believed that the deficiencies were less during the 18th century than the 19th and were growing during the 18th century [11] owing to the growth of Dissent. Birch writing in 1759 estimated that the baptismal entries should be increased by one-sixth to obtain the actual number of births, the defect in burials he believed to be considerable, but less.[12] Therefore the deficiencies were not the same at different times and they were not the same in different places. They were greater in parts of the country where Dissent was strong, they were greater in urban than in rural areas, they were greatest of all in London. The Parish Registers gave no information as to the cause of death or the age of the deceased. In London the Bills of Mortality were published regularly from 1605 onwards primarily with the object of giving information as to the existence of the Plague. The Bills were weekly, monthly and yearly summaries of christenings and burials compiled by the Company of Parish Clerks from the Registers, to which the cause of death as ascertained by the appointed searchers was added. From 1728 onwards the age of the deceased was also recorded. Graunt thus describes the procedure: "When anyone dies, then, either by tolling or ringing of a Bell, or by bespeaking of a Grave of the *Sexton* the same is known to the *Searchers*, corresponding with the said *Sexton*. The *Searchers* hereupon (who are antient Matrons sworn to their Office) repair to the place where the dead Corps lies, and by view of the same and by other enquiries, they examine by what *Disease* or *Casualty* the Corps died. Hereupon they make their Report to the *Parish Clerk* and he, every *Tuesday* night carries in an Accompt of all the *Burials* and *Christenings* happening that Week to the *Clerk* of the *Hall*." He adds that the searchers were open to bribery.

The Bills naturally reproduced the deficiencies of the Registers and, in addition, the copying was often carelessly done. There was a further source of confusion in the fact that London, then as now, was a somewhat loose term and the town proper was constantly growing. At the beginning of the 19th century some of the large outlying parishes such as Hackney, Bermondsey and Bethnal Green were still partly rural, while other parishes which had definitely become suburbs, such as St. Pancras and Marylebone, were not included.

The Parish Registers were the only source of information for the country as a whole, but several corporate towns had copied London in instituting Bills of Mortality. During the second half of the 18th century enumerations of the population were held in several of the larger towns. With regard to rural parishes, if early enquirers could invoke the interest and help of the local parson, they were often able to obtain information as to the population and as to the visitations of epidemics.

The 18th century statistician had, therefore, at his disposal in regard to England and Wales the following sources of information :—

1. The Parish Registers for the whole country.
2. The London Bills of Mortality.
3. A few provincial Bills of Mortality.
4. A few town enumerations.
5. Supplementary private information from country clergymen and other sources.
6. Certain taxation returns upon which it was possible to

VITAL STATISTICS

base estimates of population, but these estimates were the subject of acute controversy.

They had no direct information as to the total size of the population, very little as to the size of the population in particular districts, only local information as to the cause of death and no information as to the age constitution of the population. A good deal of their work was concerned with calculations as to the increase or decrease of the population, for which purpose they were forced to assume that the birth rate or the death rate was constant in an altering population. Dr. Price's errors largely arose from his assuming a constant death rate at a time when it was falling rapidly and thus arriving at the conclusion that the population was decreasing. Most authorities held the birth rate to be a better guide and they were supported by later investigators and by foreign experience based upon more reliable data. Contemporary authorities were well aware of the deficiencies of the Registers and always made allowance for it in their calculations. So long as there was no direct information as to the size of the population it was, of course, impossible to calculate birth and death rates for the country as a whole, since it would only have been arguing in a circle. Where there was local information as to the size of the population such rates were sometimes calculated and the ratio between the number of births and deaths was also calculated for many districts. The results of this latter calculation were apt to be misleading unless allowance was made for migration, since a district losing population by migration would tend to show a favourable proportion between births and deaths and a district gaining by migration an unfavourable one. Though many of the calculations made by 18th century statisticians are now of little or of doubtful value their work is by no means without importance for the historian. For one thing, these early writers did an enormous amount of spade work in the collection and preservation of material and secondly, owing to the exiguous nature of their purely statistical material, their work is illumined by descriptive matter and personal impressions which are of very great value.

The modern student, however, is not totally dependent upon

contemporary records and writers for his knowledge of the 18th century. It was possible in the early 19th century to know a great deal more statistically about the 18th century than the 18th century knew about itself. The census returns of the 19th century made it possible to calculate the population throughout the 18th century with a greater degree of accuracy than had been possible by contemporaries. Rickman first calculated the population of the 18th century for decennial periods by assuming the birth rate to be constant and by calculating from the ratio of births to total population on the basis of the census of 1811. He made an allowance for the deficiency of the registers. Rickman's method of calculation contained two sources of error. Firstly, in calculating the births he took the decennial year and not an average of the decade. The decennial year might happen to be an exceptional one and some authorities believe that the decline in population shown in the decade 1700–1710 in Rickman's table is due to this cause. Secondly, the assumption of a uniform birth rate with a growing population is obviously false. If a population is growing it must be due either to immigration or an increase in the excess of births over deaths. In either case the make up of the population will be altered and therefore the crude birth rate will be altered. Finlaison accordingly made another calculation based upon the same data as Rickman's but making an allowance for the alteration in the birth rate and, on this calculation, made the population of 1700 about 350,000 less than Rickman's figure and the subsequent increase, therefore, by that much the greater. Taking a very broad view of the growth of population in the 18th century the difference in these two results is not important.

Secondly, the invaluable Carlisle Tables compiled by Dr. Heysham of that city and annotated by Milne [13] were published by the latter in 1815. In 1763 a census had been taken in Carlisle by order of the Bishop. In 1780 and in 1787 further enumerations were made and the information required included the age of the enumerated. Dr. Heysham saw that the registers of death were kept with accuracy and from these two sources of information he compiled the famous Carlisle Tables. For a number of years these Tables remained the only accurate source of information as to the relative mortality at different ages in this country. Heysham's statement also included the cause of death and gave a vivid picture of the mortality due to different diseases, particularly smallpox. The accuracy of these Tables can be gauged from the fact that they were used for Life Insurance purposes until the middle of the 19th century. Finlaison's study of the Government annuitants was published in 1829. Lastly, in the early 19th century the science of statistics was making great strides in England and still greater on the Continent. The works of these early 19th century writers are important sources for the modern historian; the writers had more information than those of the 18th century, their methods were superior and they were sufficiently near the period to have some personal or hearsay knowledge of its general conditions.

To the modern student, therefore, the following sources are available for the vital statistics of England during the 18th and early 19th centuries :—

1. Estimates of population, of which those of Rickman and Finlaison are generally accepted as approximately accurate.

2. Compilations, criticisms and deductions from the Parish Registers and the London Bills of Mortality by various contemporary writers.

3. A certain amount of scattered information about various towns.

4. The Carlisle Tables and Finlaison's study of Life Annuitants.

5. A good deal of information of a quasi-statistical character scattered in the writings of medical men, especially in regard to the mortality from certain diseases.

It will be gathered from what has already been said that only very broad deductions can be drawn from these sources. Data on many important points is non-existent and none of the data possess a high degree of accuracy. Nevertheless, the movements recorded are so large that no one could imagine them to be due to inaccuracy or accident; the fine lines of the miniature are lacking, but with the broad sweep of impressionism the truth is delineated in a manner which is incontrovertible.

CHAPTER III

POPULATION STATISTICS, BIRTH AND DEATH RATES

ESTIMATED POPULATION OF ENGLAND AND WALES

000 omitted.

1688	5,500	G. King		in Davenant's Works.	
1700	5,475	Rickman		5,134*	Finlaison
1710	5,240	,,		5,066	,,
1720	5,565	,,		5,345	,,
1730	5,796	,,		5,688	,,
1740	6,064	,,		5,830	,,
1750	6,467	,,		6,040	,,
1760	6,736	,,		6,480	,,
1770	7,428	,,		7,227	,,
1780	7,953	,,		7,815	,,
1790	8,675	,,		8,541	,,
1801	8,892	(deficient) Census	1800	9,187	,,
1811	10,164		,, 1810	10,407	,,
1821	12,000		,, 1820	11,957	,,

* This column includes Army, Navy, and Merchant Seamen.

Gregory King's estimate of the population of England and Wales is the first upon which any reliance can be placed; it was probably an over-estimate, but the computation was extraordinarily accurate considering the meagreness of the data upon which it was based. The general opinion is that the population of England and Wales increased, though but slowly, during the 17th century. Farr considered that the population in 1600 was probably about five million, other authorities have put it at four million. It may, therefore, be concluded that the increase during the 17th century was at the highest not more than a million and was very probably a good deal less; perhaps even under half a million. The 17th century was a period of civil war and disorder, many severe epidemics are recorded, including visitations of Plague. Though a beginning had been made in the improvement of agriculture and of other arts, it was but a beginning, small and local, having little effect upon society as a whole. *A priori* there is nothing in what we know of the general conditions of the 17th century to lead us to expect anything but a very moderate increase in population, and this is borne out by such statistical guesses, for they are little more, that can be made.

The computations show an estimated decrease for the first decade of the 18th century, but, as already stated, these estimates were based on the entries for the decennial years and not on the figures for the whole decade. The year 1710 happened to be one of harvest failure and acute distress so that it is possible that the decade as a whole was not one of declining population; the period was, however, one of war and harvest failure and consequent fever and therefore may have been one of continual decline. The first fifteen years of the 18th century were bad years but after that a period of prosperity set in, for the next forty years the harvests were extraordinarily good, only three years of bad harvests are recorded and even in these years the failure was not acute.[1] The years 1715–1739 were years of internal and external peace and the country was also free from Plague and from other violent epidemics. Under these favourable conditions the population increased by one million during the half century 1700–1750. At this rate of growth the population would have doubled in something under 200 years, but in fact it doubled in the seventy years 1750 to 1820. The population increased by one-fifth during the period 1700–1750, it increased by one half during the period 1750–1800 (Finlaison's figures).

The increase during the first half of the 18th century was not in any way extraordinary. It was probably proportionately greater, but not remarkably so, than the increase in the 17th century. This increase in the rate of growth is readily explainable by the natural phenomenen of a series of good harvests coupled with political stability and a relatively long peace. To this must be added the absence of Plague and some improvements in agriculture, particularly in gardening. Had no new factors appeared it seems possible that this rate of increase would not have been maintained in the second half of the century, which suffered from many bad harvest failures and was, in addition, a period of war and moreover of war which was carried on with ever growing intensity. The latter part of the century was one of rising prices and social dislocation in agriculture, the main employment. The towns also were growing rapidly and town conditions were notoriously less healthy than those of the country. Yet the population continued to grow and at an increasing rate. This rate of growth continued during the 19th century, in spite of the sufferings in the latter part of the war and during its aftermath and of the still further dislocation of life by economic and social change. It is this new and rapid growth in face of conditions superficially so unfavourable that has puzzled historians and for which no very satisfactory or rational explanation has been suggested. In seeking an explanation the first necessary step is to find the proximate cause of the increase.

An alteration in the rate of growth of the population must be due to an alteration (1) in the birth rate, (2) in the death rate, (3) in the migration rate. The problem as to which of these is mainly operative is complicated by the fact that a growth of population from any cause will alter the age composition and possibly the sex composition of that population and that this will react on the crude marriage, birth and death rates.[2] In a rapidly growing population a change in the crude rates is, therefore, only a very imperfect indication of a change in the corrected rates. It follows also that the ultimate rate of growth of population will differ according to the reasons for the primary increase, i.e. if we know why population grew between 1750–1800 we may to some degree explain the growth between 1800–1850.

Returning to the period under discussion it may be assumed that the growth of population was mainly or entirely a "natural" one, i.e. there was no appreciable immigration. Such immigration as occurred was balanced, or more than balanced, by emigration. It therefore becomes necessary to examine such statistics as exist in regard to birth and death rates. As the population of England and Wales and of London during the 18th century was calculated from the birth rate it is not possible to make any calculation of that rate, since to do so would simply be to argue in a circle. On the Continent, however, rather more material was available. Benoiston de Chateauneuf estimated that round about 1780 the birth rate in most European countries was about 1 in 27·7 (36 per 1000), though Necker had estimated the French birth rate at this period at 1 in 25·7

(39 per 1000). About 1825 de Chateauneuf estimated that the birth rate in north-western Europe had fallen to 1 in 30·1 (33 per 1000) and in France to 1 in 31·7 (31 per 1000). Though these estimates are extremely crude and are most probably underestimates throughout, they are based upon the best material available and embody the belief of those best able to judge that the European birth rate fell appreciably during the period in question.

The statistics of the marriage rate confirm this view. De Chateauneuf calculated the marriage rate of Europe in 1780 at from 1 in 110–115 (8·8 to 9·1 per 1000), in 1825 at about 1 in 123·3 (8·3 per 1000). In England the marriage rate was estimated to have been in 1760, 1 in 116 (8·6 per 1000), in 1796–1800 (England only) it was 1 in 123 (8·3 per 1000), in 1826–30 (England only) it was 1 in 128 (7·8 per 1000). It has to be remembered that the population figure for 1760 is only an estimate based on the assumption of a constant birth rate. However, that the English rate in 1825 was below the Continental rate is confirmatory evidence of a fall. Though a fall in the marriage rate is likely to be accompanied by a fall in the birth rate *pari passu*, it is not absolutely certain to be so, as there may be an alteration in the average fertility of marriage. It need hardly be said that no exact information on this subject existed until modern times. Such figures as exist are generally only a crude ratio between the marriages and births in the same year,[3] a very inexact method if these rates are changing ones. De Chateauneuf believed that the fertility of marriage had remained about constant at 4 during the whole period 1780–1825.[4] Necker, however, calculated it at 4·4 in France in 1780 and it was calculated by a later writer at 3·96 for that country in 1825. Farr calculated it at 4·2 for England and Wales for the ten years ending with 1830. In 1876 the English figure was 4·63. It is impossible to say if this rise is real or simply due to an insufficient allowance for the deficiencies of the registry of births in the 1830 computation. On balance there does not seem any evidence of an alteration in the fecundity of marriage in this country and a mean of 4·5 would probably not be grossly inaccurate.

The startling statement that the birth rate probably fell during a period when it is often stated to have been rising rapidly need not, however, lead us to suppose that there was any widespread change of social habit causing a fall. It was believed at the time, and no doubt rightly, that the fall in the crude marriage and birth rates between 1780 and 1825 was mainly a result of the great saving of child life that had taken place during the period; the existence of a greater proportion of children in the population naturally leading to a fall in the number of marriages and births relative to the whole. The great wastage of male life in the wars and the consequent relative shortage of adult males was an additional adverse factor in regard to the crude marriage and birth rates during this period. It is even possible that these alterations in age and sex composition were great enough to mask some increase in the corrected birth rate, but this supposition is incapable of proof or negation. It has been assumed by many writers that the growth of towns necessarily led to increased natality. There is little or no confirmatory evidence of this view. One or two contemporary writers refer to a high marriage rate in the new towns of the north, but this was mainly, if not entirely, accounted for by the influx of young adults. The effect of an unusual age composition upon the crude birth rate has often been overlooked. For example, Chadwick, in illustration of the high birth rate of towns, compared the birth rate of 1 in 37 in London with that of Herefordshire which was 1 in 44. But another writer showed that the difference was largely explained by the fact that, while the population between 20-40 years of age was 36% of the total in London, it was only 28% in Hereford.[5] In Ireland in 1881 the crude birth rate was 24·5 per 1000 as compared with 33·9 in England and Wales, but the standardized rate for Ireland was 35·2 and that for England and Wales 34·7. There is, in fact, little evidence to support the contention that the growth of towns *per se* leads to a higher birth rate. Little can be argued from present day figures owing to the disturbing factor of the use of contraceptives, which are likely to be more widely resorted to in towns. But if we take the figures for about 1881, a date when statistics were tolerably reliable and when, outside France, contraception was an unimportant factor, the standardized birth rates were distinctly lower in towns than in rural districts.[6] For 1876 the fecundity of marriage was calculated at 5·15 for Italy and 4·84 for Sweden, both at that time predominantly rural countries, while in England it was only 4·63.

Farr and McCulloch quote with approval the following passage from a report on Friendly Societies by Griffith Davies published in 1827 :—

" About 100 years back if any dependence can be placed on the registers the number of annual births did not exceed the number of annual burials, so that the population could not then have been on the increase. The increase since that period must, therefore, be attributed to an increased fruitfulness of the female sex, to immigration, to a diminution in the rate of mortality or to two more of those causes combined. *But it does not appear that the first of these causes had any sensible operation,*[7] and the second can have had none, otherwise the number of burials must have increased in comparison with the number of births, which is contrary to the fact : the increase of population must, therefore, be entirely attributable to a diminution in the rate of mortality." [8]

To assume an increase in the birth rate as the cause of the increased population we have to assume :—

1. That the surviving statistics are utterly valueless.

2. That able writers near the time not only were foolish enough to believe these absolutely unreliable statistics, but invented reasons to account for them.

3. That numbers of other writers on other subjects invented incidental corroborative evidence, especially as to diseases.

4. That at the same time a great increase in the birth rate was not only unrecorded in any official returns, but was totally unnoticed by numbers of competent observers.

5. Lastly, that a decrease in the death rate shown in all surviving statistics and alluded to and explained almost *ad nauseam* by contemporary writers was purely illusory.

Turning to such statistics of the death rate as are available we find that de Chateauneuf (in 1826) comparing the average rate of mortality of Europe about 1780 with that about 1825, calculated that the average proportion of deaths to the whole population about 1780 was 1 in 32·2 (31 per 1000). In 1825, from the 40th degree of latitude to the 65th, the proportion of deaths was 1 in 40·3 (24 per 1000). He estimated the mortality of France for an average of ten years ending 1780 at 1 in 30·2 (33 per 1000) and for an average of seven years ending 1825 at 1 in 39·9 (25 per 1000). De Chateauneuf based his estimates for the earlier period upon the calculations of Necker, Moheau and Pommelles in France, Short and Price in England, Süssmilch in Germany and Wargentin in Sweden.[9] McCulloch considered that, though de Chateauneuf's estimates were necessarily loose, in general they seemed accurate and that those for France, in particular, could be relied upon.

There is no statistical information as to the death rate of the whole of England and Wales until the 19th century. The first absolutely reliable information we possess is that of the Carlisle Tables (1779–1787). These show an annual average death rate for all ages of 25 per 1000. Carlisle was a small, relatively healthy town. The death rate would have been lower in a healthy country parish and a great deal higher in larger towns. The Carlisle figure has sometimes been accepted as typical of the whole country, but it was probably rather lower than the average. Finlaison's calculations based upon the accurate data of the Government Tontines and Life Annuities gave approximately the same result. From this Finlaison concluded that mortality must be about the same in all classes since the Carlisle tables represented a general population and the Government figures related only to the " higher and more affluent orders of society ".[10] In further support of this contention he quoted Blane's statement that the mortality in his private practice was about the same as that at St. Thomas's Hospital (1 in 10). Case mortality is, however, a very different thing from general mortality. The rich man may not have had a very much better chance of recovery if he contracted typhus, but he was very much less likely to contract it than was the poor man. The similarity between Finlaison's results and the Carlisle Tables was no doubt due to the fact that a large number of Government annuitants spent the whole, or a large part, of their lives in London where the general death rate was much higher than that of Carlisle.

Contemporaries generally believed that the death rate fell remarkably during the period under discussion. Farr stated, " there cannot in fact be a doubt that the value of life in England and Wales regularly increased from 1740 or 1750 down to 1815 and there are good grounds for thinking that it then exceeded its value in any other country with the exception of Scotland." [11] Milne in his Treatise on Annuities in 1815 says, " the truth is that the ratio of the annual excess of the births above the deaths . . . has been increasing throughout these 30 years and that increase has been accelerated within the last ten principally by the practice of vaccination." The context shows that he was alluding to a decreased death rate. Another writer says in 1818 [12]: " It cannot be doubted that the general healthiness of Great Britain has increased within the last fifty years, that the rate of mortality is greatly abridged and that the standard population is rapidly augmenting." This writer adds that the fall in the death rate was probably somewhat exaggerated owing to insufficient allowance for the increase of Dissenting burial grounds and for the large number of men dying abroad in the army, navy or commercial establishments.

Short in 1750 estimated the death rate of a healthy country parish at 30 per 1000, the death rate of London at that time was estimated at 50 per 1000. For the whole country, which included malarious districts and smaller towns, some of which were nearly as unhealthy as London, an estimate of 35 per 1000 does not seem improbable. With a birth rate of 39 per 1000 this gives an annual increase of 4 per 1000 or $22\frac{1}{2}\%$ in 50 years, the actual estimated increase for the period 1700–1750 being 20%.[13] For the fifty years 1750–1800 there was a total increase of 50%, i.e., a mean annual increase of 8·4 per 1000. The Carlisle table gives a death rate of 25 per 1000, but by that date there had been considerable improvement and even in 1780 the rate for the whole country may well have been higher. The mean annual death rate for the whole period was, therefore, probably over 25 per 1000 but, since the birth rate was probably under 40, the death rate, including war losses, was probably under 30. That is to say, a mean death rate for the whole country, for the whole period, of about 28 per 1000 may be assumed with some degree of likelihood. And probably the death rate fell from 35 per 1000 in 1750 to 25 per 1000 in 1800 and fell again to about 20 per 1000 in 1815. These figures are little more than guesses but they tally with such facts as are available and they indicate the direction of change, though they are not put forward as exact measurements.

Though there seems reason to suppose that there was some general improvement in health throughout the country and at all age periods, yet the greater part of the fall was due to a decreased town death rate and to a decreased infant mortality. The fall in the infant mortality rate was common to the whole of north-western Europe, though it seems to have been greatest in this country. For Europe, de Chateauneuf estimated that in 1780 about half of the children born (more exactly 49·9%) died before reaching the age of 10 years. In 1825 the corresponding figure was a little more than one-third (38·3%). In France the corresponding figures were 50·5% and 43·7%. A writer in the *Lancet* for 1835 [14] deduced the following figures from the London Bills of Mortality. The proportion of those born in London dying before five years of age was:—

	%
1730–49	74·5
1750–69	63·0
1770–89	51·5
1790–09	41·3
1810–29	31·8

The Carlisle Tables (1779–87) shewed a mortality of 82·3 per 1000 living between ages of 0–5, while the figure for deaths in England and Wales of females under five for the seven years 1818–24 was calculated at 45·6 per 1000.[15] This latter figure was no doubt grossly underestimated. The defect in the registration of deaths (estimated at about 14%) was greater at the earlier age period than for later life. A correction for this brings the figure to about 50, a further correction for sex to 55, but even this is doubtless too low. The death rate under 5 for 1841–50 was 66 per 1000 and, as the general death rate had changed inappreciably since 1830, we may perhaps accept a death rate of 66 per 1000 under 5 as approximately accurate for the whole country in 1830. [The corresponding figure for Belgium in 1829 was 65%.] If, however, the accurate Carlisle figure was ever in any degree representative of the whole country, we still have a remarkable diminution, even supposing we take 66 per 1000 as the correct figure for 1820. The corrected calculations for Glasgow, London and Six Large Towns [16] for about 1830 show a mortality under 5 equal to the Carlisle figure. These were all places where infant mortality was notoriously high and it argues great improvement in the interim if this rate had been reduced to that of a small healthy town forty years earlier. The London figures afford, however, the most startling and conclusive evidence. However inaccurate the figures may be, their comparative value remains and no difference in accuracy could account for alterations upon such a scale.

If the Carlisle Tables be compared in detail with the corresponding figures as calculated for England and Wales for the years 1818–24 and 1818–30 it will be seen that the improvement is mainly confined to the age groups of 0–5 and 5–10, at some other ages there is even retrogression. This accounts for the fact that the Carlisle Tables could still be used in 1837 for life insurance business, a fact which might at first sight seem to argue a stationary death rate, since the lives of non-adults are normally unimportant in life assurance. For a similar reason Finlaison's study of Life Annuitants threw no light on the decrease of infant mortality, as he says " I have never had any means of knowing from facts the mortality from birth to one year old and very imperfectly under the age of three, because people do not nominate lives in extreme infancy as the subject of tontines ".

The great reduction of infant mortality was ascribed by contemporaries to the better nurture of infants and to vaccination. Vaccination was not generally introduced in this country until 1805 even among the well-to-do.[17] From that date onwards it became increasingly effective among the mass of the population.

But by 1805 the proportion of burials under 5 to baptisms in London had been reduced from 74·5% to 41%. Though a large part of this improvement was probably due to a general amelioration of conditions, a portion may be ascribed to the general improvement in infant nurture due to the teaching inculcated by the medical profession and spread among the mass of the people by the numerous hospitals and dispensaries. The infant death rate is much less susceptible to general conditions of public hygiene than is the death rate at other ages. It is significant that the sanitary reforms inaugurated in 1848 began to affect the general death rate in 1874, but the infant mortality rate remained almost stationary until 1906, when an era of remarkable reduction set in. This reduction is generally ascribed to improved infant hygiene, knowledge of which has reached the poorest mothers by means of baby clinics and similar institutions ; in fact, by the methods by which a similar result was achieved over 100 years ago. For the infant personal and household hygiene is more important than public hygiene. A reduction of mortality under 5 is profoundly important. Once passed the perils of infancy the future citizen enters a favourable period from the point of view of mortality and has a good chance of surviving to become an active member of the community and a parent. Such a reduction has, therefore, more than its immediate effect on the growth of population. The resultant modification in the make up of the population will also have important social and economic reactions. The reduction of infant mortality was thus in itself of profound importance but the fact that this reduction was effective in towns and great cities was equally significant.

Towns and cities from 1800 onwards began to grow by natural increase and not merely by immigration. This fact was not only of great social significance but was an important factor in the growth of population, since the unhealthiness of the towns, and particularly of London, had kept down the population as a whole, both directly and indirectly. The population of London during the 18th century has been calculated upon the assumption that the registered births bore the same relation to the total population as they did in 1800 and the death rate has been computed by comparing the figures of the Bills of Mortality with the estimated population. According to calculations based on the Parish Registers and the Bills of Mortality the death rate in London in 1700 was 1 in 25 (40 per 1000) : this was probably an under estimate ; the general calculation at that time was that the death rate in great cities was about 1 in 20. It is possible, however, that London in 1700 was slightly healthier than other cities since a large part of it had been recently re-built and it also enjoyed a relatively good water supply. The death rate in London rose during the first half of the 18th century, reaching its greatest height between 1727 and 1750; it was calculated at about 50 per 1000 for 1750. This retrograde movement was generally ascribed by contemporaries to the orgy of spirit drinking which took place in the Metropolis between about 1720 and 1751. That this opinion was correct seems probable, firstly because there is no other discoverable cause, secondly because the set-back was peculiar to London, to which place excessive gin drinking was mainly confined.[18] The Act of 1751 effectually checked this extreme drunkenness and from that time onward the Bills of Mortality point to improved conditions. During the first half of the century the burials were to the christenings as 3 to 2, from 1740–42 inclusive they were more than 2 to 1. In bad years the excess of deaths over births rose to over 15,000. Taking the ratio of 3 to 2 and a death rate of 50 per 1000, the birth rate would have been 33 per 1000. The birth rate for the whole country at this period was generally calculated to be about 35 per 1000 and was probably higher, but it was believed to be very low in London compared with other places. On this basis an immigration of 17 per 1000 per annum, namely about 10,200 persons, was necessary in order to maintain a stationary population. That is to say, speaking very roughly, London destroyed half a million population from the rest of the country during the first 50 years of the 18th century, without making any allowance for the destruction of potential descendants.

After 1750 there was an improvement in the London figures, slow at first, but becoming more definite after 1775. The burials decreased and in 1790 for the first time were actually fewer than the births. The following years were not so favourable, but on the average for the five years 1795–99 the christenings and burials were equal. In spite of a bad season in 1800, the average number of baptisms exceeded that of the burials for the five years 1800–04 and after that date the excess grew rapidly. The estimated death rate for 1801 was 1 in 35 (29 per 1000) that for 1811 was 1 in 38 (26 per 1000) ; that is to say, between 1750 and 1811 the death rate of London was halved. During the ten years 1801–10 the annual average excess of births over deaths was probably about 5,000.[19] The population grew during this decade from 900,000 to 1,050,000, an annual increase of 15,000. The average net immigration into London was therefore about 10–11,000, actually a smaller proportion of the total population than the estimated immigration for the period 1700–59. This decreased proportionate immigration has been ascribed by some authorities to the reform of the settlement laws and the lavish relief given in the southern rural counties.[20] But the natural increase in London must have been a factor and of course, the immigration into the great towns of the north was growing rapidly.

In the first half of the century the deaths as a rule exceeded the births in towns, while in the second half the reverse was true. Thus in York in the period 1728–35 the burials exceeded the births by 98 per annum (total burials 3,488), but in the period 1770–76 the births exceeded the burials by 21 per annum (total burials 3,175).[21] Howlett writing in 1781 [22] quotes the registers of Norwich (which included all denominations) : In 1729 the baptisms numbered 877 and the burials 1,136, while the annual average for 1775–80 was baptisms 1,157 and burials 1,176. In Manchester during the six years ending 1786 the registered births exceeded the registered deaths by an annual average of 433. There is a considerable amount of scattered evidence to the same effect.

It may be objected that all these conclusions are based upon the notoriously inaccurate Bills of Mortality and Parish Registers. No one would base an argument upon a small variation of the bills, but the movements here recorded are too big to have been the result of accident or error. Moreover, the broad truth is corroborated from a number of other sources. An experienced doctor writing in 1808 summed up the question of the credibility of the Bills (and incidentally of the Registers) in the following words " The Bills of Mortality have often been objected to as erroneous and imperfect sources of information and unworthy of credit. This charge is not without foundation though by no means to be admitted to its full extent. For what they want in accuracy is in a great measure supplied by their magnitude, the large scale upon which they are constructed making their smaller errors inconsiderable. But the surest testimony to their credibility was afforded by the Bills themselves ; whose agreement with each other is quite inexplicable upon any other supposition than that of their being drawn from the uniformity of nature and truth." [23]

This diminution of the death rate took place in a period which has been generally considered to have been one of increasing degradation among the mass of the people ; during which, moreover, social effort has been presumed to have been at a minimum owing to the acceptance of the doctrine of laisser-faire. It is not safe, however, to measure achievement solely by the Statute Book, especially in Great Britain. Active social effort can exist apart from legal enactment, and as a matter of fact the period in question was one of enterprise and experiment in social betterment in many spheres, but more especially in the domain of Public Health.

CHAPTER IV

INDIVIDUALISM AND LAISSER-FAIRE

The 18th century is not altogether sympathetic to modern minds. An age that believed in reason is distasteful to one which teaches that emotion is the source of all human actions. An age which believes in communal effort as the remedy for all ills is impatient with one that pinned its faith to individualism. To understand the 18th century faith in Reason we must remember how near it was to the ages of unreason, how new was the conception of order and unalterable cause and effect in nature. Only a few short years before, poor old women had been burnt as witches, not by an ignorant mob but by the order of educated magistrates. The 18th century gentleman looked back over the mental gulf which separated him from his grandfather and praised reason and science which saved him from the emotional follies and superstition of his forbears. If he pinned his faith to individualism, it was because he lived in a period when regulative machinery whether of the State, the corporation, or the guild had fallen into corruption and decay. Progress in every sphere he found to be due to the initiative and enterprise of individuals, in most communal institutions he found only the dead hand of a bygone and unenlightened age. The theory of laisser-faire was it is true in harmony with the general philosophical views of the period, but Englishmen have always been swayed more by practical considerations of the moment than by philosophical harmonies. It was the actual success of private enterprise and the inefficiency and corruption of Government control that caused laisser-faire to be an acceptable policy. As the educated man at the end of the 18th century looked round his world, he saw that the agriculture of a large part of the country had been revolutionized by the private initiative of the landowners. He rejoiced in the marshes that had been drained, in the barren sandy soil that had been made fruitful. If he looked at commerce, he saw it pushed by private enterprise into every quarter of the globe. If he looked at industry, he saw the iron industry resuscitated by private initiative, he marvelled at the new steam engine, he admired the new cotton fabric. But if he turned to Government activity, he found inefficiency and corruption. The Government was engaged in a long and costly war, financed with the aid of the private enterprise of the banks and the stockbrokers. If success crowned some of the military and naval efforts, he knew it was mainly due to the exertions of individuals of force and character, who were generally engaged in a heart-breaking struggle with the inefficient bureaucracy.

Arthur Young well summed up the point of view of the typical educated Englishman of his time when, in reply to a Frenchman who had expressed astonishment that the diarist's travels were not subsidized by a public authority, he said, " everything is well done in England, except what is done with public money." [1] Nor was this attitude confined to satisfied supporters of the ruling classes. Modern historians have tended to blame the Regency Government for a laisser-faire attitude, but contemporary critics rather blamed it for sins of commission than of omission. They pointed out that the Government had involved the country in a long and terribly costly war for objects of doubtful importance to the nation at large and that the financial policy of the Government had brought upon the people all the complicated ills due to a period of inflation, followed by the inevitable deflation. These were the fundamental ills from which the nation suffered, but they were added to by a badly administered Poor Law and a criminal law which was at once uncertain and harsh. Mr. Cole points out in his recent biography of Cobbett, that the latter said little about machinery or enclosures as a cause of the misery of the poor but constantly inveighed against the war, the currency policy and the Poor Law administration. Cobbett was endowed with a shrewd native common sense which doubtless helped him to his conclusions, but in this connection he was expressing no isolated opinion, but that of some of the acutest thinkers of the time.

The doctrine of laisser-faire and individualism was also in harmony with the general economic conditions of the country. It is hard to realise that the England of the late 18th and early 19th century was in many respects a new country. Great tracts of moor and fen were being brought under cultivation by new settlers. It is related of the father of one of the well known agriculturists of Northumberland that when he first settled in Glendale, at the end of the 18th century, " the plain was a forest of wild broom. He took his axe, and, like a backwoodsman, cleared a space on which to begin his farming operations." The Cheviot herdsmen at this period were described as fierce and sullen, the people as uneducated, barbarous and ill-clothed ; the country was wholly unenclosed, without either roads or sign-posts, and the cattle were often lost for days in the forests of wild broom. Men of the same stamp as the Messrs. Cullely settled in its fertile vales, and by their spirited farming revolutionized whole districts which, like the rich vale of the Till, were wildernesses of undergrowth.[2] In the same way miles of rabbit warrens in Norfolk and Lincolnshire were developed into rich wheat lands. These pioneer conditions were, of course, only to be found in certain districts of the North and the East, but they were also found to a marked degree in the new towns. These new urban communities grew with the rapidity which is now associated with the New World. A writer in 1778 speaking of the Soho district of Birmingham said, " eight years ago (it) was a barren uncultivated heath, it now contains many houses and wears the appearance of a populous town."[3] The early manufacturer who established a new town was compelled to engage in many subsidiary enterprises. Samuel Oldknow of Mellor for instance not only built a cotton factory but supplied his employees with houses, coals, and meat and established a shop. He was also compelled to repair roads, construct bridges and was active in forming a canal company. Some of his workers showed equal versatility, a certain employee of his was, in turn, a cotton spinner, a miner, a farm labourer, a road mender, a builder, a gardener, a woodman.[4]

It was a period of freedom, the old guild restrictions had broken down and effective Trade Union restrictions had not arisen.

It is not true, as has so often been alleged, that the period was one during which it became increasingly difficult for talent to rise in the world. Never were the barriers so down. The period of transition offered great opportunities to a man clever with his hands. Early machinery was primitive and clumsy and only replaced mechanical and routine processes. There was great opportunity for skilled men in constructing and repairing machinery and in finishing processes. The majority of the workers, however, were only competent to do routine work in an unthinking way, and were unused to regular hours or sober habits. Wedgwood, Boulton and other pioneers constantly lamented the difficulty of obtaining skilled and sober workmen. The few who possessed skill and diligence must have been too valuable to be anything but well treated, and it was easy to turn from one trade to another. Those who had a little education or initiative also found it easy to rise through the avenue of small shop keeping or through the numerous openings in management and agency work. The mass of the people, however, possessing neither mental nor manual education, undisciplined and ignorant, could not avail themselves of the many chances which offered, and this fact made the rewards the greater for those who had had the opportunity to acquire skill or were possessed of exceptional natural ability. Life offered golden opportunities to the versatile, the pushing and the strong, it was apt to be hard on the unenterprising and the weak. The successful of all classes desired naturally to be " let alone ".

It is a mistake to suppose that industry became impersonal at this period, this development is due to joint stock enterprise, which did not become predominant in most branches of industry until the 20th century. Men like Wedgwood, Boulton and Peel knew their workers personally and their attitude to them resembled that of the old time squire to those who lived on his estate. Moreover, owing to the shortage of skilled and directing labour of all kinds these men were compelled to take a very minute and active interest in the actual technique of their business. If this was the case with these large enterprises it must have been much more so in the ordinary small business. Gradually, with the evolution of a professional managing and technical staff on the one hand, and of company organization on the other, the personal touch has been lost over a large part of industry, but this development must not be read into the earlier period. On the contrary, there was, perhaps, never a period when organization counted for so little and personality for so much as the end of the 18th and the beginning of the 19th centuries. This applies to every aspect of life and is the key to much that is difficult for modern students to understand. It is not astonishing that preachers and moralists laid stress upon character training and sought to impose a stern self discipline upon all those called to positions of responsibility. The power of the individual of the governing classes was potent for good or evil. If often this power was misused it was also often well used; the stimulus of freedom and the possibility of achievement being to some a great incentive to activity.

It is not safe to measure social achievement by the activities of the central government. Government activities were a very small part of life in those days. The Home Office consisted of the Home Secretary, a Permanent Secretary and twenty clerks and its function was mainly advisory. It is unnecessary to say that the other great departments which now deal with social administration did not exist. Internal Government was essentially a local affair; the country, apart from a few towns, was ruled by the magistrates with a stern paternalism which was honest if narrow-minded. The close corporations in the towns were often corrupt but not necessarily inefficient according to the lights of the time.[5] At this period the actual government was necessarily left mainly to the local authorities. The size of the unit of government is dependent upon the means of communication and the development of administrative machinery. Before the days of railways, telephones, telegraphs, typewriters, calculating machines, card indexes and other similar inventions and devices, decentralization of government was a practical necessity. Great latitude was of necessity given to the man on the spot, even though he might be appointed by and dismissable by the central authority. But in England even this control did not exist, since in practice local government was vested in the local owners of property. This complete local autonomy left room for considerable local divergence. Some magistrates were slack, others were harsh but many were conscientious, hard working and philanthropic. No one can doubt that the best magistrates made great efforts, in their official capacity, to improve the conditions of the poor, either through the agency of the poor law or otherwise. The extreme individualism and the decentralization of such government activity as existed makes it extraordinarily difficult to generalize about the period. In the Middle Ages manorial and guild customs had a great similarity over the whole country and imposed certain common conditions. At the present day central legislation, the activities of Trade Unions and the dissemination of knowledge, impose a certain minimum standard. But in our period great differences could exist in adjoining parishes, owing to the personality of the resident magistrates, and extraordinary differences could be found in neighbouring factories. The worst employers were unchecked in their neglect and cruelty, but the best were also unchecked in well-doing by a satisfied feeling that legal enactments were being obeyed.

Not only was such government activity as existed mainly local, but the sphere of government, including local government, was very narrow. The ruling classes wished to keep it narrow, not because they believed in inaction, but because they believed in private enterprise. Neither were they so foolish as to ignore the necessity of co-operative effort in many enterprises. But they believed in free co-operation. The 19th century was to teach that in many matters compulsion is necessary, but the 18th century achieved much by voluntary effort which probably could not at the time have been achieved by other means. It is, indeed, a narrow view that the use of the machinery of the national executive is the only possible form of corporate effort. A reaction from that extreme view is already noticeable in current political thought.

In the free co-operation of the 18th century, the machinery of the joint stock company was much used. By this machinery the roads of the country were largely re-made, and in spite of some failures, in a few years roads which had been some of the worst in Europe became some of the best. By joint stock enterprise, the country was intersected by a network of canals which were invaluable in developing its production. By joint stock enterprise towns were supplied with water and town improvements were carried through. Most of these enterprises were run on profit making lines, though not always successfully. It cannot be doubted, however, that the main object of many of the promoters was not to make a profit on the shares. The landowner was thinking of his comfort and convenience and the value of his land when he helped to promote a Turnpike Trust, not of the possible interest from the investment. Josiah Wedgwood was thinking of the benefit to his Potteries, not of dividends, when he promoted the Grand Trunk Canal. The objects aimed at may have been mainly selfish, but neither are the promoters of government enterprise necessarily purely disinterested. The reasons for which a man desires a good road are the same, whether it is made by a Turnpike Trust or a Local Authority. The method by which he is most likely to attain it will differ according to the general social and political environment.

The co-operative effort of the period was not, however, limited to profit making and selfish ends. It has been too readily assumed that laisser-faire was a do nothing policy, that it envisaged a society of economic men, each fighting blindly and ruthlessly for his own hand, while a complacent state looked on, " keeping the ring " in the form of the laws of property, imagining that an all wise providence would in time evolve harmony out of the chaos. Certainly the classical economists believed and taught that men pursuing their own economic ends generally benefited the community at the same time. Perhaps they underrated the cases in which the reverse is true but the error tends now to be in the opposite direction ; many modern writers seem to overlook the fact that most of our common economic wants are supplied because the supplier wishes to satisfy his own. Nobody ever believed that the world would be a very pleasant place if each individual thought only of his own economic good. Very different motives were presumed to inspire dealings within the family, but even outside the family it was held that the economic motive should be joined with those of philanthropy and benevolence. Never were these duties more assiduously preached than in the 18th and early 19th centuries and that it was not all preaching and no practice the numerous and varied philanthropic efforts of the age bear witness. The organization of the philanthropic societies was similar to that of a joint stock company, except that dividends were replaced by letters of recommendation and votes. The objects were wide spread in their scope : hospitals and dispensaries, institutions for the blind, orphanages, charity schools, while early in the 19th century private effort tackled general elementary education.

The causes of the great growth of English philanthropic enterprise, especially in London, were various. In the first place it was due to the increasing wealth and prosperity of the upper and middle classes. Some of the money made in trade and finance found its way into charitable channels. Thomas Guy, for instance, founded the hospital which has perpetuated his name, out of the proceeds of successful speculation during the Bubble. The growing wealth increased not only the means but the will to give. The previous century during the Plague of London, had revealed an extraordinary callousness upon the part of the governing classes, while the majority of the clergy and the doctors considered their own safety rather than the alleviation of suffering.[6] This callousness, so shocking to modern eyes, was the natural result of familiarity with suffering and of powerlessness to give any adequate relief, coupled with a very real danger to any who attempted to give aid. The war showed us how easily our sensibilities are blunted to suffering. Life was uncertain even for the upper and middle classses in the 17th century. Smallpox, malaria, rickets and other illnesses made it difficult even for the well-to-do to rear children ; political changes might cause exile and loss of fortune. The charitable foundations of the 17th century were largely for the benefit of the middle and artisan ranks and simply filled the gap left by the relative break-down of the Guild organization. Trade was subject to extraordinary risks and wealthy merchants might, in a short space of time, be reduced to a debtor's prison by some event outside their control. This insecurity did not make these classes more sympathetic to the poor but less so. Drowning men will fight ruthlessly for a plank, but those who are secure on the deck of a ship will be of extraordinary inhumanity if they will not trouble to throw a rope to the strugglers in the water. The growing wealth and security of the upper classes during the 18th century was, therefore, one cause of their growing charity. But charity was not only growing during the century, it was becoming more organized. There had always been a great deal of indiscriminate charity, the existence of hordes of professional beggars in itself proves this fact. Such charity, however, tends to benefit mainly the professional beggar and the 18th century began to appreciate this fact. Hence the attempt to organize charity so that it reached the deserving poor and discouraged pauperism and begging.

The growth of philanthropy was also closely associated with a changed religious outlook. The 16th and 17th centuries had been periods of fierce religious disputes and intolerance, in which matters of dogma rather than of conduct were fundamentally in controversy. Though the 18th century was not tolerant according to modern notions, it was so compared with previous centuries. Political disability, rather than prison or the stake, had become the ordinary penalty for religious Dissent. It would not be true to say that dogma formed no part of the 18th century religion, but it had become largely a matter for academic argument by divines. The vast majority of the people took the accepted dogma for granted and a dogma that is not disputed is profoundly uninteresting. It is significant that the great secession of the 18th century rested not on a difference of opinion about dogma, but upon questions of organization and practical Christian conduct. The Wesleyan movement, and the Evangelical movement within the Church which resulted from it, is not altogether sympathetic to modern minds. It asked altogether too much of human nature, it insisted too much upon the sterner virtues of sobriety, continence, hard work and thrift. It banned too many innocent amusements along with many, it is true, which were not innocent. It was too apt to look upon suffering and poverty as disciplinary dispensations of Providence. No one, however, can read the letters and memoirs of the time without admitting that at any rate verbal resignation was applied to the personal misfortunes of the rich. We should too be unjust if in spite of our prejudices we fail to recognize the part which charitable effort played in the religious revival; the duty of charity was, indeed, insistently preached and practised. This charity was not confined to the mere giving of money, the gospel behest was literally obeyed and the poor, the sick and the prisoners were visited in their affliction in a way that had been unknown since the early days of the friars. Personal risk and inconvenience were not considered by those ardent souls who staffed the Dispensaries or taught in the slum Sunday Schools, but it must be confessed that their charity was of a different *genre* to that of the Middle Ages. Almsgiving was not merely an end in itself, beneficial to the soul of the giver, it must show results. The deserving poor must be aided to escape pauperism, the thriftless and drunken must be disciplined into better ways. Both the religion and the philosophy of the period discouraged emotional pity. Evangelicalism and Utilitarianism both imposed a stern discipline upon their followers. The adherents of these creeds worked long hours, saved and gave away a large proportion of their incomes, lived simply, " took their pleasures sadly " and expected the poor to do the same. Their life and creed did not encourage imagination, and the notion that it was not very easy to work hard and keep sober on insufficient food or to be chaste under the housing conditions of the poor, would have been rejected as weakly sentimental. At the end of the century charity took on a coldness and an efficiency that had been unknown to the urbane, easy going Pagans who had directed the earlier efforts. The French Revolution also, had been a shock to the complacent paternalism of earlier years. The poor were no longer mere objects of pity, to the sternness of an austere creed was added an element of cruelty begotten of fear. This cruelty, however, was mainly reserved for " agitators and dangerous characters "; all through the worst period of repression charitable effort was continued on behalf of the "deserving poor".

The enterprising, inventive spirit of the age was not, as has so often been alleged, directed solely to self seeking ends. At first sight the growing social conscience may seem to have been out of harmony with the general spirit of the age, but, in fact, it was part of the general desire for efficiency. Despite its narrowness, the philanthropic effort of our period achieved much. Not only did charity to some extent bridge the chasm between classes, but it was by no means unfruitful in relieving suffering. This philanthropy may not have been so acceptable to some of the recipients as the old haphazard almsgiving, but in fairness it must be remembered that to the donors it entailed giving work and thought as well as mere money. The 18th century saw the birth of modern philanthropy with its organization and its definite aims. This movement, indeed, has had its faults and limitations, yet few would be found to deny that it has played its part in the betterment of the lot of mankind.

CHAPTER V

THE GROWTH OF COMMERCE

IN endeavouring to elucidate the ultimate causes of the reduction of the death rate we may perhaps roughly classify them under the heads 'increasing wealth' and 'increasing knowledge', though these two are obviously mutually interdependent. The main cause of the increasing wealth was undoubtedly the growth of commerce and, as far as this country was concerned, the growth of the commerce of London. It is significant that it was in London, where the wealth and commerce of the country were largely concentrated, that town improvement and the great hospital movement had their origin. The commerce of London re-acted upon agriculture, providing it both with a market and with capital, and thus it was an important factor in a remarkable increase in both the quality and the quantity of the food supply. The wealth of London encouraged improvement in industry and in medicine. But wealth and commerce alone could have achieved nothing if they had not been able to draw upon an ever growing stream of knowledge in every sphere, in science, in agriculture, in navigation, in industrial technique, in medicine. The growth of commerce itself had its origin in the great geographical discoveries of the 15th century, which also placed this country in a favourable position in regard to foreign trade.

Up to the middle of the 16th century England was a poor and backward country, her finance and foreign commerce in the hands of foreigners, her natural resources largely undeveloped. The discovery of the New World and of the ocean routes to the East inevitably shifted the world's economic centre of gravity; the prosperity of the Mediterranean countries tended to decline and that of the Atlantic countries to rise. England shook off the foreign yoke and began to attempt long distance foreign trade and to be less dependent upon foreign finance.

Slow, but perceptible, progress was made under the Tudors and Early Stuarts but then came civil disorder, disastrous foreign wars, plague and fire. All this held back economic development, though some progress was made in spite of adverse circumstances, but it was not until 1688 that continuous advance was possible. The 18th century may be said in many respects to have begun in 1688 ; 18th century writers date everything from " The Revolution ". In that year the constitutional question was settled in a manner favourable to the only class that counted politically and internal peace was only slightly interrupted after this date. The national finances were placed upon a secure basis ; the device of a perpetual national debt, the interest upon which was a first charge upon national revenue, not only added elasticity to the State finances but educated its citizens in investment. The foundation of the Bank of England (1694) and its successful management, gave additional stability to both public and private finance. There can be no doubt that the Dutch connection was extremely advantageous to England at this juncture. Holland was at that time the leading commercial and financial nation of Europe and was viewed by Englishmen with jealous admiration and dislike. Nevertheless they learnt much from Holland in agriculture and in gardening, in commerce and shipping, but more especially in finance. Moreover, Dutch investors contributed substantially to the successful launching of the Bank of England and otherwise supported English government borrowings.

Two important financial devices were developed in England in the first part of the 17th century and substantially improved after 1688, namely banking and joint stock trading. Both these devices were dangerous in ignorant and inexperienced hands, and numerous banking runs and crises on the one hand, and commercial crashes, from the famous Bubble onwards, on the other, proved this to the full during the next two hundred years. Yet without these devices it is difficult to conceive of modern commerce and industry. They are an essential part of the world as we know it. The first successful application of the Joint Stock principle was to distant and foreign trade, of which the East India Company was the most famous example. Such

GROWTH OF COMMERCE

an enterprise would have been impossible for the individual merchant. The possibility of distant trade was also dependent upon the development of sea transport. By 1760 land transport had improved little but sea transport had already made considerable advance. The mariner no longer, as in ancient and medieval times, had to hug the coast nor seek a port at night nor lay up his ship in winter. Sea transport continued day and night, summer and winter. Great improvements in ship building and the art of sailing enabled the sailor to contend against tempestuous seas and contrary winds. The adoption of the compass and the invention of the quadrant,[1] the log line and, at last, the chronometer [2] enabled him safely to leave the sight of land and to find a path across vast oceans. The development of foreign trade directly stimulated many branches of industry while the profits from it were largely invested in land and so indirectly stimulated the improvements in agriculture.

Joint Stock enterprise was centred in London and trading by joint stock and regulated companies tended to the concentration of commerce in that city.[3] London was never so predominant as during the 17th and the first half of the 18th centuries. Greater London contained one-tenth of the total population of the country and probably over half of the urban population.[4] The major proportion of the foreign trade passed through London; Bristol and Norwich were stationary and Liverpool had hardly begun to be, at a time when the capital was developing rapidly. London was the great collecting and distributing centre for the foreign trade of the country and in the 18th century she further developed a great entrepôt trade for the Continent. As a result of these activities London possessed a great shipping and ship building industry. The East Indiamen, the largest merchant ships afloat, were built on the Thames. In connection with the flourishing commerce, banking and finance developed. Until the second half of the 18th century nearly all the banking of the country was concentrated in London, Burke stated that in 1750 there were not twelve banks outside London but by 1793 there were over 400 country banks. In the 18th century London began to rival Amsterdam as the financial centre of Europe. A specialized class of stock jobbers arose and insurance for sea, fire and other risks was also developed. London was also the administrative centre of the country and, though the Civil servants at that date were an extremely small body, yet Parliament and its numerous hangers on and the administrative branches of the Army and Navy formed a not inconsiderable body. As the seat of government London was necessarily, in the absence of police, a large garrison town. Lastly, it was the centre of the world of fashion and of the intellectual and artistic activities which were dependent upon the patronage of that world. A large part of the great population of London consisted of persons employed in subordinate capacities in these various activities. There must have been a very large army of porters, warehousemen, lightermen and clerks attached to shipping and commerce and numerous clerks and messengers in finance. Shipbuilding gave employment to various subsidiary industries such as rope making, barrel making and so on. Shipping provided for all those who live, honestly or dishonestly, by the sailor, from the marine storekeeper to the crimp. As to the world of fashion, moralists were never tired of inveighing against the armies of idle footmen it supported and, in addition, there were more active domestics and hosts of chairmen, link boys and hangers on.

London was also a great industrial city. Besides shipbuilding and its numerous subsidiary industries, it was a great centre of luxury trade which had naturally developed near its market. Apart from the important silk industry it was famous for watches, leather goods, jewellery, furniture, plate, coach building and so on, not to mention such obvious things as the various branches of the clothing industry. Concentration of population is cumulative; all this mass of persons needed an army of traders to serve them, from the high class shop-keeper to the petty huckster, from the wealthy wholesale merchant to the pedestrian market woman, there were also the carters, horse tenders, road menders and scavengers who directly or indirectly assisted in transport. There were besides the various branches of the building trade which provided it with shelter. Lastly, London like other great cities, supported a large number of parasites; prostitutes, beggars, thieves and rogues of every description.

This great city, containing one-tenth of the population of the country and a considerably greater proportion of the wealth, had to be fed and provided with the fuel and raw materials necessary for its industry. The repercussion of the necessary organization upon the economic life of the country as a whole was far reaching. The economic life of the country immediately surrounding London was subordinate to it. In the immediate vicinity prosperous villages depended upon market gardening, which by the middle of the 18th century had reached a very high standard; while in Middlesex many farmers devoted themselves to producing hay upon an intensive system for the numerous London horses.[5] The farmers of Kent, especially those near the river, raised fruit for the London market. All these persons had to buy corn, meat and other necessaries, London had made specialization in agriculture lucrative. Less beautiful than the market gardens were the numerous brick fields to be found in many directions, on the outskirts of the town. Timber mainly came by sea from Scotland or the Baltic, coal by sea from Newcastle, this latter being a highly organized and lucrative trade. Corn was brought in by river or sea; poultry was brought by cart from as far as Norfolk, geese are even said to have been driven in flocks from that county. Milk, notoriously adulterated, was supplied by dairy farmers, whose herds grazed in Hyde Park and other open spaces, but less perishable dairy produce came from a distance. The meat trade needed an elaborate organization. Cattle walked from all parts of the country, even from the Highlands of Scotland, to be slaughtered in London. On the cattle routes many farmers made a lucrative living by letting temporary grazing for the travelling droves, while fattening them after their long trek was another paying branch of the trade. Adam Smith mentioned the importance of the London meat market in improving Scottish agriculture, and the part which it played in Highland farm economy has been well brought out in a recent study.[6] By relieving the extreme poverty of the Highlands it was, perhaps, a factor in their final pacification.

At any rate it gave the Highlands, what they had not possessed before, an economic interest in the English connection. The repercussion of the London market on English agriculture is dealt with more fully in the next chapter.

As London grew in wealth and population, so her needs led to greater calls over wider areas upon the agriculture and industry of the rest of the country. As the rest of the country grew in wealth, it made greater demands upon the luxury products of London and upon the foreign products for which London was the distributing centre. In the second half of the 18th century, when the new industries of the North and the Midlands were developing, the London market was of great importance. It was that market which stimulated the early cotton industry [7] and gave an outlet for the products of Birmingham, Sheffield and of the Potteries. London merchants, instead of expecting credit from the manufacturers, appear to have given it and, in some cases, the London banks also gave credit to provincial enterprise. The country banks, which developed after 1750 and which did much to finance improvements in agriculture and industry were themselves very dependent upon their London agents and upon the Bank of England. Thus the foreign trade of London caused the growth of that city in wealth and population and that growth in its turn stimulated improvement in the rest of the country.

There was, however, another stimulating influence which acted upon certain industries, especially in the second half of the 18th century, and that was war. The war demand had an important reaction upon agriculture,[8] and also upon that typical war industry—iron making. Iron making in the 18th century was even more dependent upon the demand for armaments than it is to-day. The multifarious modern uses for the metal had not arisen and, apart from armaments, the sole demand was for a few tools and domestic utensils most of which required little material. Domestic utensils were generally of wood, pewter, bronze or copper, though iron pots were used to a limited extent. Ships were built of wood, bridges of stone, water pipes were of wood, such simple machinery as existed was made of wood and most tools were of the same material.

than with a factory system. The factory, indeed, in the long run probably tended to mitigate these evils rather than to increase them.

The growth of towns showed itself before the advent of the factory or machinery. The changes in transport led to a rapid increase of trade and facilitated localization of industry. The towns as distributing centres, therefore, increased in importance. There also seems to have been some concentration of hand workers in the towns. In the old days the workers necessarily lived near the sources of food and fuel and the more portable manufactures were transported. Increased transport facilities made it more economic to employ the worker near the market for raw material and finished goods, since it was possible to bring food and fuel in large quantities to the towns. Though the use of water power was a factor tending to the decentralization of industry, the centralizing forces were sufficiently strong to lead to a rapid urban growth in the second half of the 18th century.[15] But though the towns were growing their condition was not, as is often supposed, deteriorating. Insanitary towns are not an invention of modern times. On the contrary, the towns of the Middle Ages were disease ridden and insanitary to a degree that is indescribable. Those of the 17th century were little better. Far from the middle of the 18th century marking the beginning of an era of town degradation, it marks the beginning of the era of town improvement. Incredible as the statement may appear to many persons, the towns, particularly London, were becoming more healthy in the second half of the 18th century. Streets were being widened and paved, drains covered in, water supply improved, houses re-built, with an astonishing effect upon the death rate.

Growing commerce led to the demand for wider and better paved streets, it also provided the money for these improvements. Growing commerce had led to improved transport, improved transport led to cheaper paving stones and building materials. The substitution of brick for timber was a factor favourable to health, tending to a more hygienic architecture and giving less harbourage to vermin. Bricks were sometimes transported by canal, but as a rule, brick works were established in close vicinity to the district which they served, coal however had to be carried to them. Improved transport led to cheap and plentiful fuel which, besides cheapening many industrial processes, made possible better warmed houses, better cooked food and greater cleanliness. Cleanliness was also aided by iron pipes and steam pumps which made possible a plentiful, if often impure, water supply. The development of the cotton industry also tended in the same direction. At first this industry was a luxury one, catering only for the well-to-do, but the rapid cheapening of its product by the application of machinery, soon led to production for the masses. Cotton cloth was a cheap material suitable for women's dresses and for body and household linen; it wore less well than stout woollen material but that was advantageous from the health point of view since it could be cheaply renewed. Cotton washed easily and therefore its use much encouraged cleanliness.[16] The cheapening of iron led to cheaper household utensils, while the substitution of the iron bedstead for the old vermin-ridden wooden one was important from the hygienic point of view, though, at first this change was mainly confined to institutions. The substitution of china crockery for the old wooden, earthenware or pewter utensils was generally held to have led to greater cleanliness. Even the cheap china ornament may have had its uses in fostering house pride among the very poor.

The growth of foreign trade had directly added two very important items to the national food supply, namely sugar and tea. The native country of the sugar cane is unknown but it was cultivated in Asia from great antiquity. It was introduced by the Arabs from Persia into Egypt, Sicily and South Spain. As early as 1319 a Venetian merchant shipped 100,000 lbs of sugar to London, but it remained a costly luxury and an article of medicine in this country until the 18th century. The Spanish and Portuguese colonists had introduced the plant to the West Indies and to the American continent and it was from the West Indies that 18th century England drew her supplies. The growth of the trade can be gauged from the fact that in 1700 the import into Great Britain was only 10,000 tons but that in 1800 it was

150,000 tons.[17] Pringle [18] believed that the increased use of sugar had been a factor very favourable to public health and apart from anything else its increased use must have encouraged the consumption of fruit, much of which never becomes pleasantly sweet in this northern climate. It also made possible the preservation of fruit for winter use in the form of jams and conserves.

Tea was brought by the East India Company from China. In the middle of the 17th century it was still an expensive luxury and by the end of that century the annual import was only about 20,000 lbs.; but by the end of the 18th century the rate of consumption exceeded two lbs. per person per annum. The importance of tea lay in the fact that it was a substitute for alcohol and it must have been an important factor in the increased sobriety, which all authorities are agreed took place at the end of the 18th century and the beginning of the 19th century. Though both these commodities were dear according to modern notions, yet early 19th century writers always considered both tea and sugar to be necessaries of life for the working classes. They were, apparently, consumed by all classes, though doubtless in small quantities by the least well off.[19]

The most important effect of the growth of commerce was, however, upon the home food supply. A new demand for agricultural products was created which stimulated agricultural improvements and the improvements in transport helped both to create and to satisfy this demand. The agriculture of the country passed rapidly from being largely communal and for subsistence to being almost entirely capitalistic and for a market. Whatever may be thought of the social consequences of these changes the effect upon agricultural output was entirely favourable. The high death rate of the Middle Ages was very largely due to the frequent recurrence of famines and food scarcities: deaths from actual starvation being added to by those from disease due to the consumption of unsuitable food; while the general malnutrition increased the numbers of victims of epidemic disease, so prevalent from other causes. A subsistence system of agriculture is not only necessarily unprogressive but also necessarily insecure. This insecurity is the more serious in so far that a community that is normally self sufficing will have great difficulty in obtaining supplies from the outside. Trade and transport will be unorganized and moreover the community will have nothing to offer in exchange for food. A community which normally imports its food supply can turn with comparative ease to other sources should the normal source fail. The wider the area from which its supplies are normally drawn, the less the inconvenience which will be felt from the failure of one source. On the other hand, a community which normally exports food can cease to do so, temporarily, in case of harvest failure and, should the failure be severe, the normal lines of trade and transport for export can be utilized for import and the future crop can be mortgaged in payment. It is commonly represented that international interdependence in regard to food supply represents insecurity. This is only true from a military point of view and even in this respect there is perhaps a tendency to over-stress it. Apart from war, international trade in food has enormously increased the security of mankind. Few countries are large enough to give security from famine by home trade, since weather conditions tend to be similar over wide areas. If this is the case with modern countries it was still more so with the smaller national units of the Middle Ages, and much more so of the economic units, which were often only tiny villages with their surrounding fields. The natural hindrances to territorial exchange were added to by the foolish policy of local exclusiveness which often prevented the transport of food between neighbouring areas. So that in addition to the great and widespread scarcities and famines which were frequent in the Middle Ages, local famines and acute scarcities often occurred. The growth of commerce thus directly added to the security of the national food supply but it also led to a revolution in agricultural organization and production.

CHAPTER VI

AGRICULTURE

THE organization of English agriculture in the Middle Ages under the Manorial System has been described almost *ad nauseam* in text books of economic history and there is no necessity to repeat the description here. It suffices to remind readers that the same or similar systems were found in many parts of Europe and Asia and that, from the economic point of view, the fundamentals of the organization were that the agriculture was mainly carried on in common and that it was very largely self-sufficing. The communal aspect of the organization, coupled with the legal institution of serfdom, gave to the economic life that freedom from change which can be called stagnation or stability according to political bias. Whichever name is preferred, it is certain that the system was relatively inelastic and could not have been adapted to a rapidly growing population. The system itself, it may be argued, provided against such a contingency by ensuring a heavy death rate from famine and disease, indeed instability arising from a decrease of population was to be feared rather than instability due to an increase. There is no reason to suppose, however, that agricultural production would have been better under a different system, given the general economic conditions of the time. Owing to the lack of transport and the small development of industry and commerce the agricultural population was bound to be mainly self-sufficing and the communal organization, at a time when the stimulus of money making and competition was necessarily absent, did ensure a minimum of efficiency. It must be remembered that the system connoted a certain level of achievement and the very trammels that later on hampered improvements did also prevent undue deterioration. The supervision of the manorial lord and his officers undoubtedly did a great deal to make medieval agriculture as good as the knowledge of the time allowed and in some directions the breakdown of that supervision led to retrogression in agricultural practice. The system was conservative and unprogressive, but the whole of society was the same and there was no outside stimulus to new methods. When society as a whole became unstable and susceptible to new ideas the system was doomed.

Medieval agriculture, like other medieval activities, worked in ignorance of the laws of nature, according to a traditionalism based on immemorial custom in which lingered some faint echoes of classical civilization. Crops were limited in number, implements were crude and inefficient, and the fact that the soil was merely scratched rendered the harvest very susceptible to weather conditions. Worst of all no root crops were known, which meant that in Northern Europe the winter feed for the cattle was woefully insufficient. It consisted in fact of a very limited supply of ordinary meadow hay. This entailed a drastic slaughtering in the autumn of all beasts not required for breeding or draught purposes, so that during the winter only salt meat was available. The few ill-nourished cows could give little or no milk in the winter and so a supply of butter was also salted down. The absence of fresh animal products in the winter was not the only evil of the slaughtering, it also entailed a permanent shortage of beasts for draught and for manure. The small range of crops and the ignorance of any system of rotation, rendered fallowing necessary. Thus a third of the arable land was always lying idle, yielding nothing except a little rough grazing for cattle. In good years the food supply, though rough and unvaried, was sufficient; but bad years came frequently. Harvest failure is not infrequent even in modern times, but in the Middle Ages the poor cultivation and the lack of variety in crops were additional factors of uncertainty, since a good wheat year is often a bad root year and vice versa. In times of harvest failure, not only was the food supply deficient in quantity, but its quality was often such that it would now be declared " unfit for human consumption ". The consumption of rotten and putrid food naturally led to disease.

The English medieval agricultural system gave place to a different one by very slow degrees. On its legal side the manorial system showed signs of change in the 13th century, a tendency for the lord to be transformed into the landlord and for the serf to become a free tenant or a wage earner. The change was, no doubt, hastened by the Black Death and the disturbances which followed it but the fundamental factor was the profitableness of sheep farming. For sheep farming the landowner needed wide stretches of land untrammelled by the grazing rights of others, at the same time the forced labour of serfs became valueless to him. Serfdom rapidly diminished and for all practical purposes became extinct in Tudor times. Status had given place to contract and though agriculture, apart from sheep farming, still remained mainly for subsistence and largely communal, yet the way had been paved for momentous changes in the future. Gradually agricultural production became for a market instead of for subsistence and at the same time communal production was displaced by individualism and capitalism. These changes in organization were accompanied by no less momentous changes in agricultural technique. The change from communal to individual farming is known to historians as the Enclosure Movement. This movement was two-fold, it connoted on the one hand the passing into individual ownership of the great common grazing grounds or wastes and, on the other, the consolidation and hedging of the individual holdings of the arable common fields. The two aspects of the process were closely related, since "the waste" (or common grazing ground) was an integral part of medieval agricultural economy, the inhabitants depending upon it not only for summer grazing for their animals but for fuel and building material. The waste was often wooded and yielded not only fuel and timber but food for swine in the form of acorns or beech nuts. The enclosure of the waste would have made the old system impossible and it was, in fact, generally accompanied by the enclosure of the common fields. But the converse was not true, a considerable enclosure movement of the common fields, carried out by agreement and exchange, went on throughout the 16th, 17th and early 18th centuries and did not necessarily entail enclosure of the common grazing grounds, though it certainly tended to lead to it.

The enclosure movement of the 15th and 16th centuries was

mainly for sheep farming and in Tudor times caused a great outcry. It was feared by the Government and denounced by the Church and was the subject of popular execration both by contemporaries and historians. Modern historical research has shown that though much suffering may have been caused to individuals, the extent of the movement was grossly exaggerated in contemporary popular estimation. According to some authorities, between 1455 and 1607 under 9% of the land was enclosed in the four counties where enclosure was most prevalent,[1] and many parts of the country were hardly touched by the movement.

Any unpopular movement tends to be exaggerated in extent in popular imagination, moreover the movement was concentrated in certain counties and therefore loomed large in those counties. Though some arable was destroyed to " pasture sheep ", the major portions of the huge flocks of the 14th, 15th and 16th centuries must have grazed on land that had never been cultivated, and which was not " enclosed " in any but the technical sense that one man had established grazing rights upon it to the exclusion of others. Sometimes this entailed very serious hardship, but there must have been much rough grazing in excess of manorial requirements, especially after the Black Death. The wars, famines and pestilences of the 14th and 15th centuries, coupled with the progress of the woollen industry both at home and in Flanders, inevitably led to a great increase of pasture farming in this country. A large portion of the land of Britain is better suited, both for reasons of climate and soil, to pasture than to arable but much of it can be used for arable when the necessity arises. Thus every time that there has been a long period alteration in the mutual values of animal products and that of corn, there has been a large scale shifting from arable to pasture or vice versa. Since different types of agricultural organization are adapted to different types of agriculture, so these widespread changes have tended to be accompanied by revolutions in organization.

With the slow restoration of internal peace and good order during the course of the 16th century the pendulum began to swing in the opposite direction. The numerous manor houses, farms and even cottages which survive from the Tudor period point to a re-settlement of the land at this time and it is significant that many of these farm houses and cottages are isolated. This not only marks the restoration of good order but a breaking away from the village community organization. Nevertheless, as late as 1685 three-fifths [2] of the cultivated land of the country was under the open common field system and the enclosure movement was slow for the next eighty years. The land already cultivated in severalty at the end of the 17th century was in part, no doubt, original demesne land which had been so cultivated from medieval times; in part land originally enclosed for sheep farming which had reverted to arable; and in part land which had become separate by the slow process of exchange and agreement and finally " enclosed ". There were also new settlements mainly on the borders of the great moors or " forests " which had never formed part of the manorial system.

The late 16th and the 17th centuries were periods of slow revival in English agriculture. The growth of population both at home and in neighbouring countries led to a reversion to tillage. The small but prosperous towns demanded an increasing quantity of meat, dairy produce and corn. The art of gardening, which had decayed after the break up of the manorial system, revived and was improved under Dutch influence. Prosperous merchants bought country estates and began to instil into the occupation of landowning some of the enterprise of trade. It began to be worth while to write text books about Husbandry and Estate Management, and Norden's Surveyors' Dialogue (1608) [3] had a host of successors. It must not be supposed that the progress was rapid, it was extremely slow and very localized; even at the end of the 18th century Arthur Young found agricultural practice primitive and unenlightened in many parts of the country. The adoption of improvements depended mainly on accessibility to markets, but it also depended upon the nature of the soil and its suitability for particular methods of cultivation, upon the form of land tenure and also, very largely, upon the personality of the influential men of the district.

The 17th century witnessed the re-introduction of marling

and liming, practices which had been common in the Middle Ages but which had fallen into disuse during the period of chaos which followed the Black Death. Renewed attention was also paid to manuring with various materials and two important new plants, the potato and turnip, were introduced, mainly or entirely, it is true, as garden crops, but the way was being prepared for the startling developments of the next century. The greatest agricultural achievement of the 17th century was the large scale draining of marshes. There is a large amount of marsh land in this country some of which had been systematically drained from Roman times. Under the medieval system the necessary dykes were maintained by a special organization and the monasteries in some cases had the work under their care. During the period following the break up of the feudal system many of these works were less well tended and the condition of the Fen country in particular deteriorated, the floodings being made worse by a blocking at the mouths of the rivers. During the Tudor and early Stuart reigns several abortive attempts were made to re-drain the Fens but these attempts were frustrated not only by natural difficulties, but by the determined opposition of the Fen men. These men hated the thought of the wild haunts in which they lived, and from which they obtained a precarious but free living by snaring wild fowl and cutting osier, being turned into fertile fields, the object of laborious and regular toil. However, in 1653 the great scheme of the Dutch engineer Vermuyden was brought to completion and many thousands of acres were added to the cultivated land of the country. The scheme was not entirely successful, much of the land was still liable to frequent bad flooding and the full benefits were not obtained until the end of the 18th century.[4] Nevertheless, some land was reclaimed wholly and some partially, not only in Lincolnshire but elsewhere, notably at Hatfield Chase in Yorkshire. A real beginning was thus made in the movement of marsh draining which went on steadily throughout the 18th century and not only added to the available productive land by thousands of acres but reduced the scourge of malaria to insignificant proportions.

Modern research has shown that, contrary to previously

held opinion, the enclosure movement did not cease during the 17th and early 18th centuries but went on, slowly but steadily, and was, indeed, the object of considerable controversy during that period. Moreover, this enclosure, particularly in the Midlands was, in spite of the growing profitableness of corn growing, mainly for pasture and not for arable. The enclosure, however, was not for sheep but for cattle raising in enclosed fields. At first sight this seems surprising but the fact was that agriculture was being increasingly carried on for a market and in consequence a process of differentiation was setting in. Under the old subsistence farming each district, as far as possible, grew everything it required; under the new system districts more and more specialized upon products for which their soil or the available means of transport rendered them suited.[5] The predominant factor was the London market. Much of the heavy soil of the Midlands was well suited to permanent pasture and the cattle could walk to London independent of roads. On the other hand it was easy for the maritime and riverine counties to transport corn to London or overseas. The common fields could not be turned into permanent pasture without enclosure, but there was no widespread change in the method of arable farming until the middle of the 18th century and, therefore, no overwhelming reason for changing the old organization of that branch of farming. Though corn growing was encouraged by the Corn Bounty Act and there was a good market for corn in London and a fair export trade, cattle breeding was a very lucrative branch of agriculture. London required a large supply of meat and the growing shipping took immense quantities of salted meat, the principal food of the sailor at this period. Moreover, the industry and commerce of London gave a lucrative market for hides, bones and other offal.

In the second half of the 18th century the technique of English agriculture was revolutionized by the introduction from Holland of root crops and clover. The clover rotation abolished the necessity for fallow and, in effect, added one third to the arable land. Turnip husbandry abolished the autumn slaughtering of cattle and fresh animal products became available in the winter. Better farming was rendered possible by an adequate supply of animals for draught purposes and for manure ; selective breeding coupled with good feeding improved both sheep and cattle, while the binding properties of the turnip revolutionized the cultivation of light soils. Under turnip husbandry the great sandy wastes in Norfolk were transformed into some of the best wheat land in England and the promoters of the reform are said to have, in effect, added a province to their country. The new methods spread very slowly in the first part of the century but rapidly in the latter part, a remarkable fact when the notorious conservatism of those engaged in agriculture is remembered. The rapidly growing population provided the necessary stimulus ; in the North, the agriculturists found new and lucrative markets springing up at their doors, in the South, London continued to grow in size and wealth. In both cases canals made easier the transport of agricultural products. In the later part of the century the demands of the army and navy became an important element and, to the natural stimulus of a population growing in numbers and wealth, was added the artificial stimulus of inflated prices and a war demand. The land owning class was keenly alive to its own interest and to what it believed to be the interest of the country, and its political, economic and social power enabled it to push through the changes with rapidity. Good farming was a fashionable and patriotic occupation in which the king himself (" Farmer George ") took part and the landowners by example and precept, and by selection of tenants, introduced changes with a rapidity which would have been impossible with a peasant proprietary. Upon one thing the agricultural reformers were agreed. The old open field husbandry, where it still continued, was an insuperable obstacle to the new methods and that the preservation of the common grazing grounds was a sinful waste. The revolution in agricultural technique was therefore accompanied by a great enclosure movement. Between 1761 and 1801 there were 2,000 Acts affecting about 3 million acres,[6] besides which much land was enclosed by agreement. Private Acts continued until 1845 when a general enclosure Act was passed, but broadly speaking by 1815 the old order had passed

AGRICULTURE

away and the ancient communal subsistence farming had been finally displaced by individualistic capitalistic farming for a market.

Few historical changes have been the subject of so much controversy as the Enclosure Movement. It was the subject of fierce dispute among contemporaries and the occasion of numerous partisan pamphlets and tracts. Nor has the matter by any means yet been translated to the Olympic calm of historical criticism, the rights and wrongs of the long dead actors still seem capable of arousing as much, or more, passion than they did in the hearts and minds of contemporaries. Contemporary controversy raged round every aspect of enclosure, it was even debated whether it increased the food supply or not. Here, at least the historians of all schools of thought are agreed, enclosure undoubtedly increased agricultural production to an enormous extent. The enclosure of the commons and waste, whether for arable or permanent pasture, quite obviously did so. Land which had formerly supported only a few half starved animals was turned into rich corn fields or filled with sleek well fed animals. The productive land of the country was, in fact, added to by many thousands of acres. It is true that the movement was in many cases pushed too far, especially during the war years, and much useless common land was enclosed at great expense, land which was doomed to revert to furze and heath in a few years. This kind of mistake is made in all new movements, it was analogous to the overbuilding of canals and railways. It was largely due to the pressure of the war demand and the stimulus of inflated prices ; under the war conditions it paid to cultivate land which did not feel the plough again until 100 years had passed and war again brought a general dislocation of economic life. The enclosure of the common arable fields also undoubtedly led to increased production. The common field production, with its numerous field paths and boundaries, was wasteful and it tended to a general level of inefficiency, since ill cultivated and dirty land freely infected neighbouring land with weeds. Moreover, any introduction of new crops was very difficult owing to the practice of throwing open the arable to grazing at a fixed date. The introduction of the turnip was particularly hampered by this custom and, as "turnip husbandry" was the battle cry of the agricultural reformers, it is not surprising that they waged war against the common fields. As it was found difficult, if not impossible, to adapt the old organization to the new method of rotation of crops, the new technique seemed necessarily to entail a new organization.

It may be accepted as no longer controversial that enclosure led to a greatly increased production, but here agreement ends, its effect upon the general well being of the people always has been and still is the subject of fierce debate. One school of thought draws a heart-rending picture of thousands of self respecting and prosperous yeomen reduced to penury and subservience and of yet greater numbers of independent cottagers reduced from earning a comfortable living with their cow and geese, to semi-starvation and pauperism. The other school of thought alleges that the commoners were semi-pauperized long before enclosure and that the bulk of them lived a shiftless life, their scanty living often eked out by poaching and petty thieving. And, while the disappearance of the yeoman farmer is, as a rule, regretted, this school of thought holds that it resulted rather from the general trend of economic forces than from enclosure itself. Closely allied with the controversy as to the social effects of enclosure is the question as to whether it led to a decreased rural population. Of contemporary writers, Dr. Price held firmly that it did, while Howlett and Wales held as firmly to the opposite opinion. Dr. Price's opinion that enclosure led to depopulation was part of his general thesis that the population of England was decreasing; in the light of subsequent knowledge Dr. Price was proved hopelessly wrong in his main thesis and therefore his statements and arguments inspire less confidence than those of men who proved to be right in their main contention. The scientific method and careful statements of Howlett and Wales also inspire confidence. Howlett collected statistics of baptisms for two sets of parishes, one set recently enclosed, the other not lately enclosed, each for two periods of five years each, the first period beginning in 1760 and the second in 1775. He found that in 89 parishes recently enclosed the births in the first period numbered 10,804 and in the second 13,138, while in 490 parishes not recently enclosed the births in the first period numbered 52,731 and in the second 57,984 ; in other words the increase of births in the parishes lately enclosed was in the proportion of 100 : 121 while in the other parishes it was only 100 : 109.[7] Howlett published a letter from the vicar of Donington, a village in Shropshire. This was a purely agricultural village which between 1688 and 1782 had grown from 138 to 263 inhabitants. During the period 442 baptisms were recorded and only 263 burials, so it was estimated that 54 persons must have migrated to other parishes. The vicar says that according to " the tradition and testimony of the inhabitants . . . a considerable part of the parish now (1782) in cultivation was formerly overgrown with underwood, broom, furze, etc." The increase in tillage was owing to the increased populousness of the surrounding country and, since the land was better tilled, there was more work. Turnip husbandry had been introduced about 20 years previously and enclosure took place about 12 years before the time of writing. The enclosed common which previously " bore little and bad grass, now produces turnips, clover and grain and cannot be managed without an increase of labour and hands ". Four houses had been erected since the enclosure and their inhabitants represented an additional population of one-tenth.

Of course not too much can be argued from one case and Howlett himself admitted that individual cases could be cited to the contrary, but he thought that they were exceptional. Much depended upon the nature of the enclosure and the purpose for which it was made. Some enclosures were undoubtedly made in order to establish great grazing farms, and where the land had previously consisted partly of arable, such enclosure doubtless led to a decreased population. On the other hand, the enclosure of large tracts of moor, fen and waste must have led to increased population in those areas. It seems likely that the enclosure for ordinary mixed farming also led to an increased population. Enclosure caused additional work in hedging and ditching, and the introduction of turnip husbandry led to a smaller proportion of the land being under grass and to the abolition of fallow. Briefly, enclosure usually had for its object more intensive cultivation and in those days more intensive cultivation meant more labour. Labour saving devices and machinery did not invade agriculture until the middle of the 19th century. Though many agricultural machines were invented at the end of the 18th century, they were not satisfactory and improved models were not brought into general use until 50 years later.[8] During the war, there was undoubtedly an increase in arable farming and this always means a relatively larger rural population. There was some reversion to pasture at the peace, but since a rapidly growing urban population was fed practically without the aid of import or of labour saving devices, the rural population must have been increasing, though of course at a slower rate than the town population. In the decade 1821–31 (one of depression in agriculture) the rural population (including towns under 10,000 inhabitants) increased by $13\frac{1}{2}\%$,[9] that is, by at least as great a rate as the whole population increased when it was mainly rural. The rural population only showed an actual decrease with large scale food imports and the introduction of labour saving devices in agriculture, but even so the actual decrease has been small. The town population has grown while the rural has remained stationary, the decrease of rural population has been *relatively* large but actually small, indeed the population of the agricultural districts increased by roughly one half in the period 1801–61.[10] Since 1861 there has been a small decrease.

It is a fallacy to suppose that the new urban population grew at the expense of the countryside. The migration to the towns is no new phenomenon of the 19th century. Laments as to the consequent depopulation of the countryside go back as early as the 16th and 17th centuries in England and far earlier on the Continent.[11] That the evil was not entirely imaginary is proved by the fact that in all cities up to the end of the 18th century the deaths largely exceeded the births and yet the cities did not decrease but grew, while the total population grew very slowly. Graunt estimated that the annual immigration into London in his day was 6,000 and though too much cannot be built upon this estimate it is not an impossible one. Mr. Weber points out that if it is correct the relative immigration into London was larger in the 17th century than in the late 19th century. Part of the excess of the deaths over births in the cities was due to the growth of the cities by migration; that is, people died in the city who had not been born there. On the other hand the fact that most of the migrants were young people must have swelled the birth rate. Graunt, it is true, says that "few bear Children in London but Inhabitants, the others die there", but this seems far too sweeping a statement to be accepted as even roughly true. It has, however, to be remembered that London in Graunt's time was possibly a malarious city and the greater fatality of malaria to immigrants from non-malarious districts is well known. Smallpox and enteric would also be very fatal to persons coming from districts free from these scourges.

Migration from the village was thus not a new phenomenon, but by the end of the 18th century a very much larger proportion of the migrants survived and produced children who also survived, than in previous centuries. This survival was partly due to the better available food supply resultant on the improvements in agriculture and transport, but it was also due to improvements within the towns, particularly in London. For if it is true that medieval agricultural organization spelt frequent Famine, it is equally true that medieval town organization spelt Pestilence.

CHAPTER VII

Improvement of Towns

It is fashionable to praise the superior civic virtues of the Middle Ages, and on some sides of life medieval civic economy perhaps surpassed the modern, but on the side of cleanliness and convenience such economy can scarcely be said to have existed. In many respects the towns of the Middle Ages were rural communities and, just as the politics of their citizens were often largely concerned with grazing rights and common fields, so the sanitary habits of backward rural communities continued almost unquestioned in their midst. The idea that practices which might be comparatively harmless in a small isolated hamlet, were absolutely fatal to health in a town, was of course totally beyond the ken of their inhabitants. It sometimes seemed unpleasant and inconvenient to kings and rich merchants that the streets should be blocked by acccumulations of garbage or that pigs should run between the legs of their horses, and ordinances would be issued accordingly, but the consequent improvement, if any, seems generally to have been of short duration. To the ordinary citizen such ordinances probably appeared yet another instance of the tyranny of the rich; should the poor man be deprived of his pig to make way for the horses of the wealthy? should the poor man be forced to spend his time carting garbage in order that lords and ladies should not soil their costly garments? The primitive sanitary regulations of medieval towns had arrayed against them that unanimous popular disapproval, manifested by a dogged and persistent passive resistance, against which the strongest government beats itself in vain. Civic sanitation which had died in the dark ages, like so much other knowledge, had to wait until modern times for its re-birth; the horrible conditions of the early 19th century towns were not a result of the new order but a terrible relic of the old.

The streets of medieval towns were generally little more than narrow alleys, the over-hanging upper stories of the houses nearly meeting, and thus effectually excluding all but a minimum of light and air. In the 17th century Bristol, which still remained typically medieval, the average breadth of the streets was under 20 feet and only trucks and sledges were allowed for transport in the centre of the town. In most continental towns and some English ones, a high city wall further impeded the free circulation of the air. The main streets might be roughly and ineffectually paved with cobbles, the rest of the streets, or rather alleys, would be totally unpaved. Rich citizens might possess a court yard in which garbage was collected and occasionally removed to the suburbs, but the usual practice was to throw everything into the streets including the garbage of slaughter houses and other offensive trades. Bye laws against this practice were quite ineffective, as were the regulations ordering citizens to scavenge the street in front of their houses. Filth of every imaginable description accumulated indefinitely in the unpaved streets and in all available space and was trodden into the ground. The water supply would be obtained either from wells or springs, polluted by the gradual percolation through the soil of the accumulated filth, or else from an equally polluted river. In some towns, notably London, small streams running down a central gutter served at once as sewers and as water supply. The dwelling houses of the well-to-do would be of timber, or timber-framed upon a foundation of brick or stone. Even these, picturesque as they appear to a modern eye, seem to have been designed to admit a minimum of light and air. The dwellings of the poor were mere hovels, built of unseasoned wood and with tiny windows. In 17th century London, which before the Fire largely remained a medieval city, the poorer class house had only a covering of weather boards, a little black pitch forming the only water proofing, and these houses were generally built back to back. Thousands of Londoners dwelt in cellars or horribly overcrowded tenements. A small house in Dowgate accommodated eleven married couples and fifteen single persons. Old mansions had been converted into 20 or even 30 tenements.[1] It is possible that the over-crowding was worse at this period than during the Middle Ages but there is no proof of this. Another source of unhealthiness were the church vaults and graveyards, so filled with corpses that the level of the latter was generally raised above that of the surrounding ground. In years of pestilence recourse had to be made to plague pits in order to dispose of the harvest of death. It is not surprising that the deaths in all medieval towns largely exceeded the births, so that the towns only survived by constant recruitment from the country; this drain on the country was supportable, since the town population was relatively very small. But the towns also indirectly decreased the population by acting as forcing grounds for pestilence which spread over the country side.

Early 18th century London was described as a great vortex which annually consumed thousands of persons from the country;[2] another 18th century writer graphically described great cities as the graves of mankind. Yet by this time improvement had begun. As early as the 16th century ordinances as to street cleansing, pig keeping, etc., became more frequent and more drastic. The 17th century discovered that the only way to keep the streets scavenged was to appoint public scavengers and the larger and more advanced towns took this course. The scavengers were generally too few in numbers, did their work inefficiently and probably only attended to the main streets, but the reform was better than nothing. More attention began to be given to the paving of the main streets, though only with cobbles, and lastly and most important of all, attention began to be given to an adequate water supply. The efforts in this direction will be described in the following chapter.

The crucial event of the 17th century from point of view of the public health was the Fire of London. The importance of the Fire has been overestimated in regard to the extinction of Plague but grossly underestimated from every other public health aspect. According to the official report 13,200 houses were destroyed, a large proportion of these being wholly or mainly built of wood; on the same site rather over 9,000 houses were built, all of brick. Before the Fire much had been done to encourage the use of brick, indeed under an ordinance dating as far back as 1189, all party walls in London were supposed to be of brick or stone, as a precaution against fire. But this rule, like so many medieval enactments, was never properly enforced. In the 17th century, however, the growing shortage of timber led to a severe discouragement of new timber buildings and the reign of brick began. Under the London Rebuilding Act of 1667 the city was accordingly rebuilt entirely of stone or brick " as being not only more comely and durable but also more safe against future perils of fire ". The clause, in fact, only re-enacted the Royal Proclamation made immediately after the Fire that " no man whatsoever shall presume to erect any house or building, great or small but of brick or stone ". The different types of houses allowed were strictly laid down in the Re-building Act and the opportunity was taken to widen many streets and to abolish alleys. As is well known, Wren, among others, prepared plans for a stately, model city with wide streets and noble buildings, and the citizens of London have been subjected to much ill-informed criticism for not carrying out this plan. The fact is, that though no doubt physically it would have been easy to rebuild the City upon entirely new lines, financially London was never so little able to undertake grandiose schemes as immediately after the Fire. The country had not recovered from the effects of the Civil War, it was engaged in a disastrous foreign war and the City had just been scourged with a terrible visitation of Plague. Then came the Fire. There was in those days no fire insurance, the loss of his house property and valuable goods fell upon the individual merchant with terrible results ; many persons formerly wealthy were forced to hire themselves as servants, others, less fortunate, languished in debtors' prisons. The great City Companies were bankrupt and only able to rebuild their Halls by selling portions of their valuable land. The Corporation itself was in severe financial straits, unable to pay its debts or the Royal Aid, and even the impecunious Charles was obliged to remit this payment for three years. Indeed the position of affairs was such that some pessimists thought the glory of the City had departed for ever and, though the dogged determination of the citizens refused to harbour such pusillanimous views, it was impossible to contemplate other than a modest scheme of rebuilding. There was no money for large compensation for street widening and from another point of view any large scale scheme was ruled out, it would have meant delay in rebuilding. As it was, the questions to be settled by the special Fire Court were complicated enough ; large scale expropriation and a totally new street plan would have inevitably meant long drawn out negotiations and consequent loss of time. The citizens were most anxious to get to work and earn money as soon as possible and the Corporation was anxious for another reason. The movement westward had already begun, a new residential neighbourhood was growing up, near the Court, in the Covent Garden district and a new shopping centre was forming in the Strand to serve it. Many enterprising shop keepers who had saved something from the Fire immediately opened shops in this district and the City feared that they would never return and that its trade would depart permanently to its hated rival, Westminster. At first there seemed some justifications for this fear ; many of the shop keepers seemed loth to return, in 1672 whole streets of new houses were standing empty ; this reluctance being partly due to the jealous guarding of the privileges of the freemen and to the lower taxes in the out parishes. But the fears were groundless, the geographical advantages of the City, in particular that of accessibility to the shipping below the Bridge, were too great for any disaster to destroy permanently. Though industry tended to move to the out parishes, though the Strand shops managed to survive, the City retained its pre-eminence in the staple trades and in finance. The new City, indeed, was to enter upon a period of pre-eminence undreamed of by the old for, from being the capital and leader of a proud but small and backward nation, it was soon destined to become an Empire City, the world centre of commerce and finance.[3]

The new London which arose slowly and painfully after the great Fire must have served as a model for the whole country. Many a citizen must have returned to his native town dissatisfied with its narrow streets and its over-hanging houses, after a visit to the metropolis with its new imposing public buildings and its neat new brick houses. As a writer in 1801 said, " in a few years the new town rose up like a phoenix from the fire with increased vigour and beauty. Nor did the benefit end there, for it produced in the country a spirit of improvement which had till then been unknown but which has never since ceased to exert itself." [4]

The new City was never quite so unkempt as the old. In 1671 was passed " An Act for the better paving and cleaning of the streets and sewers in and about the City of London ". Under this Act the sanitary responsibility for the City was taken from the parishes and transferred to the Commissioners of Sewers with power to levy a City rate for the purpose. The Fellowship of Carmen undertook the sweeping and cleansing of the streets of all filth which was fortunately at this time becoming a valuable product owing to the extension of market gardening in the environs of the metropolis. The City, in spite of its financial difficulties, spent £80,500 in converting the stinking Fleet river, which had degenerated into an open sewer, into a wide and navigable New Canal.

But in spite of all this, for the next half century the health of the area included in the Bills of Mortality did not improve. Indeed most authorities consider that the death rate of London rose during the first half of the 18th century. There is no reason to believe, however, that the sanitary conditions grew worse, except in so far as the houses in the re-built area were growing older and that, as the City prospered it demanded more workers and therefore over-crowding was probably again on the increase. Contemporary authorities all ascribe the increased death rate, the extent of which was probably exaggerated, to the orgy of spirit drinking which took place during this period. But if there is no evidence of sanitary deterioration there is also very little of improvement before the middle of the century. By then greater London was a rich city, a great centre of wealth and fashion as well as of trade and finance. Widespread reform began and London obtained the reputation which she has never since lost, of being healthier and more convenient than the great cities of the Continent even if inferior to them in beauty and public buildings.

G

Westminster obtained an Improvement Act in 1762 and the City followed suit in 1766. " Fleet ditch was then first covered in : the streets were paved with squared large stones, the sewers and drains were improved ; . . . openings were made in the incommodious parts of the streets ; and cleanliness still further promoted by the more active employment of scavengers, the increased supply of water, etc.; which system has been pursued and is still continued to the great ornament of the town, as well as the substantial benefit of its inhabitants." [5] An earlier writer, discussing the alleged diminution in population suggests that "the London inhabitants are now more widely dispersed . . . formerly the city was close confined and unhealthy". He adds " London streets are now widened, the inhabitants live less crowded together, the houses stand upon double or treble the ground which they formerly occupied, ventilation is freer, the city is more plentifully supplied with water and fuel, both extremely necessary in preserving health . . . the streets are better paved . . . sewers and drains are made to carry of moisture and corruption . . . the better and middling classes of people at least, drink less than formerly." [6]

William Hutton, a native of Birmingham who visited London in 1785, was astounded at what he saw, the lighting seemed to him marvellous, "not a corner of this prodigious city is unlighted." The spectacle at night overwhelmed the provincial with amazement at its marvel and beauty, he wonderingly counted " twenty two candles in one little shop ". He admits, however, that in the daytime, some of the narrow streets with high houses were dark and the light was further obscured by smoke. Nevertheless he says " the stranger will be astonished at the improvements which have been introduced during the last 35 years and how money could be procured to complete them. He will find during that small space, three grand bridges erected, each of which is an honour to the place, and would cost an immense sum. That besides many superb edifices, of a public and private nature, every street and passage in the whole city, and its environs has been paved in one regular and convenient stile ; an expence equal in value to the whole dominions of some sovereign princes . . . As the connexions of the people of Birmingham frequently draw them to London, where they must observe the conveniency arising from open streets, the centers of which are regularly paved and the sides, from one foot to sixteen, according to the width of the street, laid with flat stones, for the benefit of the passenger, it is surprizing they do not, at a humble distance, wish to imitate the Metropolis ".[7]

In reading local accounts of street improvements and so on it is striking to find how London was the criterion; the streets are cobbled, not paved like London, the scavengers do not do their work as it is done in London, and so on. And when Englishmen went abroad, even to the Metropolis of Europe, they could still speak of the superiority of London. Writing from Paris in 1787 Arthur Young says, " this great city appears to be in many respects the most ineligible and inconvenient for the residence of a person of small fortune of any that I have seen; and vastly inferior to London. The streets are very narrow and many of them crowded, nine tenths dirty, and all without foot pavements. Walking, which in London is so pleasant and so clean, that ladies do it every day, is here a toil and a fatigue to a man, and an impossibility to a well-dressed woman . . . I . . . have been myself many times blackened with the mud of the kennels. . . . all persons of small or moderate fortune, are forced to dress in black with black stockings." Arthur Young was speaking in no spirit of blind patriotism, he found much to like and admire in France and goes on in this very passage to say that the social and intellectual life of Paris was far superior to that of London.

Soon many English towns began, in Hutton's phrase, at a "humble distance" to follow London. Between 1785 and 1800 211 Acts for Paving and other Parochial Improvements were passed.[8]

Manchester obtained a Street Improvement Act in 1776 for widening several streets in the centre of the town, for which purpose a public subscription was raised. It was said that the " streets which were then improved had long been a disgrace to the town. They had often doomed the unwary passenger to broken limbs, and sometimes to death; to say nothing of the unwholesomeness of so confined a situation;

for our ancestors had seemed solicitous to shut out the wholesome air of heaven from their habitations." [9] The streets of Manchester in 1775 according to another writer were "no better than a common Dunghill . . . our very churchyards are profaned with filth . . . they are rendered no better than errant draught houses ".[10] But in spite of these conditions there was improvement, or at least no retrogression, the streets were wider, the new brick houses healthier than the old. A writer in 1786 says the relatively favourable conditions would have been even better if the high price of timber and consequent check of building during the American war had not led to severe over-crowding and a consequent increase of contagious fever. But in spite of this set-back he says, "Within these few years also the great alterations that have been made in the town by widening and providing for the ventilation of the streets, together with the commodiousness of our modern houses etc., may have contributed to restrain the increased mortality which might otherwise have been apprehended from its enlargement." [11] About 1780 some improvement was made in the quantity and quality of the water supply and in 1791 an Act of Parliament was obtained for lighting, watching and policing the town. Under this Act the streets were swept and the soil carried off twice every week.[12]

In 1786 Liverpool obtained an Improvement Act under which £150,000 was spent upon opening and widening streets. The Corporation of Liverpool was extremely wealthy, since it owned the manorial rights and therefore was the owner, not only of a considerable amount of land, but also of the port dues. In spite of this the streets in 1760 are described as being narrow, mean, dirty and badly kept. But in 1795 they are described as being well paved, though with cobbles, but the lower part of the town was said to be often flooded. The scavenging was well done, but the soil was raked into heaps and not at once carted away, as in London, but left in great heaps, often for eight or ten days.[13] The lavish expenditure upon public buildings is contrasted with the lack of a proper water supply, the nuisance of projecting cellars and the absence of any expenditure upon education. The amount spent upon public buildings was certainly large but in 1833, when, with the rising tide of democracy, the Corporation was at last called upon to give account of its stewardship, it strenuously defended itself, alleging that all the sums at its disposal had gone in the public service; that between 1773 and 1832 the total expenditure upon public improvements had been £4,439,000 and that the net expenditure upon opening and widening streets had been £645,891.[14] These erections had certainly made Liverpool, compared with other modern English towns, a fine city with noble public buildings and, human motives being notoriously mixed, there can be no doubt that the Corporation felt pride in the achievements and was animated by patriotic zeal. Yet the cynical may reflect that no form of public expenditure gives such scope for the less crude forms of graft as does street improvements and the erection of public buildings. The Corporation was not, however, altogether unmindful of the claims of the poor, it gave large sums to the Infirmary and the Free Schools and lavish charity to relief funds and to individuals.[15] It even attempted to deal with the evil of cellar dwellings. These were considered to be a scandal in Liverpool, even in the 18th century, the projecting entrances being a nuisance that perhaps appealed to some more than the condition of the poor, though a writer in 1810 [16] speaks of the labouring poor " who are almost deprived of the common blessings of light and now languish in noxious cellars ". As early as 1786 the Corporation Council enacted the following order " that in all Leases to be hereafter granted by this Corporation there shall be a proviso to make void such Lease or Leases in case the tenants under such Leases shall let or demise the Cellars thereof as separate dwellings ". This clause remained a standing clause in Corporation Leases but its efficacy was more than doubtful and of course it only applied to buildings upon Corporation land.[17] It was doubtless upon Dr. Currie's suggestion that in 1802 the Corporation attempted to obtain a building Act [18] to regulate the dwellings of the Poor. In this proposed Act there was to be a clause to prevent any cellar being inhabited in which the ceiling was not raised three feet above the curb stone and the door, and to compel white-washing and proper ventilation.

The Bill was lost, possibly because of these clauses so alien to the individualistic spirit of the age. The disgrace of the cellar-dwellings rested with the private citizens and not with the Corporation. In the matter of water supply Liverpool also lagged behind other towns. This was partly due to natural disadvantages (there was no really suitable supply near at hand), partly to legal difficulties caused by an old contract and partly, perhaps, to indifference. In 1786 Liverpool had a population verging on 50,000 and its sole water supply was a few unsatisfactory wells and even these showed signs of exhaustion. Water was brought into Liverpool by carts and sold to the inhabitants and it was stated that "there was often not a gallon of wholesome water for a whole street".[19] The Corporation did not use the powers obtained under the Act of 1786 until 1798. After that there was some improvement but the problem of the water supply was only really solved by the Rivington scheme of 1847 which took ten years to complete.

An Act for "Enlightening and Cleansing the Streets" was brought forward in Birmingham in 1765; it included plans for demolition and there was great opposition by interested persons. Only after a great controversy and numerous public meetings was the Act finally passed in 1769. Under this Act scavengers were appointed and a rate levied; extended powers were obtained in 1773 and 1780. William Hutton alleged that nothing was done by the Commissioners, but he had quarrelled with them over the demolition of some of his property so his testimony is hardly unbiased. It seems probable that like many other persons his zeal for public reform dwindled rapidly when his own purse and convenience were touched.[20]

A Bristol Guide Book of 1794 says "the streets are well paved on each side from street to street". The streets were cleaned twice a week and the footways swept every morning and the Corporation had a full time Inspector of Nuisances. Much of the old town remained, many of the houses being of wood or plaster but all new buildings had to be of brick or stone by Act of Parliament and already some of the most ancient streets had been widened and improved.[21]

if not abolished, malaria and lessened dysentery, while the drier, airier houses had decreased many other diseases. If the death rate was high, it was considerably lower than it had been fifty years earlier, for whereas normally the death rate had always largely exceeded the birth rate in towns, the birth rate at the end of the 18th century in most towns equalled or even surpassed the death rate. The whole position is admirably summed up by Thomas Bateman, who, writing in 1819, brought together the observations of the many able writers of the preceding fifty years :

" In comparing the catalogue of diseases, and the extent of the ravages occasioned by them, as exhibited in the Bills of Mortality, and the writings of physicians of our own times, with those contained in the Bills of the 17th century and in the works of Sydenham, Morton and Willis, to whom we are indebted for the first accurate and comprehensive accounts of the prevailing diseases of London, we are naturally struck with the great diminution of the fatality, and with the total disappearance of some of the most formidable of human maladies, and the comparative rarity of others, in our present annual Bills. While the Metropolis has extended itself in all directions, and multiplied its inhabitants to an enormous amount i.e. while the apparent causes of its unhealthiness have been augmented, it has actually become more favourable to health. In the year 1697, for example, the total mortality in London was 20,970 : whereas the total mortality in 1797 amounted only to 17,014 : and when we take into consideration the great increase of the population of the Out parishes at the latter period, the comparative healthiness of London will appear in very strong colours. But the healthy condition of the metropolis seems to have been more particularly produced within the last 50 years, during which period it has most rapidly increased in extent and population. Until nearly the middle of the 18th century, the mortality kept pace, in some measure, with the advancing population : the average number of deaths annually, from the year 1720 to 1730 was 27,492 ; and the average number from the latter year to 1740 was 26,492 ; but so late as the year 1746 the annual number of deaths was

28,157 . . . The real sources of the unhealthiness of London, at the period when Willis and Sydenham wrote, eluded the observation of those sagacious enquirers, and remained for development by the gradual experience of a more enlightened and scientific age; although, perhaps, that experience has been, in a great measure, the unforeseen result of the necessities of increasing commerce, and of the contrivance of increasing wealth and civilization. This subject may be illustrated by a reference to the condition of an army in camp. The diseases, by which London, in common with all large towns, was almost constantly invested during and previous to the 17th century, were, as we have seen, the plague, malignant, intermittent, and remittent fevers, and dysentery. Now these very diseases, according to the concurring testimony of all military physicians, are the regular endemics of camps, especially in the autumnal season, if they continue for a short time stationary, or are situated on damp or swampy ground . . . . Now a large town is but an extensive camp, so constructed as to be destitute of the means of changing its situation, and therefore liable to be invested with the same diseases, as are endemic in camps, unless the precautions just alluded to be fully adopted. Hence the necessity for the construction of privies, drains, and common sewers, and the advantages of a flowing stream, by which all impurities may be carried off, as well as of an abundant supply of water, for the purposes of cleanliness, and of a hard and regular pavement preserved in a cleanly condition by proper scavengers, etc,, in every crowded town . . . "

" It will not, however, be difficult to prove . . . that those precautions of cleanliness . . . were not sufficiently attended to in London before the great fire nor till upwards of half a century subsequent to that calamitous, though, ultimately beneficial event. And, what is not less convincing as a proof of the pernicious consequences of such inattention, we shall find the health of the inhabitants improving, *pari passu*, and exactly in proportion as these causes of their unhealthiness were removed, while the damps and colds of spring return as heretofore, and the rains and heats of autumn continue ".

" The accumulation of filth and moisture in the streets,

especially the narrow ones, for a considerable period after the great fire, was aided by various circumstances; bad and ill-repaired pavements, obstruction to the free current of air, water from the spouts, the habit of throwing all the refuse of victuals, etc., into the streets, of feeding animals, such as goats, hogs and poultry, in them, etc. Northouck affirms, that no considerable reformation had taken place in the pavement since the fire of London, when the improvements were commenced about 60 years ago in Westminster. The high streets had indeed flat pavements on each side for foot passengers, but these were very negligently repaired. Projecting spouts in narrow old streets still poured their collected rain from the roofs of the houses, impetuously upon the dripping passengers [25]; while in all the streets, large signboards hung across by irons fixed to the fronts of the houses, which, in proportion to the abilities of the shop-keepers, were carried to extravagant degree of ostentation and not only obstructed the view, but also the free circulation of the air: grating the ear with most discordant creaking, as they swung to and fro in windy weather. The middle of the streets were paved with large pebbles, of all sizes and shapes, rough to the horse and uneasy to the rider, which, continually worn by carriages into dangerous holes, the mud lay in too great quantities to suffer the streets to be called clean, except in extreme dry weather, when the dust was as troublesome as the dirt, while wet. Many of the narrower streets continued altogether unpaved, until after the occurrence of the fire; the sewers, at the same time, were in a very neglected state, and the drains all ran above ground. And although the water of the Thames had been partially conveyed to the city, so early as 1582, by a machine erected in one of the arches of London Bridge, by a German engineer, and that important acquisition, the New River, had been brought to the Metropolis in 1613; yet the supply of that great necessary of life, which is now conveyed into every house, continued to be but scantily obtained for many years subsequent to those periods. But if in these general and external circumstances, the Metropolis was in a condition to generate the miasmata, which whether in camps or towns, are exciting causes of endemic diseases; the internal economy of the dwellings was calculated at once to give efficiency to those causes, and to aggravate the diseases which they produced. Indeed, when we compare the domestic habits of our ancestors, with those in our contemporaries, and consider their respective notions in regard to the importance of cleanliness, ventilation, and the close or open situation of their houses, we can no longer be surprised, that the former suffered almost constantly from some endemic or epidemic disease, and that in the 14th, 15th and 16th centuries, (to say nothing of the 17th) few years elapsed, without the occurrence of a considerable pestilence. Erasmus, in a letter to the physician of Cardinal Wolsey, ascribes the Sweating Sickness, and the frequent plagues with which the English were visited, to the slovenly habits of the people and their filthiness both without doors and within. ' The floors ' he says, ' are commonly of clay, strewed with rushes, which are occasionally renewed, but underneath lies unmolested, an ancient collection of beer, grease, fragments of fish, spittle, the excrements of dogs and cats, and everything that is nasty.' In what comparative condition of filth (if a degree of comparison lower than this can now be conceived) must the poor have lived in these times ; the poor who now occupy, in separate apartments, the very houses in the courts and alleys of London, which were formerly inhabited by the rich, even by the Comptrollers of the King's Household !

"After the contemplation of such facts, not a doubt can remain, it is presumed, of the existence of these causes, which the experience of physicians, in camps and hospitals, in ships and prisons, has proved to be adequate to the production and actually to accompany or precede the appearance of the acute diseases in question . . . the gradual and happy amelioration of the health of the metropolis which has been synchronous with the changes of the circumstances above described not only here but in every large town in Europe." [26]

In estimating the achievements and failures in civic administration it must never be forgotten that the rise of the new towns brought with it entirely new problems. Critics of the period generally speak as if virtues formerly possessed had been lost, and as if all sense of civic pride and responsibility was totally lacking in the new communities. This was not true; moreover, medieval cities had never had the same problems to solve.

The city of medieval Europe was not only small but of very gradual growth. The cathedral, the school, the University buildings, the Town Hall, like the spirit which inspired them, grew slowly and unhurriedly through decades and sometimes through centuries. With a stationary, or very slowly increasing population, the necessary institutions for distressed citizens, for education and so on, could be leisurely provided from the bequests of pious and wealthy citizens. Towns which doubled their population in twenty years could not meet their problems upon the same lines. Churches and civic buildings must be erected in months whereas in the past years had sufficed. There was no time to evolve a school of architecture which should be the expression of the new age and its wants and it was, on the whole, a sound instinct which made the best builders of the period turn to the simple, clear cut Greek architecture. After all, the new age was the child of Greece and not of the Middle Ages. The element of hurry meant also that the citizens had to be accustomed to give during their lives and to give continuously, instead of being charitable and public spirited at the expense of their heirs. The difficulties were no doubt added to by the lack of a proper machinery of town government, but the effects of this lack may be easily overestimated. The machinery of administration is no doubt important but its importance can be exaggerated, especially in an undemocratic system. When active members are few and imbued with the right spirit it is possible to achieve a good deal with unwieldy and even with corrupt machinery. It is also possible with an effete machine to have considerable enterprise outside of it. It is not true that the leading citizens of the new towns showed a complete lack of interest in anything except money making or that they were utterly wanting in civic pride. Many towns had grown from an ancient nucleus and civic pride survived amid all the difficulties of the new age, others prided themselves upon newness and freedom. In either case a study of contemporary records shows that pride was there and its work survives. Churches, municipal buildings, hospitals and charitable foundations arose in a short space of years. Nor were the things of the mind entirely neglected, most towns possessed philosophic and literary societies, lending libraries and other institutions for promoting knowledge. It is true that no modern English city has produced an outstanding school of art or literature, but this was also true of the English medieval town. Geographical conditions, even in the Middle Ages, made it inevitable that London should draw to itself the intellectual life of the country, thus making that life national and not local. Modern transport simply confirmed and emphasized this ancient tendency.

But, say the critics, what of the miles of mean insanitary streets, of the gaunt factories and warehouses, of the mass of the citizens untended in body or mind; did the leading men of the transition do anything to prevent these things? This question may be countered by another, what of the dwellings of the poor in the Middle Ages? Cramped, evil smelling, unlighted, hidden in some noisome alley that only a sentimental romanticism could find beautiful; in these dwellings the poor died like flies, their race only surviving through the constant influx from the country. If the men of the new age did not trouble about the dwellings of the poor they were only following in the footsteps of their fathers. But in the medieval town the beauty of the great cathedral hid under its wing the noisome alleys and putrefying rubbish heaps, while in the 19th century town the miles of mean streets swamped the attempts at beauty and dignity in public architecture. Slowly, however, new civic ideals arose in response to the new circumstances. As the population became increasingly urban the heavy death rate in the towns could no longer be a matter of indifference, moreover science was teaching that disease was not a visitation of the Almighty, but largely preventable. In the 18th century came the beginnings of preventive medicine. Wide and well paved streets, at first a matter of civic pride and commercial necessity became increasingly advocated from a public health point of view. Fever hospitals, smallpox prevention, water supply all began to be matters of concern. In the second half of the 19th century civic enterprise, whether corporate or voluntary became more and more a matter of sanitation in its widest aspects, even religious organizations taking part in the sanitary battle. It has been said that in the modern city " large provision is made for health, convenience and education. But ugliness remains a quality of the modern city ". Broadly this is true ; the ugliness is partly the result of size and youth, for our modern cities are still very young and beauty is of slow growth, partly of that very necessary preoccupation with problems of sanitation. Cleanliness may be next to godliness but it is often its rival; we have built drains instead of cathedrals.[27]

CHAPTER VIII

WATER SUPPLY AND DRAINAGE

ONE of the first requisites of public health and convenience is an adequate and pure water supply. Early settlements no doubt were always made at places where drinking water could be obtained easily from springs or rivers; but, as communities grew, they tended to outgrow the local water supply, and the cities of antiquity, like those of modern times, were compelled to bring water from a distance. The remains of great waterworks still exist in Egypt, Mesopotamia, Mexico, Peru and India, but probably these works were primarily for irrigation purposes. Carthage possessed an elaborate system for water supply and the aqueducts of Rome are too well known to need description. Their total length was 381 miles and Rome was supplied by them with water until the 14th century, when they were allowed to fall into decay. Four of them, however, have been restored and supply the city with water at the present day. In two important particulars the problem of the modern water engineer differs from that of his ancient prototype. The ancients had no pumping machinery and no cheap material for pipes capable of withstanding high pressure, they were therefore compelled to find a source of supply at a higher level than the place to be supplied. This often meant a distant source. The advantage of this was that the distant and high source was likely to give pure water and ancient cities were not tempted, as many modern ones have been, to obtain their water from the nearest polluted river. Secondly, the water had to be brought in open conduits, rounding hills (unless the rock was non-porous enough for a tunnel to be possible) and either brought to the head of the valleys or carried across them in aqueducts. The inverted syphon principle, though known, could not be used, since bronze, the only available material capable of withstanding high pressure, was far too expensive

WATER SUPPLY AND DRAINAGE

to be used for such a purpose. The water supply, therefore, was necessarily brought a long distance by circuitous routes, and in spite of relatively cheap labour, at enormous expense.

Medieval cities were small and, except where the Roman works survived, were generally content with a local supply. If the town were situated by a river, as was often the case owing to the importance of water transport, water would be supplied to the town by water carriers. In some places wells and springs were plentiful or small tributary streams ran through the town, other places less fortunate were partially dependent upon rain water stored in cisterns. Water supply must often have been inadequate in quantity and highly deficient in quality in medieval towns, but their inhabitants had not a high standard of cleanliness and had no knowledge of the dangers of pollution. The ancient medical writers, though unaware of the part played by water in spreading epidemic disease, had yet taught that a plentiful supply of clear, sweet tasting water was necessary to health, but this teaching had been forgotten. With the medical renaissance it was revived and re-inforced by contemporary experience. All the 18th and early 19th century writers on public health insist on the importance of a good water supply, though of course the dangers of a polluted supply were very imperfectly apprehended.

Long before the 18th century, however, progressive cities had begun to bestir themselves in the matter of water supply. Even the slow growth of medieval towns tended to outrun the local supplies, wells began to give out, the tributary streams to be choked with filth and garbage and, even in medieval eyes, to become more fitted for sewers than water supply. Open stone or brick conduits were therefore constructed to bring water from some outside source. As early as the 13th century water was brought to London in a conduit from the Tybourn and in the 16th century other conduits were constructed from Dalston and Bloomsbury. Bristol also had an elaborate system of conduits from Brandon Hill, which property had originally belonged to the Carmelite Friars and passed into private hands at the Reformation but was seized by the Corporation in 1654.[1]

Water had to be carried from the conduits to the houses by water carriers, though occasionally a rich citizen would convey water by pipes from the public supply to his house. This was usually detrimental to the public supply and often led to protests. Town records are full of accounts of quarrels as to water rights and wrongs. Another source of complaint was that thoughtless persons found the conduits a convenient dumping place for rubbish, sometimes even to the point of blocking them. About 1660 the Bristol Corporation made four disbursements in three months " for taking dead cats out of conduit head " and this was not an exceptional occurrence; in 1670 a conduit house was built to protect the Head from this nuisance. Conduit water must always have been of doubtful purity in view of the dirt and ignorance of the population, but it was perhaps no worse than much river water.

Some towns were early forced to look far afield for an adequate water supply. In 1240 the Countess of Devon brought water by an artificial channel five miles in length to Tiverton and in 1376 water was brought to Hull from the Aulaby springs. A far more ambitious scheme was successfully carried through by Sir Francis Drake in 1591, when the Leet was completed and presented to Plymouth. The Leet is an artificial channel running from Sheep's Tor to Plymouth, a distance of seven miles but the necessary détours made the channel 24 miles long.

By the end of the 16th century the question of the water supply of London was becoming pressing. An effort had been made to relieve the situation by pumping water from the Thames. The pump was worked by a water wheel fixed to one of the arches of London Bridge; this contrivance, which was a great obstruction to navigation, was the invention of Peter Morice a Dutchman. It was evident, however, that no pumps then invented could supply London adequately from the plentiful waters of the Thames. It was fortunate from the public health point of view that 17th century London, like ancient Rome, was compelled to seek additional water supplies from a distant and high source. After many initial hindrances and financial difficulties Hugh Myddleton successfully carried out in 1613 the long projected scheme of bringing water from Chadwell

Hertford to London. The rejoicings of the projectors and of the citizens of London upon the completion of the New River have often been described. The New River was an artificial open channel which generally crossed valleys at their head, though aqueducts were also used. The springs at Chadwell still form part of the water supply of London, but the New River is now carried in an iron pipe and its length has been consequently shortened from $38\frac{3}{4}$ miles to 27 miles.

Seventeenth century London enjoyed a water supply which, judged by the standards of the time, was good and plentiful. A considerable portion of the city was still supplied with Thames water but the Thames at this period was far less contaminated than it became later. During the 18th century London continued to grow, not only in population but in extent, the New River Company could not serve many of the new districts and numerous new undertakings were formed for the purpose. Though the New River project had been fostered by the City Corporation the undertaking was ultimately carried through by a joint stock company and this precedent was followed ; the water supply of London remaining a matter of private enterprise until the 20th century. Supplying water was not always the profitable undertaking that its promoters had hoped and the shortcomings of many of the water companies were partly due to financial difficulties. These difficulties were enhanced by rivalries between the companies and foolish attempts at competition, but they were primarily due to technical difficulties which were only slowly overcome.[2] Between 1669 and 1806 nine water companies were founded to deal with the water supply of the greater London of that period, of these all but two drew their supply from the Thames. This was made possible by the improved pumps which by 1800 could be entirely worked by steam,[3] the supply of water from a lower to a higher level, of course, connoting pipes instead of open conduits. The original water mains were made of hollowed elm trunks fitted end to end, the length and straight growth of the elm making it peculiarly suitable for this purpose, besides which elm wood withstands the action of water much better than most timber. There was, however, enormous leakage at the joints and these mains could never have withstood a pressure sufficient to maintain a constant supply over the total area supplied. In 1800 the usual system was that each house connected with the mains would be supplied with water for two or three hours on about three days of the week, when tanks and cisterns would be filled. To people at the time this did not appear as unsatisfactory as it does to us. A guide book writer in 1802 says with pride, " Water is conveyed three times a week into almost every house by leaden pipes and preserved in cisterns or tubs in such quantities that the inhabitants have a constant and even lavish supply." [4] In better class houses with adequate storage facilities the system was possible, but the condition of affairs was different in poor districts where one tap probably served a whole court or street and where proper storage facilities would be lacking. Contemporaries, however, were more exercised by the danger of the system in case of fire. If a fire occurred in a district not being served with water at the moment, a messenger had to be despatched to the water company, whose officials then shut off the supply from the district where it was running and turned it on to the district where it was required. By the time the water arrived the house was probably burnt down.

The dry periods had the further disadvantage, from a technical point of view, of shortening the life of the mains. The perpetual difficulty with the mains and the uncertainty of the early steam engine led to constant breakdowns even in the intermittent supply enjoyed by most householders. Evidence was given to the Parliamentary Commission held in 1810 that in the west and north west of London the water supply sometimes failed for two or three weeks in succession. It is to be hoped that the owners of private wells came to the assistance of their less fortunate neighbours during these periods. Industrial change, however, had made a new material available for mains. Iron pipes were first used about 1746, and the Chelsea Water Company, one of the more progressive of the London companies, introduced iron mains between 1756-60. The New River Company was still employing wooden mains in 1802, but the pressure in this area was less

WATER SUPPLY AND DRAINAGE

since the water was brought in an open conduit to the Head at Sadlers Wells and the mains only had to distribute from there to districts at a lower level. In 1802, however, the Company was attempting to supply some new districts lying at a higher level than the Head and for this purpose employed one water and two steam engines. Later a new basin at a higher level was constructed to supply Marylebone and the Tottenham Court Road, which lie higher than the Head at Sadlers Wells, and by 1821 the New River is stated to have had "some iron mains".[5] But as explained, the problem was less urgent in the case of this company and iron mains may be said to have become general between 1810 and 1820.[6] In 1817 an Act was passed requiring that after ten years all new mains should be of iron.

The new iron mains, though an improvement, were by no means perfect, the jointing was very defective and hence there was still enormous wastage. This wastage made an intermittent supply a necessity in places where the sources of supply were limited; even in the middle of the 19th century many water authorities after attempting a constant supply were compelled to abandon it owing to the wastage. From a technical point of view alone a constant supply was desirable, since an intermittent supply means unequal pressure and is an additional strain on the joints, while iron pipes corrode much more rapidly if not kept filled. But only in the second half of the 19th century was a satisfactory system of jointing evolved and a practical system of waste detection devised. Unless, therefore, a water authority had at its disposal a very abundant source, an intermittent supply was a necessity, and with the rapidly growing towns of the mid 19th century an abundant source was by no means the rule. The consequent intermittent supply led to the impossibility of the free and plentiful use of water, so necessary for public health, and also to the frequent possibility of the contamination of the water during the necessary storage by the householder. It also held another danger, which was not appreciated at the time. When the defective mains lay empty, water from the surrounding soil often percolated into them; this water was often contaminated surface water, it might even be the overflow of a cesspool. When water drainage became general it was no uncommon thing for the sewers and water mains, both defective, to run near to one another and for water from the sewer to find its way into the water main.

In London, however, the supply was so contaminated at the source that any further contamination might appear immaterial. Even the New River was far from perfect. Probably the open channel had always been used by the people living near it for bathing and washing clothes, but the 17th and early 18th centuries were not pernickity in these matters. By 1800 more enlightened persons began to object to this contamination, which had doubtless become worse owing to the growth of a populous district to the north of the Head. A writer of that date complains that the water was polluted by bathing and by the throwing of filth into it, especially in the neighbourhood of Islington, and adds that the New River Company ought to take steps to prevent the scandal.[7] The New River Company might, perhaps, have retorted that their water was clean compared with that of the Thames, with the water of which the majority of Londoners were supplied; the New River in 1821 supplying 50,000 houses out of an estimated total of 160,000. To understand the terrible condition of the Thames during the first half of the 19th century it will be necessary to consider the history of the problem of sewage disposal and to treat that not very savoury subject with some degree of frankness.

Drainage is concerned with three problems: (1) the reclaiming of marshes and fens, (2) the disposal of storm and flood water, (3) the disposal of liquid refuse, both human excreta and the waste of certain industries.

In modern times the two last objects may be achieved by a common sewerage system and the third has become the predominant problem; but this is a development of the 19th century.

Many cities of antiquity had elaborate systems of drainage. It is possible that, as in modern times, a system originally designed to deal with flood water was afterwards utilized for other purposes. But though the draining of the cities of antiquity is interesting the modern historian can ignore it, for, as in so many other spheres of human endeavour, the problem had to be solved afresh. In the drainage of the marsh lands, however, the lessons taught by the Romans seem never to have been entirely lost in this island. It seems probable that parts of Romney Marsh and the Lincolnshire fens were continuously drained from Roman times. It was only in the 17th century, however, that large scale draining was attempted upon Dutch methods, and this form of enterprise continued throughout the 18th century. It added thousands of acres of fertile land to the country and reduced malaria to negligible proportions. Where the marshes had existed near towns the draining, of course, added to the healthiness of the town population.[8]

Until modern times floods were a serious problem to all riverside populations. Though the English rivers were not capable of the wholesale and dramatic slaughter of those of China and India, yet they could sweep away hundreds of fragile homesteads, drown cattle (and occasionally human beings) and destroy property. Moreover, when the floods subsided the undestroyed dwellings were left damp and noisome. The citizens of the larger riverside towns, for example London and Bristol, early devised elaborate schemes for dealing with flood water. The use of these sewers for any other purpose than the disposal of rain and flood water was never contemplated by their constructors, indeed such a use was originally illegal. These early sewers were not as a rule capable of effectively protecting from flooding low lying portions of the town in the time of exceptional rain or tides. Only with the invention of the steam engine was it possible to achieve a satisfactory sewerage system in low lying places and even to-day occasional flooding occurs in some towns and districts. Until modern times even the disposal of ordinary rainfall in towns was most unsatisfactory. The gabled medieval houses had no gutters, the side streets and alleys were often totally unpaved, only the principal streets being cobbled. Down the centre of the street ran the street gutter, which was often the course of a rivulet or stream. Since the cobbles were generally kept in ill repair and since all kinds of refuse was thrown into the street, clogging the central channel, the condition of affairs during or after wet weather can be easier imagined than described. Pools of stagnant water formed happy breeding grounds for the carriers of malaria and enteric and even contemporaries occasionally complained of the stench and dirt. The introduction of the house gutter with a proper gully pipe enormously eased the problem, also a better arrangement of street channels accompanied the improved paving of the mid 18th century.

The last problem, that of the disposal of sewage in the more modern and restricted sense was infinitely the most difficult and its solution was protracted. In the Middle Ages the administrative problem was simply one of scavenging, since *all* refuse, including human excreta, was thrown into the street. The town authorities sometimes forbade this practice, but such bye laws were generally a dead letter since no alternative method of disposal was provided, except that rich citizens possessing a yard or court sometimes accumulated refuse in an open cesspool which was emptied at very infrequent intervals. Citizens were admonished to sweep the portions of the street in front of their houses, but these orders also were treated with contempt. In 14th century Paris everything was thrown from the window to the cry of " Garde l'eau." This practice was forbidden in 1372 and again in 1395. In 1513 the Coûtume de Paris ordered that every house should have a privy and this ordinance was frequently re-enacted up to 1700. Similar orders are to be found in the Coûtumes of other French towns. But even in the 18th century in many Continental towns everything was still thrown into the street and in Madrid the royal residence had no privies in 1773 ; a contemporary writer asserting that the sanitary arrangements of the Spanish Royal Palace were inferior to those of many savage tribes.[9]

In England in the 18th century, judging from literary references, privies seem to have been usual in better class houses, even in country districts, and in London an elaborate system of emptying had been developed. Pringle writing in 1752 said the privies of London were well regulated ; he was speaking, of course, according to the standard of his time. This relatively good regulation was due mainly to the fact that, owing to the increasing profitableness of growing vegetables and fruit, 18th century London was surrounded by market gardens. These market gardens required a large quantity of manure and it was no longer necessary to pay scavengers and night soil men ; contractors were eager to obtain the privilege of collecting the valuable refuse matter. By the middle of the 18th century the better parts of London were tolerably scavenged and in better class houses the privies were emptied at night by the night soil men. Even in the poorer districts the value of all refuse probably often led to its removal, even if at irregular and too infrequent intervals. In any case, horrible as the arrangements, even in wealthy households, would appear to a 20th century Englishman, England in the 18th century was ahead of her neighbours in sanitation. Smollett complains of the filth of the French privies where they existed, and of their frequent absence. In Edinburgh privies were unknown and the good old medieval custom of throwing everything into the street to the cry of " Gardy Lo " still flourished. It is a relief to hear that there were public scavengers.[10]

If properly carried out the best methods of the mid 18th century were not necessarily insanitary. It is not pretended that they ever were well carried out, except perhaps in a few well to do districts in London, but it is suggested that the next apparent advance was probably in reality retrogression and that an improvement of the old methods might have been better. In the latter half of the 18th century a crude form of the water system was introduced in London. It was apparently cleaner, the best sanitary opinion of the time applauded and wealthy householders and enlightened institutions hastened to adopt it. Howard (Lazarettos, 1791) frequently mentioned water closets in connection with hospitals, sometimes noting their non-existence sometimes their existence, satisfactory or otherwise, but evidently he considered them a necessary part of the equipment of a well managed hospital. He noted that the new wards at Guy's possessed water closets of the best construction and " not in the least offensive ", and that by opening the door the water was turned into them.

The improved water closet was the invention of Joseph Bramah

(1748–1814), the inventor of the Bramah lock. His biographer states that " Part of his business consisted in putting up water closets, after a method invented or improved by a Mr. Allen but the article was still very imperfect ".

Bramah being laid up by an accident had the leisure to think out a better method, which he patented in 1778; later he improved his invention by the addition of a water cock, patented in 1783. " The merits of the machine were generally recognised and before long it came into extensive use continuing to be employed with but few alterations until the present day." [11] His circumstances improving with the increased use of his invention, Bramah proceeded to undertake the manufacture of the pumps, pipes, etc., required for its construction. As usual the patent was attacked by pirates as soon as it became productive, but Bramah successfully defended it in the Courts. At first the new closets emptied into underground cesspools or, in the case of large buildings, vaults. This method avoided the trouble and inconvenience of frequent visits of the night soil men, who were often dirty and inefficient, but the stagnant filth in cesspool or vault, which were only emptied at very infrequent intervals, became a source of infection and unpleasantness. As late as 1847 a Dr. Lankester stated at a public meeting that he thought that the refuse from his own house was carried away with a drain but, some repairs being necessary, on examination, he found, to his surprise, that under his very feet was a cesspool 25 feet deep charged with decomposed matter which had probably remained in that state for 25 years. At the same meeting another speaker stated that many cesspools in Westminster were very offensive and frequently overflowed.[12] As this system spread to the country, contamination of the water supply became frequent in the neighbourhood of large houses. The difficulty and danger of underground cesspools in neighbourhoods with no main drainage remained a problem until the end of the 19th century; a problem perhaps not completely solved even to-day.

In the meantime, in cities which possessed a drainage system the custom sprang up of connecting the water closets with the drains, which of course had never been devised for that purpose.

As early as 1794 a writer on Bristol [13] says, " the ground under the surface is perforated with drains and common sewers in all directions and the two Rivers . . . receive and carry off all the filth and its noxious effluvia. Perhaps there is not a home which has not a communication with the main sewers, a possession of cleanliness, not so universal in any City in the World." It seems probable that the sewers were often used as a convenient way of disposing of filth apart from the use of the water closet. A writer on London in 1802 says " Underneath the pavements are large vaulted channels called sewers, which communicate with each house by smaller ones and with every street by convenient openings and gratings to carry off all filth that can be conveyed in that manner into the river." [14] " Each house " must not, of course, be interpreted literally ; the above description can only have applied to the houses of the well-to-do and to certain parts of the town. In the City such a use of the sewers was forbidden and often prevented, while in parts of London there were nothing but open drains or cess-pools forty years later. In Westminster, the Ranelagh [15] and King's Scholars Pond sewers were still open in 1847. Nevertheless the adoption of the water closet undoubtedly increased the tendency to use the sewers, whether open or closed, for the disposal of dejecta. A Mr. W. Haywood, engineer to the Corporation of London, stated that water closets became general in houses of the better class in London about 1828, and " the entire discharge of the dejecta from the houses in which the water-closets were fixed in many cases took place "—but this was often prevented by the Commissioners of Sewers—(the closets) often discharged into " cesspools having overflow drains just beneath their doming, by which means the solid matters were deposited and the supernatant liquid only ran off ; but gradually the mode of construction crept in and the entire refuse of the better class of new houses flowed by the drains into the public sewers." In 1849 for the first time the discharge into the City sewers was legalized and upon notice such discharge was made legally compulsory.[16]

The sewers themselves discharged into the river and the Thames, polluted for years by shipping and the inhabitants of riverside dwellings, became, under this new assault, nothing but a vast and stinking open sewer. The windows of the Houses of Parliament could never be opened because of the stench and the world of Fashion forsook Westminster and Chelsea for more salubrious neighbourhoods. The public health reformers of the mid 19th century give in their reports lurid details of the sanitary condition of the dwellings of the poor but, in the light of modern knowledge, it seems probable that the drained houses of the rich were a greater menace to public health than the primitive filth of the slums. By the "improved drainage" the water supply of large sections of the community was contaminated on a vaster scale than ever before. Unfortunately the new experiment coincided with the arrival of Asiatic cholera, a disease spread mainly by the contamination of water supply. No hospital segregation availed to stay the infection, since as Farr says, "the water closet throws into the sewer the evacuations of the sick" and it might be added the sewer threw them into the river from which the water supply was drawn. Farr goes on to say "that almost coincidently with the first appearance of epidemic cholera and with the striking increase of diarrhoea in England was the introduction into general use of the water closet system". The degree of the pollution of the drinking water of London may be gathered from the fact that until 1848 the Lambeth Company had its intake at Battersea and Charing Cross and in 1850 the Chelsea Company had its intake within a few feet of the mouth of the Westbourne, which at this time had become the Ranelagh common sewer. The Lambeth Company removed its intake to Surbiton in 1848 and in 1852 Parliament, stirred by the cholera epidemic, compelled all companies to take their waters from above Teddington Lock this Act also made the filtration of all river water compulsory. In justice to the Lambeth and Chelsea Companies it must be stated that they had filtered their water and that the filter devised in 1828 by their engineer, Mr. James Simpson, has been since only improved upon in small details. Chemical analysis however, had failed to reveal any alteration in the water owing to filtration and it was apt to be looked upon as a luxury unless the water was very dirty. It was only at the end of the 19th century that it was discovered that bacteria are stopped by the fine film of mud and microbes formed above the sand filter bed and that the worse the condition of the sand filter bed, in the ordinary acceptance of the term, the better it was as a bacteria filter. Even more important was the discovery that water is purified by storage.

The history of the water supply of London cannot be taken as entirely typical. The immense size of the metropolis and the fact that an abundant river flowed through it, made its problem to some extent unique. But it may be safely said that all the growing towns were faced with a water problem during the first half of the 19th century. If the supply were drawn from a river it was likely to be increasingly contaminated from the mere growth of the town and later from the increasing use of water drainage. If the supply were drawn from local wells or springs it was apt to run dry or to be inadequate for the growing population and was also in danger of contamination. Such towns found in their very difficulties their ultimate salvation, for like the ancients they were compelled to seek distant and pure supplies.

Broadly speaking it may be said that the household water supply was increased in quantity in most towns during the 18th century. The houses of the well-to-do were actually connected with the mains and convenient stack pipes were erected in the poorer districts. The quality of the new supply was very variable. In some districts it was contaminated at the source, in others it was superior to the old wells and springs, which, if surface ones, were likely to have been polluted in populous districts. In this connection it has to be remembered that water was not a usual beverage in the 18th century, even charity children were given small beer. It was from the point of view of cleanliness that the increased supply, even if polluted, was so important. All contemporary authorities refer to this, especially in regard to London. Sanitary arrangements also were improved during the 18th century; the water system, the early results of which were not altogether fortunate, was not general until after our period. In accordance with the general tendency of the age both the provision of water supply and the collection of refuse were matters for private enterprise. The local authorities sometimes paid street scavengers, but even this duty was often delegated to contractors in return for the saleable rights in the valuable refuse. The improved conditions were due, therefore, partly to the advance in agriculture which made all kinds of manure valuable; partly to the advance in joint stock enterprise, which enabled money to be found for water undertakings; partly to the increasing wealth, which provided money to be invested on the one hand and money to pay for decency and comfort on the other. But it was also due to increasing knowledge, not only knowledge as to steam engines and pumps but also knowledge as to the importance of cleanliness from the point of view of health. Undoubtedly many of the promoters and shareholders of the early water companies were actuated not so much by a desire for profit as by the wish to improve the water supply of the district in which they lived. That the knowledge which prompted such action was available was due to the advance in medicine, an advance which has been ignored in most histories of the period.

CHAPTER IX

The 18th Century Doctor and the British Pioneers of Public Health

" Dans mon art, je n'ai pas copié, comme on le croit, les figures des vases grecs, des frises ou des peintures. J'appris d'eux à regarder la nature ".

ISADORA DUNCAN.

MODERN medicine is a child of the Renaissance and of that independent study of science which preceded the rediscovery of Greek literature. It belongs to that great re-birth of the human intellect of which the study of Greek literature at the source was only a part; though a part which infused a new spirit and outlook into the whole. Medieval medicine, like other medieval thought, was bound fast in traditionalism, it was content to repeat very debased and imperfect renderings of the ideas of the ancient Greek physicians, with a certain admixture of Arabian ideas. The importance of the study of the ancient medical writers at the source lay, not in the recalling of forgotten facts, but rather in the infusing of a new spirit into medical studies, a spirit of enquiry and freedom, of clear cut and questioning thought, above all in a return to the observation of Nature. The cradle of the renewed learning in medicine, as in other branches of knowledge, was in Italy. In Italy important schools of medicine had existed throughout the Middle Ages, anatomy was studied in the 11th century and public dissections took place as early as the 12th century; and there too, during the Renaissance, many modern medical ideas were anticipated by Fracastoro and others.[1] In France also there were ancient medical schools that were justly famous. But though the ground was being prepared there was little change in the actual practice of medicine until the 17th century, for it was not until Vesalius revolutionized anatomy and Harvey had made possible modern physiology, that modern medicine could begin. Even then the new knowledge did not conquer suddenly or dramatically. Traditionalism and medievalism retained much of their influence in medicine during the 17th century and even in the early 18th century. In the 16th and 17th centuries thought had so broken its medieval fetters in the realms of literature that it is difficult to realize that in some branches of knowledge it was still in bondage. It was not until the middle of the 18th century that the broad conception of an immutable order in nature became part of the mental heritage of all educated persons, a conception that was of immeasurable importance in the study of medicine. Whoever glances through the index to the medical transactions of the Royal Society (founded 1660) cannot fail to be struck with the contrast between the titles of the papers of the first fifty years and those of the subsequent ones. The earlier papers are mainly concerned with marvels and curiosities while the subjects of the 18th century are similar to those which would be discussed in a modern medical society. Even in the year 1720 a woman in Godalming declared that she was giving birth to rabbits, and several doctors, including the King's anatomist, believed her story.[2] Twenty years later no doctor could have been thus deceived. The scientific age had begun. The study of anatomy and physiology proceeded apace both in England and on the Continent, but the advance in knowledge of the human frame and its mechanism did not have any immediate outstanding result in diminishing human suffering except, and it is an important exception, in the practice of obstetrics. The art of the surgeon, which was ultimately to achieve such marvels, was held back until the discovery of anaesthetics and still more until Pasteur and Lister had laid bare the cause of, and cure for, septic wounds. The earliest triumphs of modern medicine were not so much due to advance in pure theory as to advance in practice in what may be called the departments of nursing and hygiene. But none the less the advance was scientific, since it was due to correct and detailed observation, to constant endeavour to classify correctly, to willingness to break away from tradition and to experiment, all of which is the mark of the scientific attitude. Diseases, especially fevers, were diagnosed and classified and if the new methods of treatment often entailed nothing more than the application of fresh air and soap and water, this advocacy at the time, was bold in the extreme.

The 18th century doctor has some reason to complain of the historian, whose popular picture of him is of a pompous ass in a large wig, sniffing a knobbed stick, while he tries to look wise and to conceal his ignorance under a flow of meaningless technical terms. Even the medical historian dismisses 18th century medicine as making no significant contribution to medical science and as being sunk in formalism.[3] It is, however, dangerous to learn history from the satirists, the greatest admirer of Mr. Bernard Shaw would not claim that a complete picture of modern medicine could be constructed by posterity from a study of his works. The satirist speaks pre-eminently for his own time, he stresses that which the ordinary man overlooks or tries to hide; he does not profess to give the whole picture, he can leave that to his readers. The very esteem in which the 18th century doctor was held by most of his contemporaries made his shortcomings a worthy object of satire. No doubt there were toadies and fools in the ranks of the physicians of the 18th century, there always have been such in all professions at all times. No doubt many of the trappings of the medical profession seemed foolish to a rational mind, but convention is strong and, moreover, modern psychology teaches us that such trivialities are not without their uses. By methods varying from the make-up of the primitive medicine man, to "a good bed-side manner", mankind in different ages, in different ways, has been re-assured in sickness by the presence of a person who, by some peculiarity of dress or speech, is associated with the power of healing. Again, the 18th century doctor no doubt often looked wise when he felt extremely ignorant and prescribed treatment which in the light of 20th century knowledge is absurd. But is the 20th century doctor never baffled under a calm and hopeful exterior ? Will all his treatment be endorsed by future ages ? No doubt the rational and superior person would say that the doctor ought, when medical knowledge fails, to address his patient somewhat in this fashion, " My dear sir, I perhaps can give a name to your complaint but I cannot do more. I can do nothing whatever to help you, you will probably die, but Nature may effect a cure, for which, of course, I could claim no credit." The practical doctor of all ages, who has always practised much that modern psychology teaches, would know that if the patient believed such a speech it would be tantamount to murder, while if he did not he would call in another practitioner with less honesty and more wisdom. The doctor must at all costs give the ordinary patient the first requisites of recovery, hope and faith. In the 18th century, when in doubt, he prescribed to this end a nauseous mixture and a bleeding, in the 20th he gives a vaccine injection, and Nature in both cases might effect a cure or the treatment might happen, by a lucky accident, to be right. Of course the list of diseases the correct treatment of which was undiscovered was very much longer in the 18th century than it is at present, and the field for " eye wash " and quackery was therefore much larger. It must be confessed that the 18th century doctor was unduly fond of both " purging " and bleeding, but it has to be remembered that he had to deal largely with patients who had eaten or drunk too much or both.[4] To imagine, however, that these were the only treatments given by the 18th century doctor or that he was complacent in his ignorance, is only possible to those who are unacquainted with medical writings of the period. It is, of course, almost impossible to evaluate a whole profession over the course of a century, and in the 18th century the medical profession was not one, but three. The unfortunate rivalry and the difference in social status between the physician, the surgeon and the apothecary, due to historical causes, undoubtedly held back the advance of medicine. In England the unsatisfactory nature of the training received by many doctors and the corruption and inefficiency of some of the examining bodies also made the difference between the qualifications of different practitioners very great. No wonder the modern student, viewing the corruption and inefficiency of professional organization, remembering the satirists' pictures of the hypocritical fashionable physician, of the illiterate brutal surgeon, of the subservient apothecary with his rule of thumb knowledge remembering also the antiquated and inelastic theoretical framework of knowledge upon which all of them worked, has dismissed 18th century medicine as negligible. But " by their fruits shall ye know them " and the 18th century has no cause to be ashamed of these. It is true the 18th century did not produce a Vesalius, a Harvey or a Pasteur ; no genius made the dry bones of its system live, no revelation gave a new and inspiring outlook upon the problems to be solved. Its achievements were not in the realm of theory, but in practice ; but here they are unquestionably greater than those of any preceding century. An age which made a real beginning in preventive medicine, which banished plague, which wiped out scurvy, which taught the correct method of avoiding malaria, typhus and smallpox and which succeeded in checking these scourges to a considerable degree, an age which revolutionized midwifery and infant nurture, such an age has no reason to hold its head.

How came this fruit from formalism, corruption and inefficiency ? The answer lies mainly in the individualism of the 18th century. These achievements were made not because of the conditions, but in spite of them. The 19th century troubled greatly about the machinery of government, it spent a great deal of time in breaking down obstructions and building theoretically correct frameworks ; the 18th century walked round the obstructions and ignored theories when convenient. Much depended on the individual, the ambitious and the conscientious medical student worked and studied, eager for knowledge, without the compulsion of exacting examinations. This spirit was carried into life. The eager student could also find good teachers if he sought them, men as keen to teach as he to learn, and however formalistic the framework of medicine, at least the importance of clinical observations would be impressed upon him. The results show that the formalism left the best minds extraordinarily free and plastic on the practical side.

The method of clinical instruction in hospitals originated in Italy and was introduced at Leyden University by Franciscus de le Boë called Sylvius (1641-72) and was there developed by Herman Boerhaave (1668-1738) with momentous results. The little hospital at Leyden which served the medical school had only twelve beds, but it became the centre of medical instruction in Europe. Herman Boerhaave was perhaps one of the greatest medical teachers who has ever lived. Doctors and medical students from every country in Europe attended his lectures and it is not too much to say that every doctor of note in the next generation had come, directly or indirectly, under his influence. His fame was truly European, for it is said that a letter sent to him by a Chinese mandarin addressed " To the learned doctor Boerhaave, Europe ", reached him safely. Boerhaave's name is associated with no great discovery or new line of thought, his published work excites surprise in modern commentators, who seek there in vain for the cause of his contemporary fame. His gift was no doubt that of personality rather than of outstanding intellect.[5] His example should be a constant reminder to all teachers that the primary function of their art is not to impart facts, but to exercise their pupils in the difficult feat of ordered and logical thought and to inculcate a habit of mind at once receptive and discriminating. That attitude of mind which Boerhaave inculcated, which sought truth everywhere, in the writings of the ancients, in science, in history, in the experience of untaught sailors and the idle talk of ignorant dairymaids, but above all at the bedside of the patient, that attitude bore fruit ten thousand fold in the work of his pupils and his pupils' pupils. Boerhaave did not dethrone the knowledge of the ancients but he directed his pupils to regard it critically and to combine it with the new knowledge of anatomy, physiology and other branches of science which was in his time growing apace. The clinical method of instruction which he constructed and organized was continued in the noted School of Medicine of Vienna which was founded by his pupil Geerad van Swieten, and in Britain by another group of his students who founded the equally famous medical school of Edinburgh (about 1725). For the clinical method to be developed at its best the co-operation of two institutions was necessary, a University and a General Hospital, and the Edinburgh Infirmary was founded in 1736 as a necessary corollary to the foundation of the School of Medicine. In London, since there was no University there was no organized school of medicine, while

THE PIONEERS OF PUBLIC HEALTH

Oxford and Cambridge failed to develop really satisfactory schools of medicine, partly owing to lack of opportunity for clinical instruction and partly to the general state of those Universities. There can be no doubt that the progress of medicine in England was much hampered by these facts. The ordinary English method of training a doctor was by apprenticeship, and though often a conscientious and able master could and did teach his pupil a good deal of practical importance, the method at its best was not conducive to a scientific habit of mind or to the dissemination of new ideas. At its worst the apprentice spent most of his time running errands or making pills, not only learning nothing but acquiring habits of mental idleness and moral laxity. After the expiration of his apprenticeship, the budding doctor usually went to London or some other large town and became a pupil at one of the numerous private venture schools of medicine. The tuition provided very often included visits to the hospitals under the guidance of the teacher and in the early 19th century "walking the hospitals" had become in London a normal part of the young doctor's training. The quality of the instruction received at the different private schools varied very much, there were some brilliant men whose teaching and personality left a lasting mark on their pupils and on the development of medicine. Hunter the anatomist and Smellie the obstetrician may be mentioned as examples. The best of them, however, were specialists and unless a young man went from school to school his training, one suspects, was apt to be one-sided. A clever, earnest student no doubt sought out good masters and profited by their tuition but many a lazy rascal, after idling through his apprenticeship, must have idled through another year or two in London under an indifferent master and then gone out into the world to spread darkness instead of light. It is significant that practically all the British doctors who advanced medicine in the second part of the 18th century and the early 19th century received the whole, or the greater part of their training at one of the organized schools of medicine attached to a University, either on the Continent or in Scotland. Edinburgh was the Alma

Mater of a very large proportion of them and therefore, naturally, a very large proportion of them were Scotsmen though, in spite of the prejudice of the time, many Englishmen availed themselves of the advantages provided in the sister kingdom. But though undergraduate work was probably less satisfactory in London than in other centres, it was an excellent field for post-graduate work. It offered lucrative employment among the rich and opportunities in its numerous hospitals and dispensaries for observation of the diseases of the poor. The College of Physicians (founded 1520) and the Royal Society formed excellent media for the propagation of new ideas, and so in the 18th century as now, London was the Mecca of the successful doctor.

As in other spheres, personality counted for a great deal in the medical world of the 18th century. It will not be out of place, therefore, to give a few biographical details of the men to whom the advance in public hygiene was mainly due. References to their work will, moreover, recur frequently in these pages.

War was a great stimulant to advance in medical practice and the origins of modern public hygiene must be sought in the departments of naval and military hygiene. In this connection two names stand out pre-eminent, those of John Pringle and James Lind. Sir John Pringle [6] (1707-1782) was the youngest son of a baronet of Roxburghshire. After a year at Edinburgh University he went to Amsterdam to gain a knowledge of business, he being intended for a commercial career. He happened, however, to visit Leyden and to hear a lecture by the famous Boerhaave and thereupon determined to devote himself to medicine. He graduated at Leyden and afterwards studied in Paris. He then practised for a time in Edinburgh, but in 1742 was appointed physician to the Earl of Stair, then commanding the British forces on the Continent, and physician to the troops in Flanders. He served in this capacity throughout the German campaign and also throughout that against the Young Pretender. He then settled in London, was made a Licentiate of the Royal College of Physicians, became President of the Royal Society and enjoyed the patronage of the royal family. In 1752 he published his "Observations on Diseases of the Army" which attained a European reputation.

Pringle has been justly called the founder of modern military medicine. His rules for camp hygiene are in many cases still followed in army practice. He discovered that camp dysentery was spread by improper sanitary arrangements and pointed out the correct methods of prevention. He was the first to point to putrefaction as a cause of disease and he studied the subject of antiseptics. He also pointed out that camping near marsh land led to intermittent fever (i.e., malaria). He laid down sensible rules as to the clothing and diet of troops. Further he first identified hospital and gaol fever as being the same disease (typhus) [7] but he thought that the infection was spread by putrid air and therefore insisted on the importance of fresh air, rather than on personal cleanliness, as a preventive.

James Lind,[8] M.D. (Edin.) (1716–1794), Fellow of the College of Surgeons, received his medical training in Edinburgh and became a navy surgeon. He made a long voyage in his professional capacity in 1746 and 80 men out of 350 were prostrated by scurvy. In 1753 he published his Treatise on Scurvy which laid down the correct rules for its prevention, that is the proper provision of fresh vegetables or lemon juice. This was not a new discovery, sailors had observed long before that scurvy could be prevented and cured by these means, but Lind laid it down with the full authority of a doctor and naval officer. Many commanders followed his advice and in 1795 the provision of lemon juice on all men of war was ordered by the Admiralty. But Lind's work in connection with scurvy is not his sole title to fame. His rules for ship hygiene were as sensible and enduring as those of Pringle for the army. In particular he laid down correct rules for the prevention of typhus.[9] In 1757 he published "An Essay on the most effectual means of preserving the Health of Seamen in the Royal Navy." In 1758 he was appointed physician to the Naval Hospital at Haslar, where he worked out the method of preventing the spread of typhus in hospitals and so made possible the hospital treatment of this disease. Lind was also a pioneer in tropical medicine. In 1768 he published an " Essay on Diseases of Europeans in Hot Climates ". He laid down sensible rules for avoiding tropical diseases. He, like Pringle, pointed out the danger of the proximity of marshes. All his books went into several editions and were translated into French and German, attracting considerable notice on the Continent.

Pringle and Lind had many disciples, who repeated and amplified their teaching in a host of publications. Among them Sir Gilbert Blane has perhaps the best claim to be mentioned.

Sir Gilbert Blane (1749–1834) was born in Ayrshire. He took his arts and medical degrees at Edinburgh University. He obtained the appointment of private physician to Lord Rodney in the West Indian expedition of 1779, became a great friend of his commander and was made physician to the fleet. He applied the latest methods of dealing with disease and effected a great improvement in the health of the fleet, especially in regard to scurvy. He issued a printed tract to the officers of the fleet upon the care of the health of the seamen. It was through his influence that the Admiralty order as to the provision of lemon juice was issued in 1795.

In 1783, largely through the influence of Rodney, he was appointed physician to St. Thomas's Hospital, which position he resigned in 1795. His two immediate predecessors, also one of the surgeons and several attendants, had died during the year preceding his appointment of fever caught in the hospital. Blane reduced the number of patients and introduced the new methods of scrupulous cleanliness with complete success. He had now achieved a considerable eminence in the medical world. His " Observations on the Diseases of Seamen " went through several editions and became a medical classic. He received several Court appointments and was frequently consulted in matters of public health. The Turkey Company asked his advice as to the prevention of the import of plague and he was one of the medical committee which drew up the Quarantine Act of 1799. The return of the army from Egypt was carried out under regulations drawn up by him to prevent the import of plague. The return of the army from the ill-fated Walcheren expedition was also under his supervision and he, a navy officer, was called upon by the War Office to report upon the unsatisfactory conduct of the medical officers attached to the expedition. The Home Office also consulted him as to the prevention of typhus in prisons and convict ships. Nor was his advice sought only by his own countrymen; he was consulted by the Emperor of Russia, the King of Prussia and the President of the United States. Honours were not lacking, he was made a baronet in 1812, he was also a Fellow of the Royal Society and a member of the Institut de France. Blane made no striking discoveries but his books are well written and full of original observations. He was a man of great force of character with a capacity for getting things done. Perhaps this was partly due to his generosity of mind which was ever ready to appreciate and help the work of others. In particular he had a profound admiration for Lind and Jenner and the latter years of his life were largely taken up with the campaign in favour of vaccination. Blane was one of the many medical men who began to deal with the history of diseases and the statistics of public health as likely to throw light on the causes of disease.

Sir John Simon in his " English Sanitary Institutions " is the only authority, to the writer's knowledge, who places Pringle and Lind in their proper place as the precursors of the public health movement. He asserts, however, that within the reign of William IV an appreciation of the social value of the new medical knowledge had hardly begun, and that this knowledge had been applied only to naval and military undertakings where the " economy of human tools was a requisite for success . . . But in the common civil world the question had hardly yet arisen whether economies in the expenditure of human life could be made ". He bases this statement upon the fact that in 1837 the Statute Book contained no general sanitary law except a " futile quarantine act " and the only other Government " activity " was an annual grant of £2,000 towards the expenses of the Vaccination Board. "Outside these two matters the Central Government had nothing to say in regard to Public Health and the Local Authorities had but the most indefinite relation to it." Sir John Simon thus implies that the work of the medical pioneers had no results as regards the civil population until 1848. But it is never safe in English history to date a reform from the Statute Book. An Act of Parliament often only imposes upon a reluctant minority a course of action which the majority have already been persuaded to follow by voluntary effort.

In fact, attempts soon began to be made to apply the lessons of military and naval hygiene to civil life, an attempt that was obviously fraught with many difficulties. The labours, the achievements and the failures of the pioneers of civilian public hygiene will be dealt with in some detail in another chapter, but a few biographical particulars of the principal protagonists may not be out of place here. Though Haygarth of Chester, who had already conducted a vigorous anti-smallpox campaign, was the first to apply Lind's methods of fighting typhus to civilian practice, the man who has some claim to the title of the first civilian public health reformer is Thomas Percival (1740–1804) of Manchester.

Percival was born at Warrington and received his medical education at Edinburgh and Leyden.[10]. In 1767 he started practice in Manchester where he became the leading light in the Manchester Literary and Philosophical Society and thus became intimate with all the most enlightened and cultured residents of that town. Robert Owen gives a vivid little picture of a meeting of the Society to which he was introduced by Percival, then its President, and remarks incidentally that the medical profession stood high in Manchester " and its leading members were the aristocracy of the town ".[11] Percival used his prestige and influence to forward matters of public health, he was one of the prime movers in the Manchester Board of Health, a voluntary organization of which the most outstanding work was the establishment of the famous Manchester House of Recovery or Fever Hospital. Percival advocated, in numerous publications, better conditions in factories and doubtless his personal acquaintance with many of the wealthy merchants who owned the early cotton mills led to some of his ideas being put into practice. He, however, was one of the earliest to see that private effort had its serious limitations, he was in favour of public health laws enforced by paid officials and was the first advocate of Factory Legislation. His work upon voluntary lines was, however, by no means totally ineffectual and Blane [12] ascribes the relatively low death rate in Manchester to his efforts.[13] This honour, however, should be shared by Percival's friend and colleague, John Ferriar (1761–1815).

Ferriar was born near Jedburgh, Roxburghshire, and studied medicine at Edinburgh where he graduated M.D. in 1781. He entered practice at Stockton-on-Tees in 1782 but about 1785 removed to Manchester. There he became an active member of the Literary and Philosophical Society and contributed many literary papers. In 1789 he was appointed a physician to Manchester Infirmary and was one of the founders of the Board of Health. Many of Ferriar's ideas about public health have a curiously modern ring. He was in favour of the inspection and licensing of common lodging houses and of their compulsory whitewashing. He also advocated the provision of public common lodging houses or failing this their provision by charity. He advocated the abolition of night work in factories and the provision of cricket pitches for workers. He was also in favour of the encouragement of clothing and sick benefit clubs. His ideas are set forth in his Medical Histories and Reflections, the three volumes of which were published between 1792–1798 and which consist mainly of detailed clinical observations of the cases at the Manchester Infirmary.[14] Closely associated with Percival and Ferriar was James Currie of Liverpool, a man of outstanding force of character and moral courage.

James Currie, M.D. (1756–1805), was born in Dumfrieshire, when not quite 16 he emigrated to Virginia where he obtained commercial employment. His mercantile career was interrupted by severe attacks of fever and was finally terminated by the War of Independence. During the war he lived for a time with a medical relative at Richmond, Virginia, and then determined to take up medicine. For this purpose he returned to his native country, enduring on the journey numerous hardships due to the war, to poverty and to ill health. But in spite of all difficulties he achieved his object and studied medicine at

Edinburgh and Glasgow, graduating at the latter University in 1780. He at first contemplated returning to America but instead settled at Liverpool where he became a physician at the Dispensary and also obtained a lucrative private practice.

Currie was a man of warm sympathies and, when they were excited, was fearless of popular disapproval. In Liverpool, the stronghold of the slave trade, he had the supreme courage to be an ardent advocate of its abolition. Later on he espoused the almost equally unpopular cause of the French prisoners. He was anti-war and in 1793 published, under a pseudonym, several pamphlets, in the form of letters to Pitt, urging a peace policy. The secret of the authorship was divulged and Currie's practice is said to have suffered. In the latter part of his life he somewhat eschewed politics, like many others his sympathies were probably less with an imperial France than they had been with a revolutionary one. Further, his health was not good, he was suffering from the hardships of his youth and his energies were more and more occupied with questions of public health. His unremitting labours in regard to the provision of a fever hospital are described in some detail in a later chapter, he also took part in measures against smallpox. In 1802 by the request of the Corporation, he drew up a report upon the health of Liverpool and it was doubtless owing to his suggestions that the Corporation attempted to obtain a Building Act to regulate the dwellings of the poor; the Bill, however, failed to pass. As a doctor, Currie's chief interest was fevers. His Medical Reports, first published in 1797, which dealt with the prevention and treatment of fevers, went into four editions and have won praise from modern medical authorities. He was a great believer in the use of cold water in fever, both internally and externally, and was the first doctor who insisted upon the importance of thermal observations in fevers and other diseases An improved clinical thermometer was constructed by Ramsden under Currie's direction and was known by his name. Politics national and local, and medicine did not exhaust Currie's interests He was one of the founders and the first president of the Athenaeum, the first literary and scientific institution in Liverpool He was a commentator on Burns and wrote his life for the benefi of the poet's widow. To Currie these literary labours probably represented relaxation and recreation, a side of life that brought him into amicable and restful relations with his fellow men. But curiously enough it is by these that he is best remembered in his adopted city, where his name is still held in honour.[15]

Most of the British medical pioneers of the 18th century were of good birth and education, and men of high moral character actuated by a noble zeal for advancing knowledge and benefiting humanity. Their work was not unrecognized or ignored by their contemporaries.[16] Most of them enjoyed the encouragement of the learned societies of the time, and the patronage of the great in the form of lucrative private practice and Court or State appointments. Moreover, the more important of their writings went into many editions and were translated into foreign languages. That, and their work as teachers, meant that their ideas must have been rapidly and widely disseminated. In fact, like Adam Smith in another sphere, part of their greatness lay in the fact that their work was in harmony with the spirit of the age in which they lived; being marked by accurate observation, shrewd common sense and a power of lucid exposition rather than by the intuition of genius. A good deal of their theory was hopelessly wrong, but their practice was often brilliantly and triumphantly right.

CHAPTER X

THE HOSPITAL AND DISPENSARY MOVEMENT

ONE of the outstanding results of the advance in medicine during the 18th century was the foundation of hospitals and dispensaries. The medieval hospitals for the sick were swept away at the Reformation with other monastic institutions, London alone was powerful enough to obtain the refounding of the great hospitals of St. Bartholomew and St. Thomas. The medieval hospital, as the original meaning of the word implies, was not so much a place of healing, indeed it was probably rather a source of disease, as a place of refuge for the destitute and homeless sick. Under the Elizabethan reconstruction the care of sick persons became the duty of the parish.[1] Poor sick persons who had homes were given out relief and the homeless were accommodated in the workhouse or boarded out. Until the medical reforms of the latter half of the 18th century the sick were probably infinitely better off in their homes than they would have been in an institution. Probably in the rapidly increasing towns the poor law provision for the sick was less satisfactory than in the country parishes, and this, together with the growing philanthropic spirit of the times, was no doubt a factor in the movement for hospital foundation. But possibly the main cause was the remarkable advance in medical science; the foundation of hospitals was due not only to the desire that the poor might benefit from the new knowledge, but that the hospitals might serve as centres for the growth and the spread of knowledge in the treatment of disease.

In 1714 John Bellers (a Quaker) published, "An Essay towards the Improvement of Physick" in which the foundation of hospitals was advocated, particularly in connection with the two Universities, pointing out that the sick would benefit from the advance in medicine. The Universities, he said, "being the Great Nurseries of our Graduated *Physicians,* make *Hospitals* there to be absolutely necessary for their better Instruction, by adding *Practice* to their *Aphorisms* and *Theory* they will learn more in Seven years than in Fourteen Years without them. . . . At present its not easie for the Students to get a Body to dissect at *Oxford,* the Mob are so Mutinous to prevent their having one " . . . " the great Experience of the Physicians of *London* and *Westminster* makes them the most *Eminent* and accounted the *best* in the kingdom" . . . " These *Hospitals*" (i.e. the hospitals advocated) "will Breed up some of the best Physicians and Chirurgeons because they may see as much there in One Year as in Seven any where else ". Bellers, it is true, was ahead of his times, he was in favour of a parish doctor being attached to every parish, of State aid to medicine and of the endowment of scientific research. In another sphere he advocated a Council of Nations to keep the peace and to settle international disputes. However, in the matter of hospitals Bellers did not stand alone, as the list in the Appendix shows, and it is interesting to see that the Hospital at Cambridge was the first to be established, only five years after Bellers wrote. The first county hospital was that for Hampshire, it was established at Winchester in 1736. In an account of its foundation, it was stated that it was a form of charity that could not be abused or misapplied and that it relieved the " useful and industrious instead of only *the Poor*" (i.e. paupers), that it would save the poor from quacks and impostors, help the parishes and encourage religion and virtue ! Lastly, prospective supporters were reminded that " It is of infinite use to *all other* Persons as well as the poor, by furnishing the Physicians and Surgeons with more experience in *one* year than they could have in *ten* without it " and that it was " a work which in the compass of a few years will be the means of greatly increasing the number of our People ".[2]

A later writer testifies that the hope that hospitals would lead to the advancement of knowledge was not altogether vain : " The following pages contain a selection of cases and observations chiefly drawn from my practice at the Manchester Infirmary. The extended plan of that institution affords the most favourable opportunities to a diligent observer for ascertaining with precision many facts in the history of diseases, and for appreciating the value of established methods of cure. Some part of the fruits of such advantages should therefore revert to the public, in acknowledgment of the good it bestows. And something may be added to the stock of science, by unwearied attention to a considerable number of patients, indiscriminately taken, in a great town." [3]

It must not be supposed that hospitals in the 18th century were by any means model institutions from a modern point of view. In the first place, admission could generally only be obtained with a Letter of Recommendation from a subscriber and after tiresome formalities, though both these were omitted in some hospitals in the case of accidents or other very urgent cases. The admission by Letter was in keeping with the times, people liked their charity to have a personal element and they enjoyed patronage, which then pervaded every aspect of life. Moreover, it is doubtful if the subscribers could have trusted the officials with the admission of patients. Further, fees were often extracted by the nurses and porters, sometimes illicitly, it was often customary to charge for laundry and, a gruesome item, it was usual to demand a sum from patients on admission in security for burial. No doubt in many cases all these charges were met by the wealthy patron who gave the Letter. The financial position of many hospitals was insecure from the first and their administration was often hampered by the squabbles of contending factions and personal recriminations, which seem to have been the breath of life to the public man of the 18th century.

Nor would a modern visitor be better impressed by the material surroundings of an 18th century hospital. The hospital building often consisted of converted houses, ill adapted to their purpose, often not kept particularly clean, with the windows closely shut and the floors sanded. The sanitary arrangements to modern eyes (and noses!) would seem offensive in the extreme. The bedsteads were of wood, with testers, and since the patients were never washed and seldom had a change of bed linen, the beds were often swarming with vermin. The nurses were rough, untrained women and the discipline both for them and the patients was extremely lax. Alcohol was brought freely into most hospitals and Howard records that the gin shops in the neighbourhood of Guy's and Thomas's benefited from the visits of the patients of these institutions.

The hospitals, however, were not worse than the outside world. Wooden bedsteads and testers were to be found in every home and it would be safe to say that vermin would have been found in most. Clean bed and body linen were only enjoyed by the wealthy and even their standard in the matter of personal cleanliness was not high. A doctor writing in 1801 says that " most men resident in London and many ladies though accustomed to wash their hands and face daily, neglect washing their bodies from year to year."[4] Even had the hospital administrators realized the importance of cleanliness it would have been a very difficult thing to enforce it, considering the state of knowledge and the material upon which they were obliged to rely for nurses. The question of discipline also must have been a difficult one and it is significant that conditions in the naval hospitals were better than in most of the civilian ones. Howard mentions that at Haslar " there were strict rules for nurses ". It is interesting to remember that the founder of modern nursing gained her main experience as a military nurse and that she laid the foundations of the reformed profession and of the reformed hospital practice upon strictly military lines. To this day the military tradition is extremely strong in the nursing profession and in hospital routine.

Hospitals which, as a class, generally seemed to be satisfactory in the 18th century were the Lying-In Hospitals. These were usually small institutions and the nurses, who were in training to be midwives, were doubtless of a somewhat superior grade to the "watcher" in an ordinary hospital. Perhaps, too, something was due to the fact that this was the one class of hospital in which, at this time, women took an important part in the management. A committee of ladies nearly always formed part of the management, indeed maternity charities

K

were often delicately known as Ladies' Charities. A Ladies' Committee would be likely to insist upon cleanliness up to the standard of the time and one suspects that the nurses did not find them quite so easy to deal with, as were the kindly gentlemen who occasionally strolled round the wards of the general hospitals.

In spite of difficulties, however, a good deal of hospital reform took place in the second half of the 18th century. Many hospitals were re-built and upon noble lines; the influence of the classical revival in architecture was at its height and the result was lofty, airy buildings adequate to their purpose. The London Hospital was re-built in 1752 and St. Bartholomew's between 1730–53, the latter building is still in use and the writer has heard an eminent physician say that, even in the light of modern knowledge, it was well adapted to its purpose. Not all the new buildings were equal to these in style and design but at any rate all the re-built hospitals gained in cleanliness and convenience. With the work of Lind and his followers the importance of fresh air and cleanliness began to be understood. Slowly reforms spread, here testers were swept away, there floors were regularly washed; hospital clothes and bed linen began to be provided, this reform being made easier by the new cheap cotton fabric, even cesspools and privies were looked after. A frequent innovation was the introduction of iron bedsteads in place of the old vermin-ridden wooden ones, another reform in the interests of health which industrial change had made possible.

Howard added to his more famous work in connection with prisons, zeal for hospital reform. He published in 1789, in an appendix to his work upon the Continental lazarettos and quarantine systems, an extremely frank description of what he found in a tour of the British and foreign hospitals. He had very definite ideas about hospital planning, as he had about prison planning, and gave his advice freely if it were asked for or not. As one reads how he appears to have been free to enter any institution he liked, at home or abroad, and to have asked any questions that occurred to him and to publish afterwards an account and criticism ruthless in its frankness, it i difficult to know which to admire the most, the man with his simple minded honesty or the age which supported such methods.

It seems worth while to give some of the more salient points from Howard's notes, since they convey in their baldness a far more vivid impression of the hospital conditions of the time than pages of elaborate description. They indicate, too, the progress of reform, slow and unequal, but nevertheless unmistakable :—

London

LONDON.—This hospital contained 18 wards but only 7 were occupied, there were 18 beds in each ward and the medical and surgical cases were together, the wards were 20 ft. wide and 12 ft. high and were not dirty but needed whitewash. The passages were dark and there were no cisterns for water and the vaults were offensive. In a dirty room in a cellar there was a bath which was seldom used.

There were no testers to the beds. No fees or rewards were paid to nurses for admission, nor was any security demanded for burial. The Committee were exerting themselves to improve the hospital.

ST. BARTHOLOMEW'S.—The wards here were clean except the men's foul ward, where no window was open. The bedsteads were of wood and with testers. Fees were taken and security had to be given for burial.

MIDDLESEX (which had been founded as a smallpox hospital). Only four wards were occupied out of the 16, the funds being very low. The rooms were close and dirty, the bedsteads of wood and the testers old. Whitewash was needed and there was a general air of poverty.

ST. THOMAS'S.—The wards were fresh and clean except the three foul wards which were offensive and with not a window open. The bedsteads were of iron with no testers and a society engaged to supply patients with clean body linen once a week. (Here is the influence of Blane's administration.) There were, however, no water closets.

Fees were required from patients and security for burial. Quantities of beer were consumed in the hospital.

Guy's.—The wards were too low, some being only $9\frac{1}{2}$ ft. high. In the old wards the bedsteads and testers were of wood and infested with bugs but in the new wards the bedsteads were of iron and the beds of hair. The windows were open and there were also ventilators. The water closets were of the best construction and "not in the least offensive"; by opening the door the water turned into them. There were excellent baths. The alterations were to continue, each ward being taken in rotation. Fees and security for burial were exacted.

Westminster.—The wards were only 17 ft. wide, the beds close to the wall with wooden testers, the floors sanded and the walls dirty. A sum was paid every year for the destruction of bugs. There were, however, no fees and no security money to be paid.

St. George's.—The description almost identical with the last, except that there is no reference to bugs and that a good cold bath existed which was never used.

(St. George's was an offshoot of the Westminster, the result of a quarrel.)

British Lying-In.—Contained six wards each with six beds, the wards clean and quiet but the house was old and needed whitewash. No fees were payable.

"A good institution" comments Howard.

The City of London Lying-In.—Also had clean wards and beds but also needed whitewash.

Provinces

Norfolk.—This hospital was spacious, neat and clean, the wards were quiet and fresh. "A notable matron" comments Howard.

Leicester.—No windows were open and the wards were close.

Nottingham.—"A neat hospital in a fine situation." The bedsteads were of iron and the furniture was clean, there were reservoirs of water over the closets.

Oxford, Radcliffe Hospital.—The wards were close and offensive and the floors were only dry rubbed. In Worcester the conditions were the same.

SHREWSBURY.—The house was not originally built for a hospital and the wards were inconvenient. The water closets were offensive.

HEREFORD.—There were baths but the floor was not clean.

GLOUCESTER.—The wards were clean, fresh and spacious and there was a convenient bath.

WINCHESTER.—The windows of the passages and staircase were shut and the venereal wards were close and offensive. The bedsteads were of iron.

HASLAR.—" This well conducted hospital " was clean and quiet, the windows on the staircase were open, indeed Lind nailed them open in summer. The floors were washed.

The patients were provided with white linen sheets and hospital clothes, there was a good diet provided and the rules for nurses were strict.

However, the ceilings were low, and the inside sewers were offensive and there were no cisterns in the wards. (These last matters were no doubt beyond Lind's control.)

ROYAL HOSPITAL, PLYMOUTH.—" This noble hospital."

LEEDS INFIRMARY.—" One of the best hospitals in the kingdom." Great attention was paid to cleanliness, there were ventilators in the wards, there were no fixed testers and no bugs ! Howard commented " Many are here cured of compound fractures who would lose their limbs in the unventilated and offensive wards of some other hospitals."

YORK.—The wards were clean, quiet and not offensive, the bedsteads were of iron with hair beds and linen bed furniture.

CHESTER.—The wards were spacious and clean.

Howard's comments upon the Continental hospitals revealed not dissimilar conditions and the same inequality between different hospitals.

According to the rules of the Winchester hospital the following classes of patient were not admitted :—Incurables, children under 7, pregnant women, the insane or those suffering from smallpox, the itch or other infectious diseases, nor those in a consumptive or dying condition. The same or similar exclusions were to be found in the rules of other general hospitals, for obvious reasons, when the conditions of the time are remembered. The necessity for specialized institutions to deal with the excluded classes soon began to be felt. Numerous Lying-In Hospitals were established during the second half of the 18th century; this movement is described in the next chapter. At the end of the century the Fever Hospital Movement began and the new methods introduced by Lind caused many general hospitals to ignore or to modify their rules and to establish fever wards.[5] The London Lock Hospital was founded in 1746 and this institution was copied in other parts of the country. Judging, however, from Howard's report most general hospitals also had venereal wards. Even the wants of the most despised and neglected class of patients began to be considered and lunatic asylums were erected in various places. Outside London, which possessed the ancient Bethlehem Hospital, the only previous refuge for the destitute lunatic had been the workhouse and dangerous lunatics were often sent to the lock up as the only safe place for confinement. London was large enough to find room for various other specialized hospitals, a list of which will be found in the Appendix.

Many of the hospitals were founded through the efforts of individual doctors, who gave their services as well as their time and money; in other cases wealthy founders interested their medical friends or their medical attendants. From the first, therefore, the curious phenomenon arose which still exists, that the very poor, like the very rich, enjoyed the benefit of the best medical advice available, while the middle and artisan class had to put up with the second or third best. The difference was even more marked in the 18th century, when the mass of the people who could pay for medical attention could only afford the services of an apothecary.

With all its faults and imperfections the 18th century hospital movement presents a noble effort to relieve suffering, an effort that by no means altogether failed in achievement. To many a poor sufferer the old, unreformed hospital with its warm bed, its pleasantly stuffy ward and its sufficiency of rough food must have been a real harbour of refuge. It is sometimes difficult to believe in the number of cures claimed by the hospital reports of the period, but the large number of serious diseases excluded by the rules make it possible that a good many patients were only suffering from under-nourishment. These, food and warmth would cure, while in other cases nature was aided by homely remedies or rough and ready surgery. It would be interesting if we could know the comments of the patients upon the reforms of the latter part of the century. How did they view the abolition of testers, coupled with open windows, what did they think of being washed or even, horror of horrors, being invited to take a bath ? Did they take kindly to the uniform hospital clothes or appreciate the fresh air and the reformed sanitary arrangements ? Did they not regret the old small, dirty, stuffy rooms, with their homely sanded floors, and view with distaste the iron bedsteads, with their coldly clean linen or cotton sheets, and the newly whitewashed walls and scrupulously scrubbed floors ? History remains mute, but a knowledge of human nature supplies the answer. One of the difficulties of the reformer is that the persons for whose benefit a reform is desired often welcome it as little as those who will have to provide it.

A very important supplement to the Hospital movement was the Dispensary movement. The first dispensary was founded by Dr. Armstrong in Red Lion Square in 1769 for the Relief of the Infant Poor. The better known General Dispensary was founded the following year. By 1800 many dispensaries had been established in London and the movement spread rapidly. A writer in 1802 says, " The dispensaries in the metropolis are numerous. From the eastern extremity of Limehouse, to the western of Millbank and on the north from Islington and Somers Town, to the south as far as Lambeth ; and by means of the Greenwich dispensary, to Newington and Peckham, including a space of nearly fifty square miles, a system of medical relief is extended to the poor unknown to any other part of the globe. About 50,000 poor persons are thus annually supplied with medicine and advice gratis ; one-third of whom, at least, are attended in their own homes." [6]

In the provinces the hospital and the dispensary were often combined, indeed one often grew out of the other. Many provincial hospitals were originally founded as dispensaries, while in other cases hospitals started dispensaries, really forerunners of the modern out-patients' departments. The dispensary was a very much easier and cheaper institution to run than the hospital, it dealt with a large number of patients and ministered to every kind of disease. It formed an even better school for the doctor than the hospital. The dispensary doctor learnt at first hand "how the poor lived" and the writings of the London dispensary doctors in the early 19th century give us a vivid description of the health conditions of the poor and of the valiant efforts made to combat disease. They pay tribute to the courage and patience of the poor and combat the popular notion that their sufferings were due to sloth and drink. At the General Dispensary patients who were well enough to do so attended as out-patients, but those seriously ill were attended in their own homes. One dispensary doctor writing in 1774 says simply, "visiting patients at their own homes is peculiarly laborious to the physician." [7] In this unboasting, matter-of-fact spirit, the dispensary doctor took his life in his hands as he went about his duty and so little was said about his unremitting and heroic labours, either by himself or anyone else, that they were almost unnoticed by his contemporaries and totally forgotten by posterity.

The crown and glory of 18th century medicine is that it first attempted to bring such knowledge as it had to the service of the mass of the people. The rich physician, pampering the imagined ills of the wealthy, has been taken as typical of the age, but he is common to all ages; the new figure was the dispensary doctor risking his life daily in the disease-ridden hovels of the poor.

CHAPTER XI

GENERAL HYGIENE AND MIDWIFERY

EIGHTEENTH century medicine is distinguished from that of preceding centuries in that it made a definite and by no means unsuccessful effort to prevent disease, especially epidemic disease, as opposed merely to curing it. Prevention was sought along four different lines, all of which are still followed in modern practice and all of which had roots in the past. In the first place the policy of segregation was developed, systematized and applied to a larger number of diseases. Secondly, there was detailed and scientific experiment with various antiseptics and a satisfactory technique of disinfection was worked out, at any rate in regard to certain types of infection. Thirdly, the method of artificial infection was introduced in the case of one disease. Lastly, and perhaps most important, the avoidance of the conditions of life which cause disease was definitely inculcated by medical reformers. The advocacy of personal and public hygiene was in part a reflection of the general philosophical attitude of the time with its admiration and respect for nature, and in part the result of the renewed discriminating study of the ancients. Ancient Greek medicine had excelled in personal hygiene, Roman administration in public, while the Jewish religion had inculcated many excellent dietic and other hygienic rules. But most, if not all, of this knowledge had been lost in the dark ages and a distrust of and disdain for the body and its requirements had been borrowed from the East. The Hypocratic School had held strongly that the natural condition of the body was one of health and that disease could be checked and prevented by proper surroundings. The deep consciousness of sin, inculcated by religious teaching, inclined Christian Europe, however, to the idea that, since the soul of man is naturally wicked, his body is naturally diseased and, that just as frequent prayers and confessions were necessary for the guilty soul, so frequent potions and bleedings were necessary for the sick body. Only very slowly is Europe regaining the old ideal of a healthy mind in a healthy body and the concept of health as the natural and usual thing.

The importance of fresh air and cleanliness began to be preached by the best doctors in the 17th century and with increasing vigour in the 18th century. Dirt and " all nastiness " was condemned as unhealthy as well as unpleasant and the origin of disease began to be ascribed to dirt, damp situations, bad water and bad food instead of to the will of the Almighty. It would be possible to quote pages of extracts from 18th century doctors preaching the efficacy of soap and water and fresh air. If it is said that, judging by early 19th century conditions, all this preaching was wasted, the reply is that we have no conception of the Augean stables which had to be cleansed and there is little cause for surprise if the work was not finished in fifty years. It is not, of course, finished even now. The pioneers had to overcome not only the physical evil but a mass of inertia, superstition and ignorance that might well appal them; for among the wealthy and educated, and even in the ranks of their own profession, they found ignorance of some of the rudiments of hygiene. What they failed to achieve is writ large in many volumes, what they succeeded in achieving has been forgotten. It is hoped in some measure to recall it in these pages. The doctors took a smaller part in the slow recovery of civic hygiene. The first reforms, which have already been described, seem to have been due to the requirements of commerce and to obvious convenience rather than to a care for public health. But the doctors applauded these efforts and pointed out the benefit to health and it is possible that in some degree the demand for a higher standard of civic convenience may have been a natural development from increased personal cleanliness.

Naturally it was in the sick room that the doctor was best able to enforce his advice. Sydenham's famous " cool regimen " in fevers was nothing more than the enforcement of what would now be considered the ordinary rules of ventilation. Its curative success in the case of certain titled patients gave it great advertisement. Slowly, very slowly, fresh air and cleanliness became increasingly advocated, first as cures for disease and then as preventives.

The respect of and admiration for nature of the new medicine was nowhere more potent in reform than in the care of women in child-birth and in infant nurture. The art and practice of midwifery depended until modern times upon verbal tradition and personal tuition, it was essentially a craft. It is true that the doctors of antiquity had some general remarks to make on the subject and seem also to have practised some of the cruder forms of operative obstetrics, but throughout the dark and Middle Ages this branch of medicine was entirely in the hands of ignorant women. No doubt most of these women had learnt a certain traditional lore, some useful, some harmful, and may have further acquired a certain manipulative skill. The harrowing accounts which are from time to time given of the suffering of modern Indian and Chinese women through the ignorance of midwives, would apply equally to those of European women before the 18th century. Not only were the midwives too ignorant to help in cases of difficulty, they were often too ignorant to let well alone in normal cases. Respect for nature is the result of knowledge not of ignorance. A 17th century doctor says, " I wish and desire all midwives not to be too forward, or too officious in their undertakings, least they disquiet nature, whose onely work it is, and I would have them to understand, that they bee but nature's servants in all their performances and that they must attend her time and motion, as hereafter shall be shewed ". This writer cites many cases of torture by brutal ignorant midwives, including that of one who tried to remove a cancerous tumour under the impression that it was a child. The doctor at least discovered the real cause of the woman's agony and left her in peace to be eased of her " disquiets within of a few months afterwards . . . by death ".[1]

In England any woman could set up as a midwife, as the same authority says, " the meanest of women, not knowing how, otherwise to live, for the gitting of a shilling or two, to sustain their necessities, become ignorant midwives, then travailling women suffer tortures, by their halings, and stretching of their bodies, after which followeth the ruinating of their healths, and sometimes death ". In some parts of the continent the midwives were subject to a certain amount of regulation. In 18th century Paris the midwives were controlled by Royal Ordinance and had to pass an examination before they could practise, and similar regulations existed in other towns. In England the profession was totally unregulated and remained so until the 20th century.[2]

In the 16th century the doctors with their growing knowledge of anatomy and the revived knowledge of the classical fragments began to turn their attention to obstetrics. For instance, the French surgeon Ambroise Paré revived the operation of *podalic version* which had been known in classical times. During the 17th century numerous treatises were published on the subject but most of them were not the result of the observation of nature but were based on theory or conjecture or were a mere repetition of the classical tradition. Much of the literature was written for the use of ignorant midwives and was therefore purposely elementary in form.[3]

The earliest clinical work was done in Paris, and in the writings of Mauriceau and La Motte in the latter half of the 17th century the beginnings of scientific midwifery can be traced. During this period the employment of a "man midwife" became customary at the French Court. Jules Clément attended several Royal ladies, also la Vallière. Indeed, scandalous legend has it that the custom of employing a man arose through the desire of la Vallière to conceal the nature of her illness and therefore employing a physician instead of a midwife. The truth of this story seems more than doubtful; moreover, the employment of a man doctor in cases of difficulty was already well established among the well to do. At this period the appointment of an accoucheur to Royal ladies probably corresponded to the appointment of a consultant obstetrician to Royalty at the present day, that is to say, unless difficulty arose the midwife practically remained in charge. Prior to the 18th century the male practitioner was only called in as a last extremity, his work was largely destructive and his advent nearly always meant death to the child and often to the mother. Many of the male practitioners had scarcely seen a normal birth and were totally unacquainted with the normal processes of nature. Paris was ahead of other cities in this branch of study and early in the 18th century students there had the advantage of studying cases in the maternity wards of the Hôtel Dieu. The title of Father of Modern Midwifery, however, has been bestowed upon a Dutchman, the accoucheur Hendrik van Deventer, whose treatise was published in 1696. His work was the first to give a scientific description of the pelvis and further made some attempt at a scientific description of the process of parturition. It is not without significance that Deventer's wife was a midwife, so he had more knowledge of normal cases, if only by hearsay, than most male practitioners.

In the meantime Great Britain remained backward, her midwives unregulated and untrained, her doctors content to translate continental works and the facilities for training almost non-existent. Edinburgh University appointed a Professor of Midwifery in 1726, but not until 1739 was there any opportunity for the clinical study of midwifery in London. At that date a ward of the parochial Infirmary of St. James, Westminster, was set apart for lying-in women; this reform was due to the initiative of Sir Richard Manningham, at that time the leading London accoucheur. He taught his students in this ward, which was supported by public subscription. Twenty years later London was held by some to surpass Paris in its facilities for studying midwifery. For one thing there had been between 1739–59 a marvellous growth in the number of institutions devoted to this branch of medicine. The Middlesex Hospital made arrangements for receiving lying-in women in 1747 and appointed a physician accoucheur. In 1749 the British Lying-In Hospital (for married women) was founded. The City of London Lying-In was founded in the following year, the Queen Charlotte's (for unmarried as well as married) in 1752, the Royal Maternity in 1757 and the General in 1778. Not only the quantity but the quality of the instruction available in London was improving during the period and this largely owing to the exertions of one man.

William Smellie (1697-1763) was born in Lanark. Little is known of his early life, he was almost certainly trained to his profession by apprenticeship, as that was the only available method in Scotland at that period. He set up as a general practitioner in Lanark in 1720, obtained a good practice and a considerable local reputation, especially as an accoucheur. About 1738 this prosperous provincial doctor threw up his practice in order to become again a student and a beginner. He journeyed to London in order to study there the latest methods of midwifery and was extremely disappointed to find that the metropolis had little or nothing to teach him and he almost at once passed on to Paris. Here he attended the lectures of the famous Grégoire but again confessed to disappointment; in some matters the provincial general practitioner could have taught even the specialists of Paris. In 1740 he returned to London and set up in practice in Pall Mall as an accoucheur, but, until his name was made, he was obliged to pursue as well the humble activities of an apothecary.

Smellie founded scientific midwifery in England. His work was based upon the observation of normal cases, upon the application of mechanics and the laws of moving bodies to parturition and upon an exact measurement of the pelvis to distinguish between normal and contracted pelvis. He improved the forceps [4] and other instruments and revolutionized the instrumental side of the obstetric art. After him the accoucheur became the herald of life instead of death, his advent brought hope instead of despair and terror. Smellie was not only a great practitioner but a great teacher, he trained over 900 male students and an unrecorded number of women. For teaching purposes he constructed an improved " phantom " or model, made of parts of a real skeleton covered with soft leather and a little doll to represent the fœtus. He also kept a detailed case book which he had started in Lanark. But in Smellie's view no teaching could be satisfactory unless students could see and practise upon actual cases. He therefore started a scheme by which he and his students attended poor women gratis in their own homes. To induce the women to submit to his attendance they were given maintenance during their lying-in, this maintenance was provided out of a fund to which every student contributed 6s. When he began this work Smellie had to endure much from prejudice and ignorance, on more than one occasion he and his students were in actual danger from the mob. He had to face the jealous anger of the midwives, his most redoubtable antagonist, Mrs. Nihell, in particular libelled and abused him, made coarse jests about his " phantom " and called him " a great horse god-mother of a he-midwife ". Smellie, indeed, was not aided by his manner, he had not, unlike many of his countrymen, come to cities early in life, he was an uncouth 18th century provincial Scot, with personal idiosyncracies of manner in addition. Yet, in spite of all these handicaps, he won his battle ; his honesty, his faith, above all his ability, conquered. He won the guerdon he sought, not personal glory or honour, but an incalculable reduction of human suffering.[5] Smellie had many able successors, of whom William Hunter, brother of the anatomist, was the most famous. After five years' study at Glasgow University he became a pupil of Smellie, in itself a tribute to the latter's reputation, and subsequently became the leading obstetrician of London.

The numerous maternity charities benefited women of all classes by the facilities which they afforded for the training both of medical students and of midwives. This indeed was one of the reasons for their establishment, as was stated in regard to the Dublin Lying-In Hospital (1745), " one of the great objects of its founder Dr. Moss being that it might afford facilities for clinical instruction and thus save students the necessity of resorting to Paris to learn this branch of the healing art." The authorities of the British Lying-In Hospital when asking for subscriptions in 1805 pointed out that by " such institutions the physician is enabled from the number of patients under his care . . . to derive considerable improvement to his profession ".

The Lying-In Charity for delivering poor women in their own homes, which was founded in 1757, also trained midwives and is typical of this kind of charity. It gave a free training to midwives, who had to obtain a certificate of proficiency from the physician of the charity, and in return for their training they were pledged to work for two years at low fees. London had a number of similar institutions, in some cases forming a department of a general dispensary, as in the case of the Westminster General Dispensary. Taken together, the lying-in charities in the latter part of the 18th century must have aided a considerable proportion of the poor women of London. The Lying-In Charity alone delivered 5,428 women in the year 1774–5, nearly one third of the total baptisms in the Bills of Mortality. The yearly average for this institution was between 4 and 5 thousand, that of the British Lying-In between 500 and 600. The accommodation of the latter institution was reduced during the first years of the 19th century, owing to the high cost of provisions, and the number fell to between 300 and 400.

The provinces seem to have followed London but slowly in the matter of Lying-In Charities, but by the end of the 18th century either hospitals or out-patient charities had been established in most important towns. In a guide to Manchester published in 1804 there is a description of the Salford Lying-In Hospital founded in 1790 for attending poor married women in their own homes. There was a small in-patients department for cases in which difficult delivery was anticipated, where the home circumstances were unsuitable or where the patient lived outside the district served by the midwives. The charity employed 16 paid midwives and there were also attached to it three accoucheurs, who were only to be called in in cases of difficulty. The charity was a training centre for midwives and nurse tenders and also kept a register of wet nurses. Free inoculation or vaccination was performed on both women and children and the charity also provided medical attention for children under two years and for diseases peculiar to women. The house for in-patients was furnished with iron bedsteads with white curtains and coverlids, and the patients were clothed in white. In total a very large number of doctors and midwives must have been trained by the various institutions, and though no doubt many untrained midwives and half-trained doctors remained in practice, yet even they must have picked up some of the new knowledge and in most towns skilled aid could be called upon in cases of difficulty. To the poorest the maternity charities were a more direct boon; before their establishment, the only place of refuge for those who could not afford help and maintenance was the general mixed workhouse; while the only paid attention available for the poor had been that of rough, totally untrained women, who often combined the employment of midwife with that of hawking fish and vegetables.

If one may judge by the records of the British Lying-In Hospital there was a considerable reduction in both maternal and infantile mortality during the second half of the 18th century. During the first ten years (1749–58) the average of deaths among the mothers was 1 in 42 (24 per 1000), among children 1 in 15 (66 per 1000). In 1779 to 1788 the corresponding figures were 1 in 60 (17 per 1000) and 1 in 44 (23 per 1000), in 1789–98 the figures were 1 in 288 (3·5 per 1000) and 1 in 77 (13 per 1000), in 1799–1808, 1 in 216 (4·5 per 1000) and 1 in 92 (10·8 per 1000). It must be remembered in considering these figures that a maternity hospital was at a disadvantage because, in the words of the Report for 1805 of the British Lying-In Hospital, " Women who are the most deformed or who are in very bad health, in general take the most pains to procure letters of admission into this charity, which certainly must add to the number of deaths, as of those . . . many would have died of disease, if they had not been with child." The dangers from puerperal fever were likely to be greater in a hospital and, in the earlier period, also from typhus and other infectious disorders not connected with child birth. Indeed it seems more than possible that a proportion, and possibly a large proportion, of the above quoted reduction in mortality was due, not to an advance in midwifery but to the reforms in general hygiene and hospital management.

According to a contemporary description of an " unreformed " confinement, the unfortunate woman was placed in a small room with a large fire, crowded with friends, and was given large doses of strong liquor. A rich woman after delivery was " covered up close in bed with additional cloths, the curtains are drawn round the bed and pinned together,

L

every crevice in the windows and door is stopped close not excepting even the keyhole, the windows are guarded not only with shutters and curtains but even with blankets the more effectually to exclude the fresh air and the good woman is not suffered to put her arm, or even her nose, out of bed for fear of catching cold. She is constantly supplied out of the spout of a tea pot with large quantities of warm liquors, to keep up perspiration and sweat, and her whole diet consists of them." The writer says that the poor living in cellars suffered from damp and those in attics from the stifling, heated air of tenement houses, while the maternity hospitals were stuffy, over-crowded and insanitary. He adds, "This description may seem over charged for a picture of that improved practice which is introduced by modern professors of the art; but upon a close examination I believe it will appear that many of the most important errors do in reality prevail, and this I impute in great measure to the large share which nurses have in directing the management of lying-in women, to whose interference practitioners must in some measure submit, though contrary to their better judgment." The writer advocated a return to nature and in particular the application of Sydenham "cool regimen", i.e., fresh air.[6] In this connection a report of the work of the Paris Maternité in 1808 is very significant. The figures for this institution contrast very unfavourably with the comparable figures for the British Lying-In. In the Maternité for the five years ending 1808 the average mortality of the mothers was 1 in 23 (43·5 per 1000) and of children 1 in 29 (34·5 per 1000), while for the British Lying-In the average of ten years ending 1808 was 1 in 216 (4·5 per 1000) for women and 1 in 92 (10·8 per 1000) for children. In fact, the Paris figure for maternal mortality were worse in 1808 than the English figures for 1760. The British Lying-In, however, was for married women only, whereas one department of the Maternité was open to poor married women, another to unmarried girls of previously good character and another to women of the town though this last class contributed very few patients. The difference in the class of patient doubtless raised the proportion of deaths due to venereal infection but on the other hand, f the reasons quoted above, the English institution would be likely to have a larger number of malformed patients, since many would enter the Paris institutions because they had no other refuge and not because they particularly needed skilled attention. But the explanation for the remarkable difference in the figures probably mainly lies in general hospital management; the writer of the description of the Maternité remarks that the maternal mortality figures improved from 1 in 23 to 1 in 32 in the years when the hospital was free from puerperal fever, "où il ne regne que des fièvres bileuses *putrides*" (typhus), "miliaire ou autres maladies." [7] In this connection it must be remembered that Howard, that impartial and severe critic, found the British Lying-In "clean and well managed".[8]

There are no English statistics available for the maternal mortality of the whole country and unfortunately the Carlisle tables do not include any figures for childbirth but only for the sub-heading, "difficult delivery." Dr. Short calculated in 1760 that 1 in 60 (16·7 per 1000) women died in childbed but Dr. Black writing in 1781 said, "others upon better foundation" calculated 3 in 200 (15 per 1000). Such calculations had to be based upon the very imperfect registers and Bills of Mortality. If they are at all reliable the difference caused by skilled attention is startlingly revealed by comparing these estimates with the figures of the British Lying-In and also those to be found in the Midwifery Reports of the Westminster General Dispensary published by Robert Bland in 1781. Here out of 1897 women delivered only 7 women died, that is a proportion of 1 in 270 (3·7 per 1000), a very near proportion to that of the British Lying-In at the same date. Of these seven deaths, four were due to puerperal fever. In comparing these figures with those of the present day it must be remembered that this scourge was then unpreventable, as, despite detailed study, medical science had failed to find either its cause or the means of prevention. To-day it is largely preventable and yet in the year 1922 there were 1,079 deaths from it in the United Kingdom, more than one-third of the total maternal deaths. Indeed, considering the great advance in general medical knowledge and hygiene the present day figures give little cause for gratification and it seems possible to claim, that relative to it's knowledge, the end of the 18th century has a better record in this vital matter of maternal well being than the end of the 19th or even the beginning of the 20th century.[9]

The advent of the qualified doctor into the lying-in room brought with it a revolution in infant nurture. From the first the doctors protested against the excessive clothing and tight swaddling beloved of the old nurse. A story is told of one of the early doctors who, seeing the unfortunate infant nearly choking, did not stop to have it unswaddled but promptly cut off its clothes. It is suggested in the story that this drastic action was necessary to save the infant's life; it was more probably a dramatic gesture akin to that of those later doctors who broke closed windows with their walking sticks. The doctors began also to advocate fresh air, cleanliness and sensible feeding; the kind of advice which advanced doctors were giving to well-to-do mothers in the middle of the 18th century can be gathered from Dr. William Cadogan's "Essay upon Nursing" published in 1747. This pamphlet was written in the form of a letter to the Governors of the Foundling Hospital, but the greater part of it is taken up with diatribes against the over feeding and over clothing of the children of the wealthy and with sensible, if caustically given, advice as to the rearing the children of the rich. Cadogan was of the opinion that the children of the poor were healthier and had a better chance of survival than those of the rich, since the poor were unable to kill their children with mistaken kindness. He, perhaps did not know very much about the children of the poor. Cadogan thought that child nurture should be considered in the light of science and the best medical knowledge and should no longer be a matter of custom and tradition, or as he somewhat unchivalrously expressed it, " In my opinion, this business has been too long fatally left to the management of Women . . . they presume upon examples and transmitted Customs of their Great-Grand Mothers, who were taught by the Physicians of their un enlightened days." He mentions as examples of these customs that new born children were nearly choked by dabs of butter and sugar or caudle being forced down their throats, some people even gave new born infants morsels of roast pork! Cadogan protested vigorously that the only food for the infant was its mother's milk. He inveighed against the common practice of employing a wet nurse, stating it to be dangerous for the infant and deleterious to the health of the mother. " Dry feeding " he considered practically tantamount to murder. He gave sensible advice as to the choice of a wet nurse should one be absolutely necessary. He pointed out to fashionable mothers that suckling their infants need not interfere with their comfort and pleasure, since it should only be at stated intervals and that four times in the 24 hours, as a rule, was sufficient. He condemned night feeding. For older children he advocated the inclusion of ripe fruit and vegetables in their diet and combated the current notion that such food was indigestible. Cadogan advocated fresh air and cleanliness, stating that " some imagine clean linen and fresh cloaths draw and rob them " (the infants) " of their nourishing juices ". On the contrary, infants cannot be changed too often since, as he frankly says, " it would free them from stinks and sournesses." Finally, this curiously modern adviser gave his contribution to the controversy of heredity and environment, he held that few diseases were inherited except scrofula and venereal diseases and that most disease was the result of wrong nurture. Cadogan, with his evident distrust of the female sex, implored fathers to exercise their marital authority in the vital matter of the rearing of their children. Whether they did so to the extent, at any rate, of presenting their wives with his pamphlet, or whether the wives were sufficiently enlightened to buy it for themselves, the fact remains that it went into ten editions between 1747 and 1772 and presumably at least some of the advice was followed. In 1773 a Dr. Clarke published a book upon the management of children in which he gave similar good advice as to light clothing, cleanliness and fresh air. He, more tactful than Cadogan, warned his readers that they would have to contend against the ignorant prejudice of nurses who " foolishly imagine that clean linen and fresh cloths draw away and rob them (i.e., the infants) of their nourishment ". The same idea had formerly been held about sick persons and Sydenham was one of the first to combat it.

The new ideas had a mass of ignorance and prejudice to overcome, even among the well to do, but they slowly gained ground and through the channels of the maternity hospitals the trained midwives and, most of all, the dispensaries, even penetrated to some degree to the homes of the poor. In 1816 a baby clinic (though not of course so called) was actually established in London. The Universal Dispensary for Sick Children, founded in that year, had as one of its objects the spread of the knowledge of infant and child management among the poor. Bound up with its report is a copy of the pamphlet distributed to poor mothers. This pamphlet advocated breast feeding, cleanliness, bathing, loose clothing and fresh air. The mother was warned against quack medicines and told to avoid night feeding. There was another pamphlet on the management of young children with advice upon similar lines.[10]

All contemporary authorities give the better care of infants as one cause of the diminution of the death rate, another was the better treatment and partial prevention of infantile diseases particularly smallpox. Together all these improvements resulted in a reduction of infantile mortality which has only been equalled in the 20th century.[11] Dr. Lettsom wrote in 1774 " In the nurture and management of infants, as well as in the treatment of lying-in women, the reformation hath equalled that of the small pox ; by these two circumstances alone incredible numbers are rescued from the grave ".[12]

CHAPTER XII

RICKETS AND SCURVY

" For if Rome decreed the Civic Crown to him who saved the life of a single citizen, what wreaths are due to that Man who having himself saved many perpetuates . . . the means by which Britain . . . may preserve numbers of her intrepid sons". (Sir John Pringle. Discourse on occasion of presentation of Copley medal to Captain Cook, 1776.)

It has been suggested in the previous chapter that a considerable part of the credit for the reduction of the infantile death rate must be given to the medical profession. But by no means all the credit was due to the doctors, a good deal must be ascribed to the general advance of society and in particular to the advance of agriculture. Undoubtedly a great deal of the infant and child mortality was due to malnutrition, sometimes causing direct specific disease, sometimes only leading to an impaired vitality. In this connection the histories of rickets and scurvy are important, not only in themselves, but as indicators of the general condition of the food supply of the population.

Rickets is a disease of malnutrition in childhood which shows itself in the lack of proper calcification of the bones. For a very long period it has been recognised as a dietic disease and many factors have been suspected in the past, such as a lack of lime in the water, too early or too late weaning and so on. Modern research has lately revealed a close correlation between rickets and the absence of fat-soluble vitamin A, which vitamin is present in most animal fat, and, in smaller quantities, in some vegetables. Butter and milk are particularly rich in it. But it is not believed that the absence of vitamin A is the sole determining factor in rickets. Obviously bone cannot be formed without calcium and phosphorus and a deficiency of either of these or a lack of balance between the two may lead to rickets.

It happens that several food-stuffs rich in vitamin A are often also rich in calcium so that a deficiency in these two factors may be closely associated. Recent research has also shown that sunlight is an important factor and that plentiful sunlight may counteract, at any rate to some extent, the deficiency of other anti-rachitic factors. Finally, Dr. Mellanby believes that cereals have a definite anti-calcification effect on growth and that in this respect oatmeal is the worst and white flour and rice the best. Calcification is an extremely complex physiological process which has by no means been completely elucidated; but it seems probable that there is more than one possible cause for rickets and that the worst cases are often due to a combination of causes.

Rickets was first ascribed by Glisson in a treatise published in 1650 which is famous as the first medical treatise on modern lines written by an Englishman. Glisson says that he first observed the disease " about thirty years since in the Counties of Dorset and Somerset " and ... " later in London, Oxford and Cambridge in almost all the Southern and Western parts of England " but that it was very rarely seen in the north. Glisson believed the disease to be a new one but there can be no doubt that it had existed long before his time but had not been recognised as a specific disease. Rickets seems to have been very prevalent in London in the 17th and early 18th centuries but to have decreased rapidly during the second half of the 18th century. The writer J. H. alleges that Charles I had rickets and that as a child he was so sickly that he " could neither go nor speak till 7 years old and altho' the said Prince outgrew and conquered the weakness ... yet he carried somewhat remarkable both in his Mouth and Knees to the Block and Scaffold. ... He ever walked in a riding Posture; and besides most of the Courtiers, and Wealthier sort of Citizens were accustomed to walk both to Church and Exchange in Boots, as being ashamed to expose their Crooked, Ricketty Legs ".[1]

Bateman writing in 1819 says that rickets, once " a most prevailing and mortal disease " ... " although occasionally occurring at present, among the children of the poor, has no longer a place in the bills of mortality, as a cause of death;

it is said to have originated in the West of England about the year 1540; but is first noticed in the Bills of London in the year 1624, when the total number of deaths, under this head, were only 14. It appears, however, to have increased rapidly, but irregularly; for, in 1649, the deaths from rickets amounted to 190;—in 1650 to 260;—in the following year to 329;—and in 1660, 521 persons died of the disease; at the commencement of the 18th century (A.D. 1700) the mortality from this disorder was 393; and it has since been on the decrease, as we find the number of deaths in the year 1750 to be only 21, and at the end of the century (1799) the deaths from 'evil and rickets' conjoined do not exceed 7 ".[2] He adds that the disease originated, increased and declined under no observable change of circumstances with which it could be connected. The origin and increase were probably a mere matter of nomenclature and diagnosis but that cannot be the case with the decline. After Glisson's treatise no moderately competent doctor could mistake a well marked case and the decrease in rickets was remarked upon by all medical writers on the history of disease. Blane says " there is no doubt . . . of the great decrease of it in common with other complaints of children ". Black in 1781 refers to the decline of rickets and ascribes it to " more maternal attention to the rearing and suckling of children ".[3]

Does modern knowledge throw any light on the problem? It is significant that the period of the decline in rickets is also the period of advance in agriculture, particularly in the breeding and feeding of cattle and the production of root crops and winter feed for cattle which made fresh meat and butter and also milk available all the year round. It was also a period of extensive market gardening which meant more vegetables, many of which contain not only vitamin A but calcium salts. It is notorious that the animals bred during the 18th century agricultural revival were very fat; many of the famous breeds have been abandoned because modern palates do not like the coarse fat meat. But their 18th century popularity may have been due to a natural craving on the part of people who had been starved of proper fat. We may safely associate the decrease of rickets with the better and more varied diet that became available after the revolution in agricultural methods, and the lighter houses and wider streets in towns may also have been a factor. It is possible also that in London the decrease may have been associated with the extinction of malaria and in support of this view Sydenham may be quoted; he says, " except in those years where autumnal intermittents are paramount true rickets rarely occur ". It may further be noted that Glisson's observations all refer to low lying, marshy districts.

The death rate from rickets was probably never high nor, on the other hand, can we imagine that rickets was quite as rare a disease at the beginning of the 19th century as contemporary writers supposed. Mild cases would escape diagnosis with the then available methods and many cases probably never came under the eye of a doctor at all. Even to-day the apparent incidence of rickets cannot be accepted at its face value, an apparently high incidence may only mean a very well organized medical service. But the evidence is fairly conclusive that very acute rickets decreased almost to the point of disappearance during the period under discussion,[4] and we can be certain, in the light of modern knowledge, that mild rickets decreased *pari passu*. For every child that died of rickets there would have been numbers who survived with every degree of deformity and ill health and numbers more, who apparently had never had rickets, who yet suffered from ill-defined delicacy. Modern research has shown that if the anti-rachitic factors are absent during pregnancy and lactation the maternal organism attempts to supply them at its own expense, thus leading to ill health and ultimately to disease in the mother. The conditions which produced acute rickets, therefore, were probably a factor in maternal mortality. But rickets certainly added to maternal mortality in another way, for one of the results of suffering from it in childhood is contracted pelvis. Before the improvement of obstetrics in the 18th century this malformation must have meant almost certain death both for mother and child. 17th and 18th century writers on midwifery in discussing cases of difficult delivery often mention that the patient had suffered from rickets in her youth.[5]

Modern medical science distinguishes between true rickets and "scurvy rickets". Scurvy, which does not normally occur in adults in modern times, does sometimes occur in babies which have been fed on dried milk extracts. Scurvy is also a deficiency disease due to the absence of certain essential factors from the diet. Recent scientific research has established the fact that these accessory food factors, which have been christened vitamin C, are to be found in varying quantities in most raw vegetables and fruits and are destroyed, in varying degrees, by cooking and preservation processes. They are also found in small quantities in fresh meat but are destroyed in preserved meat. The exact nature and functions of these vitamins have yet to be elucidated.[6]

Scurvy is now thought of as a disease peculiar to seamen but a knowledge of its cause at once suggests that it must frequently have occurred on land before the modern developments in agriculture and transport. This is borne out by historical records of the 16th and 17th centuries in which scurvy is frequently mentioned. Hentzner [7] in his travels in the time of Elizabeth observes that "the English are often molested by scurvy" and it is noteworthy that in England the art of gardening was particularly backward. Chameau [8] writing in 1683 says "that scurvy in a particular manner is endemic with the English". However, scurvy also occurred very frequently elsewhere.

The writer J. H.[9] who published what he called a supplement to Graunt's work says, "Scorbute ... hath invaded all the Populous Cities along the Sea Coast of Germany, Holland and England". He is not absolutely reliable, as he thought, not unnaturally, that scurvy and rickets were different forms of the same disease. But he mentions a bad epidemic in Paris in 1652, due to the blockade, and a further one in 1670, which were probably true scurvy; indeed the latter epidemic is mentioned in the records of l'Hôpital Saint-Louis and is said not to have ceased until 1690. A new epidemic occurred in Paris in 1709, " par suite de la rigueur de l'hiver et de la misère qu'il occasionna ".[10] J. H. quotes the famous French physician Patin as saying " we do not meet with the Disease among the Rich Burgers, but only amongst the Poor People, which Wretches mostly drink bad Waters ." It is curious after this to read in Smollett that the French doctors of his day seemed to think that scurvy was a purely English disease. Perhaps the 17th century confusion between scurvy and rickets had survived, for rickets was always known on the Continent as the English disease, for no better reason than that an Englishman first described it. Smollett, who was himself a doctor, says that the French doctors " often confound the symptoms of it " (scurvy) " with those of venereal distemper ".[11] Pringle states that scurvy was endemic in the Baltic provinces in the late 18th century owing to a winter diet of salt meat and no vegetables.[12]

In Northern Europe it is not easy to obtain an adequate supply of fruit and green vegetables, especially during the winter months. Until the 17th century the art of gardening remained extremely backward, indeed some authorities believe that there was retrogression in the 14th and 15th centuries, at any rate in England. This retrogression, if it actually took place, may have been associated with the upheaval caused by the Black Death and also with the decay and final destruction of monasticism, since monks and nuns have always found in gardening a solace for the loss of many earthly pleasures. During this period, too, England became predominantly pastoral and gardening is seldom highly developed in a pastoral community. The women, who are the gardeners in all primitive communities, are perhaps too occupied with dairy work to undertake it. In the latter 16th century a revival in gardening began, which revival was continued during the 17th century. Wealthy persons began to take a pride in their gardens and to introduce new plants from abroad. In England the revival was much influenced by the example of Holland. This movement, however, only affected the well to do ; the poor, especially in towns, would probably have had a very inadequate supply of vegetables even in summer and would have been without in the winter, when, moreover, only salted meat would have been obtainable. But by the end of the 18th century a great change had occurred. The agricultural revolution had made fresh meat available all the year round and market gardening had so developed, especially round London, that vegetables were obtainable even by the poor. In 1758 Tucker wrote, " the price of green vegetables is prodigiously sunk to what it was in former times, and I much question whether any town of note in Scotland can now vie with the common markets of London in that respect. Certain it is that . . . about 100 years ago a cabbage would have cost threepence in London which at present may be bought for a halfpenny. . . . The common articles of pease and beans, sallads, onions, carrots, parsnips and turnips are considerably cheaper than ever they were known to be in former times, tho' the rent of garden grounds and the wages of journeymen gardeners are a great deal higher." [13] The introduction of the potato as a common article of diet was also important from the point of view of the extinction of scurvy. The potato is not rich in the anti-scorbutic factor but it does possess it and if eaten in sufficient quantities is protective. It has the great advantage of keeping and therefore being obtainable and relatively cheap in the winter and early spring when other vegetables are very dear. Its importance is proved by the fact that local outbreaks of scurvy among the poor followed failures of the potato crop in the 19th century and even, under war conditions, in 1917.[14] The use of the potato was increasing rapidly during the 18th century and as early as 1758 a writer speaks of it as " that great help of the poor ".[15]

Owing to this improved dietary, scurvy ceased to be a cause of death among the civilian population though doubtless mild cases occurred in times of scarcity. Lind stated in 1753 that scurvy was still found among the land population, though not in an extreme form. Blane says that a considerable number of deaths were ascribed to scurvy in the London Bills of Mortality of the 17th century, seldom under 50, often as high as 90 ; he adds, " we know from the description which Willis has given us that a disease having the genuine characters of sea scurvy did prevail in London in that age though now entirely extinct ".[16] Bateman was doubtful if scurvy was ever very prevalent in London, he believed that consumption was often confused with it, but the balance of evidence is strongly against this view. It is possible that some of the rickets of the 17th and early 18th centuries was really infantile scurvy. This disease can occur even in breast fed babies if the mother's diet is very deficient in anti-scorbutic factors.

Scurvy often appears in acute form in beleaguered cities or among armies imperfectly provisioned, either from necessity or from mismanagement. Several thousand Saxons died of it at the siege of Thorn in 1703, Howard found it prevalent in the military hospitals in Russia in 1790.[17] In more recent times scurvy has often been a menace to armies either on account of military contingencies or through the ignorance of commanders. There was much suffering from this disease during the American Civil War owing to the use of dried vegetables instead of fresh ones. During the late war a severe outbreak of scurvy among the Indian troops at the siege of Kut was an important factor in the final surrender. The white troops were saved by a large ration of fresh horse flesh.[18]

The reduction of scurvy on land was due to the advance in agriculture, but its conquest at sea can be ascribed to administrative action based on medical knowledge. Scurvy only became a specifically sea disease with the long voyages of modern times; the first account of the disease at sea is that of Vasco da Gama who lost by it 100 men out of 150. In the first voyage of the East India Company the four ships carried a total complement of 480 men and, when the ships were three days beyond the line, the scurvy was so bad that the merchants had to do duty as common sailors and before the Cape was reached 105 men were dead.[19] Sir Richard Hawkins said that in 20 years' life at sea he could give an account of 10,000 mariners who had been consumed by scurvy. The disease continued to be a heavy drain on the manhood of the maritime nations during the 18th century, especially in war time when vessels were kept at sea for long periods. In 1747, 1,200 men of Admiral Martin's fleet were disabled by scurvy and John Huxham of Devon (a pupil of Boerhaave) recommended that they should be put upon a vegetable diet. Lind states in 1754 that more men died of scurvy in the preceding naval war than were killed in action with the French and Spanish. The fleet was on several occasions prevented from putting to sea owing to this disease. In the ship in which Lind voyaged in

1746, 80 men out of 350 were prostrated by it and when Lord Anson circumnavigated the globe one of his vessels lost 292 men out of 506 and the other, 292 out of 374.

At first it was thought that sea scurvy was a different disease from land scurvy and that it was due to sea air and damp. Some authorities held it to be infectious, rather naturally, since whole crews would be affected at once. Lind, writing in 1753, declared land and sea scurvy to be one and the same disease and that therefore it was not due to sea air nor was it infectious since officers practically never contracted it. He found the true cause in the diet of the common sailor which consisted of salt meat and biscuit and said that the disease could not only be cured but prevented by the provision of fresh fruit and vegetables. He recommended the use of lemon juice as being very effectual and easy to carry on ship-board. Lind was not the discoverer of the anti-scorbutic properties of fruit and vegetables in general and oranges and lemons in particular. Nature gives to the victim of scurvy an intense longing for fruit and vegetables, Lind himself noted that scorbutic patients ate the oranges and lemons given to them with greediness. The almost magical effect of anti-scorbutics upon the patients could not fail to be noticed by the most ignorant and unobservant. This common knowledge was accepted by the more broadminded physicians, though others continued to advocate useless remedies. Mead, not a very original thinker, writing in 1702 thought scurvy was due to bad air, yet he stated it could be cured by fruit and vegetables, especially oranges, lemons and pomegranates. As early as 1720 Kramer, chief surgeon of the Austrian army in Hungary, after having been faced with an outbreak of scurvy in which thousands perished and in which the remedies dispatched by the Vienna College of Physicians were useless, commented in his Medicina Castrensis as follows—" The scurvy is the most loathsome disease in nature : for which no cure is to be found in your medicine chest, no, not in the best furnished apothecary's shop. Pharmacy gives no relief, surgery as little. Beware of bleeding : shun mercury as a poison : you may rub the gums, you may grease the rigid tendons in the knee, to little purpose. But if you can get green vegetables, if you can prepare a sufficient quantity of fresh, noble, anti-scorbutic juices, if you have oranges, lemons or citrons; or their pulp and juice preserved with whey in cask, so that you can make a lemonade, or rather give to the quantity of three or four ounces of their juice in whey, you will, without other assistance cure this dreadful evil." Bachstrom writing in 1734 said, " From want of proper attention to the history of scurvy, its causes have been generally, though wrongfully, supposed to be, cold in northern climates, sea air, the use of salt meats, etc., whereas this evil is solely owing to a total abstinence from fresh vegetable food and greens, which is alone the true primary cause of the disease. And where persons, either from neglect or necessity, do refrain for a considerable time from eating the fresh fruits of the earth and greens no age, no climate or soil are exempted from its attack. Other secondary causes may likewise concur: but recent vegetables are found alone effectual to preserve the body from this malady and most speedily to cure it, even in a few days, when the case is not rendered desperate by the patients being dropsical or consumptive."

Lind was acquainted with the works of both these above writers, indeed the above quotations are taken from his book. But he was no mere copyist, he had studied the disease at first hand in his capacity of navy surgeon and in 1747 had carried out a rough experiment upon twelve scurvy patients from which he had concluded that, among the various available remedies recommended by different authorities, lemons and oranges were the only satisfactory anti-scorbutics. Lind published his results in 1757 in his famous Essay on the Health of Seamen. Its importance in respect to scurvy lies in its clear and convincing exposition and the stress laid upon *prevention* rather than cure. Ships' crews should be given fresh meat and vegetables whenever possible and during long voyages a regular ration of lemon juice should be consumed daily. Lind's ideas upon naval hygiene were given a great advertisement by the experiences of Captain Cook. In a voyage of discovery ending in 1771 this famous explorer lost 30 men out of a complement of 85, mainly from scurvy. This proportion was not considered heavy at the time. Cook then became acquainted with the new methods of preventing scurvy and of general naval hygiene and applied them in his next voyage of exploration. This lasted 3½ years and was an extremely hard voyage, yet the expedition enjoyed entire freedom from scurvy and, out of a complement of 118 men, lost only one man by disease, which man is stated to have been consumptive when he embarked. Curiously enough Cook was no believer in lemon or orange juice and pinned his faith to malt, sugar and sauerkraut. Modern science only confirms his faith in regard to the first. Pringle thought that Cook's poor opinion of lemon juice was due to his having had experience of juice which had been improperly prepared. Cook, however, was careful to touch land and to obtain fresh provisions whenever possible and he carried portable soup by means of which he rendered unaccustomed green food palatable. Captain King who wrote the account of Cook's third voyage, during which Cook was killed, stated that scurvy was avoided " by availing ourselves of every substitute our situation at various times afforded. These frequently consisting of articles which our people had not been used to consider as food for men, and being sometimes exceedingly nauseous, it required the joint aid of persuasion, authority, and example, to conquer their prejudices and disgusts ". Cook also exercised persuasion, authority and example in inculcating scrupulous cleanliness both of the person and of sleeping quarters and also careful ventilation of the latter. He in fact, instituted that almost fanatical cleanliness which we associate with a well managed ship and which alone renders healthy conditions possible in a crowded and confined space. If it be considered what the condition of ships must have been before these reforms, the appalling death rate among sailors is easily explained.

Cook's achievement in the matter of health during his second voyage caused a considerable stir. He was invited to read a paper explaining his methods before the Royal Society and later the Society bestowed upon him the Copley medal, upon the occasion of the presentation of which Sir John Pringle, the President, delivered a laudatory address.[20] The new ideas, however, spread slowly; it was not until 1795 that the Admiralty, owing to the efforts of Sir Gilbert Blane, ordered the provision of lemon juice upon every ship and the issue of a lemon juice ration when at sea. This ration was served with sugar, also believed to be anti-scorbutic and mixed with the rum ration in order to ensure its being taken. The effect of correct precautions against scurvy was magical. Blane states that in 1779 the Channel fleet after a cruise of 10 weeks put on shore 2,400 men ill of scurvy. In 1800 the Channel fleet kept the sea off Brest for four months without one ship being in port and when they did return to port there were only 16 subjects for hospital. He adds, "If the mortality during the 20 years of the revolutionary war had been equal to what it was in 1779, the whole stock of seamen would have been exhausted." It is recorded that in 1797 Earl Spencer visited Haslar and wished to see a case of scurvy and there was not one in the hospital. Writing in 1813 Blane was able to say that scurvy " is now nearly as rare at sea as it is on land ".

Though the Admiralty order was not issued until 1795 many commanders undoubtedly anticipated it. Blane effected a great improvement in the health of Rodney's fleet in 1779 especially in regard to scurvy, and his tract for officers of the fleet upon the health of seamen must have been read by many Lind's much greater work went into several editions and must have been read by many young navy surgeons and officers The new movement was much helped by the new school of navy officers which was growing up. In the old days when the mercantile and navy services were not differentiated, the fighting officers were army officers detailed for the purpose, with soldiers acting under them, and the navigating officers were the ordinary mercantile captains, rough men who had generally served before the mast. As a royal navy gradually evolved the officer continued at first to be of a similar class, brave and skilful men no doubt, but like the early master manufacturers, hardened by their own early experiences, and unlikely to be amenable to new ideas. Cook, it is true, had risen from the ranks but he was in every way an exceptional man. During the 18th century the navy gradually became a profession for gentlemen and its officers began to be largely recruited from the families of the smaller squirearchy and the clergy. They came, in fact, from homes where paternal care for the poor, even if a stern paternal care, was part of the everyday work of life, and they were sufficiently educated to realize the importance of the health of seamen from a military point of view. During the latter part of the century the navy was engaged in a stern conflict which gave scope to talent and ensured that, on the whole, the officers were men of elasticity of mind. Above all there was the influence of Nelson. Nelson was the darling of the fleet, not only because of his personal daring and his success in war but because he cared for the well being of the ordinary sailor. No officer could hope for his approval who did not follow him in this in the letter, if not in the spirit. Nelson took a great pride in the health of his crews. He writes after the pursuit of Villeneuve's fleet to the West Indies, " We have lost neither officer nor man by sickness since we left the Mediterranean " (a period of ten weeks, total numbers about 7,000) ; the " French and Spanish landed a thousand sick at Martinique and buried full that number during their stay ". Collingwood writes, " I have not let go an anchor for 15 months, and on the first day of the year had not a sick list in the ship—not one man ".[21] This perfection of naval hygiene must have been no small factor in victory, for the man-of-war's man was a highly skilled person not easily replaced, moreover good health among fighting men enormously increases their military value. The honour of this great administrative achievement rests with Nelson and his band of devoted commanders, but they built upon the knowledge supplied by the doctors ; and the name of Lind, which is almost forgotten, surely deserves to be enshrined in honourable memory with that of Nelson.

CHAPTER XIII

ANTISEPTICS, SEGREGATION, LEPROSY AND PLAGUE

BESIDES the inculcation of general hygiene, 18th century medicine waged a definite campaign against disease by the use of the twin methods of disinfection and segregation. Neither of these methods was new, both, indeed, had their roots in the immemorial past, but in the 18th century they were first brought to some degree of scientific precision and applied with a considerable degree of success.

From the earliest times it had been believed that certain substances had the power of protecting from disease. Sweet smelling herbs and spices were in particular favour in the Middle Ages. The custom of sprinkling herbs in Court Houses as a protection against gaol fever survived long after its futility was known. The 18th century doctor carried herbs in the great knob of his cane as a protection against infection, though many of them in so doing were probably merely following custom. The fumes arising from the burning of these substances were held to be more effectual than the natural scent. The Arab physicians recommended burning spices and balsams and in 14th century Italy one of the measures taken against the plague was the burning of balsams and resins.[1] Fire was generally held to be a purifying agent and in the 15th and 16th centuries in times of plague it was customary to light great fires in the streets and also to burn all infected clothes. Infected houses were exposed to the air 40 days. It is said that the fumigation of infected houses and clothing was first brought into use by a Capucin monk at Genoa in 1657.[2] This invention obviated the necessity of destroying clothing, etc. a procedure which had always led to much concealment, and it also reduced the purification period for houses from 40 days to 24 hours. Many different substances were used for fumigation

Mead writing in 1720 says that making hot fumes with benzoin, frankincense and storax was often recommended but he did not see any reason to expect their virtue " to destroy the matter of infection ", but he thought " it not improper to fume houses with vinegar, either alone or with nitre " by throwing these on a hot iron or tile. He condemned fumigation with mercury or arsenic as dangerous but thought smoke of sulphur, " which is found by experience to be very penetrating and to have a great power to repress fermentations . . . may promise some service this way." Mead was obviously no great believer in fumigation, he rather tolerated it as a harmless alternative to the burning of infected goods, to which he had a great objection as he believed contagion to be spread by the flying embers. During the 18th century, however, fumigation, particularly with sulphur, steadily gained ground. Lind was a great believer in it and laid down a regular routine in connection with typhus. Hale designed an apparatus for fumigating infected clothing with sulphur and this, or a similar apparatus was part of the equipment of the earliest fever hospitals. Houses were also fumigated and washed with lime. Howard is said to have discovered the antiseptic properties of ordinary limewash. Quick lime was first used in burying the victims of the plague in the 17th century.

It would seem, therefore, that fumigation can be traced to the burning of sweet herbs or balsams which originally may have had a religious or magical significance. In the 17th century or earlier this began to be replaced by the burning of substances giving noxious vapours. This may have been connected with the belief in infection as a living thing which would be destroyed by anything which destroyed other life. By experiment the 18th century selected nitre and sulphur, particularly the latter, as being both effectual and easy to handle.[3]

Closely related, both in practice and theory, to the use of antiseptics was the vigorous segregation of infected persons, by quarantine laws and by the provision of special institutions for persons suffering from certain infectious illnesses. Both developments were dependent for their successful application upon an advance in theory as to the nature of infection.

Primitive magic or animism held that all qualities were transferable from one object to another and that such transference could be hindered or fostered by certain actions. One of the most obvious ways of preventing the transference of an undesirable quality was to avoid all contact with the object possessing it. Here is the germ of the idea of contagion and its avoidance by segregation. All organized religions, with their teaching as to an all powerful God or gods, tended to discourage this idea; disease, especially epidemic disease, came as a punishment from heaven and the only hope was to induce heaven by prayer, fasting and sacrifice to deign to remove the scourge. Modern research has shown, however, that the old animistic ideas have lingered in superstition and folk lore after thousands of years of condemnation by priests and law givers.[4] And the belief that contact with certain forms of illness was dangerous can never have disappeared completely, re-inforced as it must have been by practical experience.

Though the Greek medical writers knew certain diseases to be contagious they had no specific theories about contagion and they were inclined to associate epidemics with conditions of the atmosphere. As a matter of fact atmospheric conditions are important factors in the spread of many contagious diseases and the opinion of the ancients was therefore based on observed fact. Many historians believe that malaria was the scourge *par excellence* of Greek civilization; if this opinion is correct it would have favoured the idea of " bad air " as a cause of epidemic disease. Medical thought has always been much influenced by the nature of the disease which is attracting attention at the moment. Medieval thought, which believed in cocks producing serpents and mice being spontaneously generated in bags of corn, was not likely to have any ordered ideas about the production of disease; but with the dawn of the New Learning many curious minds turned to the problem. The Black Death and plague in general were so obviously infectious that the fact of infection began to be accepted in the case of certain diseases; and the brilliant hypothesis that disease was due to minute living beings was formulated out of due time.[5] The discovery of the parasite that causes itch, which is large enough to be visible with a strong magnifying glass, made it easier to accept the idea that other diseases were caused by parasites of a smaller size, yet the idea remained barren, it bore no fruit in the field of practical medicine.[6]

The early 17th century held almost fanatically to the belief in infection, as the Plague Ordinances showed. The late 17th and early 18th century medical writers were inclined to return to the Greek idea that epidemics were due to climatic conditions and several long records were kept of health and weather conditions in order to prove a correlation. But again the pendulum swung and by the second half of the 18th century advanced medical opinion began to look on infection as the primary cause of epidemics. It was believed that infection was conveyed in effluvia that were given off by the sick person. Some authorities believed in minute particles which conveyed infection from one person to another, but it is not clear that these were thought of as living beings capable of reproduction. The infections of different diseases were, however, believed to be distinct and only capable of producing their own disease and to differ in their method of travelling from one person to another. Some could travel through the air, some such as the typhus could not, but could be conveyed by clothing or other infected objects. According to this theory there was nothing impossible in the plague infection making long journeys in a bale of cotton. The believers in "fomites"[7] frankly confessed that they knew very little about them except that it was possible to destroy them with fresh air, soap and water, heat and the fumes of certain "antiseptics". Practice rather than theory was the mark of the age. The 18th century medical writers on typhus and other fevers devote very little space to the theory of contagion and a great deal to directions as to fumigation and hospital management. It is not certain whether the doctrine of "fomites" is a faint and debased echo of Fracastor's brilliant teaching or whether it was invented anew to explain the observed facts. Pringle quotes Fracastor in another connection, so his work was known to him indirectly, if not directly. In any case it is clear that the practice of the 18th century in regard to infectious illness was based upon the experience gained in dealing with plague and that this, in its turn, was derived from the ancient policy of the segregation of the leper, a policy which goes back to ancient times and had religious sanction, a sanction that was perhaps itself a survival of animistic belief.

Leprosy was a well known disease in medieval Europe and at one time there were as many as 95 religious hospitals for leprosy in Great Britain. There can be no doubt that a large number of the inmates of these hospitals, perhaps even the majority, were not lepers, since in the Middle Ages any disease which caused repulsive looking eruptions of the skin was apt to be called leprosy. Many modern medical authorities hold that a considerable proportion of medieval leprosy was in reality syphilis.[8] However, true leprosy undoubtedly existed in medieval Europe though to what extent it is quite impossible to say. During the 15th century the disease almost disappeared from the greater part of Europe, though it lingered in Scotland and Norway until the 19th century. Leprosy is due to a bacterial infection (*Bacillus leprae*) but the method of infection is still unknown. It may possibly be conveyed by the bite of insects or by food, many authorities have believed it to be associated with the consumption of putrid food, particularly fish.[9] Its extinction in Europe may have been due to the segregation of the afflicted persons or to some other factor; until we know the method of infection it is impossible to form an opinion, since the fact that the disease has been proved to be bacterial proves nothing as to the method of infection. Malaria is due to a bacterial infection but ordinary segregation would be useless to arrest it. The medical authorities who associate leprosy with putrid food, especially fish, are supported by the historical fact that a considerable amount of badly and insufficiently salted fish was consumed in the Middle Ages. Salt was a dear and rare article and was no doubt often used too sparingly. With the growth of commerce salt became easier to acquire and new sources of supply were discovered, inventions also appear to have been made in the process of curing fish. Anderson mentions an improved method of curing fish in the year 1220 and improvements in herring curing were made in Flanders in the 15th century. There is no reason to suppose that the death rate from leprosy was ever high and in any case the extinction of the disease in England is outside the period covered by this book. The importance of leprosy from the public health aspect lies in its influence on the development of preventive medicine, since it was the first disease in respect of which vigorous segregation was practised. Leprosy is a very repulsive disease and it is not surprising that, in the days when all illness was ascribed to the displeasure of Heaven, the leper was considered in a peculiar degree accursed of God. Plagues and pestilences showed the Almighty's displeasure with a whole community but the slow agony of leprosy implied personal moral guilt. Since many so called lepers probably were in reality the victims of venereal disease it may also have been noticed that " leprosy " often followed loose moral conduct. Natural abhorrence of so loathsome an illness and impatience with the long drawn out agony no doubt made friends and relatives easily acquiescent in the terrible verdict, " Unclean." God had cursed the leper and set him apart " outside the camp " and those who ignored the sentence ran the danger of sharing the curse; observed cases of infection would fortify this belief. The stern Mosaic Law had not troubled about the fate of the leper, but Christianity, whose Founder called sinners to repentance, coupled with the ancient sentence of expulsion the provision of shelter and sustenance. The provision of Lazar Houses became a popular form of Christian charity and with the dawning belief in infection this provision began to have a hygienic as well as a religious significance. The idea of segregation, originally religious and superstitious, resting on a belief in moral guilt and the danger of sharing a curse, took on a new aspect. The provision of special institutions for the segregation of persons suffering from one infectious disease being hallowed in the popular conscience as a religious act, it was easier to adopt the same system in regard to another disease. When the Venetian authorities (about 1484) took the momentous step of providing special pest houses the name Lazarettos clearly showed the origin of the idea.

True plague was extinct in England before the main period

of this study. But no account of the Public Health in England in the 18th century could be complete without some discussion of the reasons for the absence of plague, which had been such a terrible scourge in previous centuries. Moreover it was in connection with plague that improved methods of disinfection and segregation were developed and their apparent success in combating this dread disease encouraged their application to other epidemics.

In the Middle Ages the term plague was applied to any epidemic disease which caused great mortality. Probably many of the visitations of " plague " were typhus, others may have been influenza or, in fact, any type of infection which would spread rapidly and fatally in the absence of all hygienic and medical knowledge. By the 18th century the term plague was limited to the so called Oriental, Levantine or Bubonic plague. It is now known that the pneumonic plague is the same disease in a different form. It is probable that the Black Death was true plague in its pneumonic variety. True plague is primarily a disease of rats and the *Bacillus pestis* is conveyed from rat to rat by the rat flea. When the plague reaches epidemic height among the rat population and consequently numbers of rats are killed by it, the rat flea, which normally only bites rats, is driven to seek other hosts, including man, and these infected fleas convey plague to their new hosts. The bubonic plague is not normally spread from man to man but from rats to man and it may be spread from place to place by infected ships' rats or by fleas in merchandise. The Indian Commission on Plague held the last to be the most important method. It is also possible that bugs and lice can carry plague. The pneumonic variety can be air carried from man to man, especially in damp weather.[10] The connection between rats and plague was noticed even in ancient times. The episode recorded in I Samuel, chapter vi, shows evidence of such observation. The possibility of the conveyance of plague by bales of merchandise was well recognised in the 17th and 18th centuries; witness in the oft quoted case of the village of Eyam in the Peak district to which plague was conveyed in 1665 by a packet of clothes from London which resulted in the death of 260 of the inhabitants.

It is an extremely interesting question, both historically and medically, whether plague was ever endemic in Western Europe. Bateman says "besides these examples of extensive epidemic pestilence the limited appearance of the disease is frequently introduced in the bills of mortality within the same period (i.e. between 1593 and 1665) in fact there are few annual bills within that period in which some instances of death from the plague are not enumerated". But though the symptoms of the bubonic plague are extremely well marked, the buboes or tumours (really swollen glands) from which its name is derived being recognisable by the most ignorant, yet, unless descriptions of the illness have survived, it cannot be certain that the illness so designated is true plague, since the term originally had a wider connotation. The London outbreaks of the 17th century are authenticated by the writings of Willis and Sydenham and probably most epidemics in the 17th century so designated are true plague, while by the 18th century the limitation of the term is thoroughly well established. But though the physicians of the 17th century may have kept the term plague for one well recognised disease, it is by no means certain that the ignorant compilers of the Bills of Mortality did so, any death by a mysterious and sudden illness may have been called "plague". For the same reason the death rate may have been exaggerated in epidemic years. On the other hand, in epidemic years when extremely inconvenient quarantine laws were in force, there were strong reasons for concealing deaths from plague and for this reason Graunt believed that the deaths between 1603 and 1625 were underestimated by one-quarter. With regard to the entries in non-epidemic years they may have referred to true sporadic cases which would always be possible in a port. The 18th century medical writers and administrators held firmly to the theory of re-infection from the East and the name Oriental or Levantine plague embodies this belief upon which the whole elaborate structure of quarantine regulations was based. The fact that all recorded outbreaks of plague started in ports or trade centres supports this theory. Short says, "When the Plague made sad havock in London and some maritime places it scarce troubled the English

Continent," which moreover seems also to suggest that even the crude quarantine methods of the 17th century had some measure of success. Indeed in 1665 Scotland, which had extremely stringent quarantine regulations, escaped infection. The author of the Great Plague of London believes that plague was endemic in that city in the 17th and previous centuries. He, perhaps, attaches too much weight to the medical nomenclature of the time. To the present writer the weight of evidence appears to be in favour of periodic re-infection from the East, at any rate in the 17th century; but the question is one that cannot be answered with certainty.

Plague gradually died out in Western Europe during the 17th and early 18th centuries, the last great epidemic in France was in 1720-22. The last visitation in England was the Plague of London, the final remnants of which are believed to have been destroyed in the Great Fire.[11] The causes of the elimination of this disease in Western Europe at first sight are somewhat mysterious. It is doubtless true that the Fire of London was a factor in ending a particular visitation of the plague, probably by destroying the rats which carried the infected parasites. But the Fire of London in 1666 can hardly account for the reduction of plague throughout Western Europe and for its final cessation in France in 1722.

Some medical historians believe that there was a natural decrease in virulence in plague during the 18th century [12]; against this view there is the recorded terrible mortality of the local outbreaks in the south of Europe. For instance that of Marseilles and Toulon in 1720 with 91,000 deaths, that of Messina in 1743 with 70,000 deaths, that of Cyprus in 1759 with 70,000 deaths,

It has also been suggested that the retreat of the disease was due to an alteration in the rat population. In this connection it is significant that the old English black rat (*mus rattus*) was ousted by the so-called Norwegian or brown rat (*mus decumanus*) early in the 18th century. The black rat is small and friendly and, like the mouse, lives in houses. The brown rat is sly and fierce, its home is in sewers, docks, slaughter houses and granaries in towns; in the country in ricks, hedges and ditches. The brown rat, is, therefore, less likely to convey infection to man since he avoids him as far as possible. Why the brown rat should have made a successful invasion of this country in the 18th century is unknown. Conditions were certainly becoming, at any rate in London, less favourable to the black rat and more favourable to the brown. The new brick houses erected after the Fire gave less good harbourage to vermin of all kinds than the old rotting, timbered ones. While, on the other hand, the erection of docks and warehouses, due to the development of trade and the building of closed-in sewers gave suitable environment to the brown rat. In Bombay, at the present time, the brown sewer rat is displacing the black house rat in the Europeanized parts of the city, while the black rat holds its own in the Easternized suburbs.[13] This change in the rat population may well have been an important factor in the retreat of plague in the 18th century. Another favourable factor was the introduction of the sea route to the East.

The weight of evidence, however, suggests that it was the improved quarantine regulations which really conquered this dread infection. To those familiar with the corruption and ineptitude of most public administration in Europe in the 18th century this may seem an incredible proposition, but Plague was a word to conjure with, it roused the corrupt and inefficient officialdom of the 18th century to drastic action, in which action the support of the population was assured. The horror which a disease inspires is not necessarily in proportion to its death dealing powers, it is dependent on the repulsiveness of its symptoms, and on the rapidity with which it kills, since, though the fear of sudden death may be illogical, it is very deep seated and has religious sanction. Familiarity breeds contempt, therefore an epidemic disease is more feared than an endemic one; also the death rate of an epidemical disease is more noticeable. An illness which recurs every 25 years and kills say, $\frac{1}{5}$th of the population in one year attracts more attention than one which kills say, $\frac{1}{125}$th annually. The rapidity with which an infection spreads and the rate of mortality among the infected will also be factors in the degree of dread which a particular epidemic will inspire. The plague stands out pre-eminent in the possession of these qualities. It was epidemic in Europe, recurring in the 17th century roughly about once in every generation, its symptoms were horrifying, it killed quickly, it spread rapidly and it slew a large proportion of those attacked.

The 18th and early 19th century writers attached great importance to proper quarantine regulations for plague. Mid 19th century writers poured scorn on these methods and thought that quarantine had had nothing to do with the extinction of the disease.[14]. The reason probably was that Asiatic cholera, which was the scourge of the mid 19th century and which was only introduced into Europe in the '30's, was not contagious in the narrow sense, but was spread through the pollution of food and of water, the latter in particular. The general introduction of water drainage, often into rivers which were a source of water supply, caused this disease to spread rapidly and ordinary quarantine, if the hospitals used the common drain, was, of course, quite ineffective as a preventive once the infection was introduced into a country. It was typical of a certain lack of elasticity in early Victorian thought to condemn a method as ineffectual for all disease, because it had been found to be ineffectual for one. It was typical of the practical 18th century mind that it found the correct method of combating three great scourges, not by any application of general theory but by the correct observation of facts. There was one great advance in practice which probably contributed largely to the success of the measures against plague. The old method had been to shut the victims of the plague into their own houses, placing a mark upon the door forbidding all exit and entry; this not only condemned all the inmates to almost certain death, but placed a premium upon concealment and evasion. Attempts were also made to avoid all communication with infected districts; this policy also led to evasion. As early as the 15th century the Venetian authorities established plague "lazarettos" to which victims were removed [15] and in the 16th century substituted quarantine for prohibition of movement. This enlightened policy gradually

spread to the rest of Europe. Mead recommended it in his
" Short Discourse on Pestilential Contagion (1720) " written
by command during a scare caused by the outbreak of plague at
Marseilles. The period of 40 days was chosen for quarantine,
not from medical observation, but possibly through association
with Lent, and the fortieth day was also considered a critical one
in disease.[16]

The Venetian Government not only established quarantine
regulations for persons coming from infected ports but invented the system of Bills of Health carried by captains of ships.
Letters of Health written by the Consuls of the various nations
trading in the Levant first became customary about 1665.
Percival [17] the younger ascribes the extinction of plague
to the establishment of lazarettos and quarantine on the
Venetian model. An 18th century writer says, " Plague
now seldom gains admittance into other European sea ports "
(i.e. other than Constantinople) " and even if imported, the
wise precautions and regulations adopted by quarantines, check
its irruption : this is a most important improvement in the
police of modern states ".[18]

The enforcement of quarantine for plague was assisted by
the organization of the Levant trade, which was of an official
or semi-official character. The Ottoman Government gave
trading privileges not to individuals, but to the regulated
companies which themselves stood in a quasi-official relation
to their own governments. One of the duties laid upon the
companies was the carrying out of the quarantine laws. Since
the companies had many enemies, clamouring for the abolition
of their privileges, and since the necessity for quarantine
regulations was a strong argument for the retention of these
privileges, the companies had good cause to carry out the
charge faithfully. When in 1743 a proposal was brought
forward in Great Britain to throw open the Levant trade, the
Turkey Company in its defence stated that " the latitude given
by the Bill in exporting and importing renders impracticable
the restraints that may be necessary to obviate the dangers of
infection ". In the Act of 1754 which threw open the membership of the Company to any British subject upon a payment

of £20 and upon taking the oath of allegiance and of obedience, it was specifically stated that the quarantine regulations were to remain in force.

The French trade with the Levant was strictly regulated. The French Levant Company was under government control and all the trade had to be conducted through Marseilles. Though at one time Dunkirk and Rouen gained the privilege of importing goods direct it was only upon payment of an excess duty of 20%. In 1701 the deputies of the trading towns of the West petitioned against the privileges of Marseilles and among other arguments the petitioners stated that "the pretence of contagious distempers ought not to be made use of against the towns of the ocean to exclude them from this trade". The deputies of Marseilles said in their reply that whatever their rivals might say as to the small danger "of bringing the plague into France, it is almost certain they could not avoid it . . . the contagious distemper never ceasing to be in the Levant and Barbary . . . because in those countries they take no precautions to avoid it, these gentlemen having neither experience, nor proper places for purging the merchandizes from that evil which cleaves to them (as is found true at Marseilles, where oftentimes several die of the plague during the quarantine) would infallibly give the plague to France, which they of Marseilles avoid, by rules which are more rigorously observed there than in any city in the world".[19]

A description of the quarantine methods of the late 18th century will be found in Howard's Lazarettos (1791). He describes the plague lazarettos "as effectual for the prevention of the most infectious of all diseases". At Marseilles the quarantine was 20 days for ships with a clean bill and 31 days for ships with a foul one. In Malta the corresponding periods were 18 and 80 days. Bales of cotton goods were opened and exposed to the air. A foul bill meant that plague had been reported at the port from which the vessel came; most ports did not receive a ship upon which plague had actually occurred. Howard mentions Leghorn as an exception, this port had three Lazarettos and received ships which had the plague and they were not "chased away or burnt" as in many places. This is a tribute to the humanity and good sense of the Jewish merchants who ruled this port and incidentally illustrates the degree of general horror inspired by the plague.

Under the Act of Geo. III, Chapter 26, British ships coming from the Levant with a foul bill were compelled to perform quarantine either at Malta, Ancona, Venice, Messina, Leghorn, Genoa or Marseilles. British ships were only given a clean bill if no case of plague had been reported in Smyrna for 40 days. British merchants complained very much of these regulations, they alleged that the Greeks often gave false information that plague was raging in order to benefit themselves and the Dutch and that the cotton was often spoiled when the bales were opened at the quarantine stations. They further alleged that half the cotton manufactured in England was purchased through Holland, France and Italy and that since these nations, particularly the Dutch, did not strictly carry out quarantine regulations, the British merchants were exposed to very unfair competition.[20] Perhaps this impediment to trade was one reason for the rapid development of the American sources of the cotton supply. Howard seems to have thought that the quarantine regulations were carried out fairly thoroughly except in Venice, where, though there were elaborate regulations, there was such " remissness and corruption " in their execution " as to render the quarantine almost useless ".

Alexander Russell, who was for many years the doctor attached to the English factory at Aleppo, has left a detailed description of the measures taken against the plague by the foreign colony in that city. When the existence of plague was proved the foreign merchants isolated themselves and " an almost total stagnation of trade immediately follows ".[21] This practice seems to have been general in the Near East and in itself was a great safeguard for Europe. It is true that the natives often managed to conceal the existence of plague, but with a virulent outbreak concealment was impossible. Patrick Russell, brother to Alexander, though he says that " Bills of Health are not entitled to that degree of credit they ought to have " yet held the opinion that " the Maritime States of the Mediterranean furnish sufficient proof of the utility of Lazarettos . . . in almost

all instances the causes of failure have been traced to negligence
. . . or to clandestine infraction of the regulations of
quarantine ".[22] This same writer relates how in 1743, when the
plague was raging at Messina, a British man of war, the Scipio,
was performing quarantine in the Thames. A clerk and the
boatswain left the vessel and were tried by courtmartial for the
offence. The Clerk was committed to the Marshalsea for six
months and the boatswain was condemned to death. The
general evidence is, that though the quarantine regulations
were normally carried out with a good deal of slackness, yet
a virulent outbreak of plague at any spot led to very drastic
enforcement of quarantine in other places. For instance, the
serious outbreak of plague in 1720 in France, generally ascribed
to the folly of the physicians in Marseilles who had failed to act
drastically, though it spread to Toulon, was effectively checked
by a national cordon.

When special regulations were drawn up by Blane to
prevent the importation of plague from Egypt upon the
return of the army to this country, these measures were
successful, mainly owing to the fear this disease inspired, a
fear which still lingers in popular memory. During the influenza
epidemic of 1918 it was whispered that the illness was really " the
plague " ; this rumour was surely a faint echo of the old horror

The apparent death rate from the plague justified this horror
Howard mentions an outbreak in Spalato in 1784 which caused
1,201 deaths out of a population of 12,200. In 1743-4 Messina
was almost entirely depopulated by plague, 70,000 persons
perishing. In 1779 about 100,000 were destroyed in Constantinople.[23] The Plague of London in 1665 is said to have
destroyed 70,000 [24] persons, i.e. about one-sixth of the population of London which was then probably about 400,000. In
1605, two thousand and sixty-five died in Bristol, that is
probably about a quarter of the population.[25] In Manchester
there were 1,000 deaths in 1605 and the same number in 1645.
We do not know the population at these dates but it was
estimated at 8,000 in 1717 and had no doubt increased since
1645. In fact, death rates of 25% do not seem to have been
uncommon, but, though the plague often lingered for several

years, it was most fatal at the first outbreak and the greater number of deaths were usually at the beginning of the epidemic. Short says, "the Plague that began in *London* in 1602, was not quite out before 1611; and that which broke out in 1637 was not extinct before 1647. In the first year died of it above 10,000, in the last 3,597." Up to 1665 the plague seems to have returned very roughly every 20 years and each outbreak to have lingered about 5 years. Petty said plague recurred about once in 20 years and commonly killed about one-fifth of the inhabitants. Graunt estimated that 25 years in a century were plague years in London and states that there were outbreaks in 1593, 1603, 1625, and 1638.[26] Short said that in Freiburg plague returned five times in a century and in Augsburg about the same.

If we accept the mortality as 20% to 25% the killing power of the plague was equal to an annual mortality of 10 to $12\frac{1}{2}$ per 1,000, the higher estimate being almost equal to the total mortality at the present day! London rates do not seem, however, to have reached these figures. Graunt extracted the deaths from plague as recorded in the Bills of Mortality and found them to equal 81,549 between the years 1604–59. He estimated the population as 400,000 and he calculated that the deaths from plague were underestimated by one-quarter. On this basis the annual death rate from plague in London was about $4\frac{1}{2}$ per 1,000. Moreover, in the 17th century the plague never spread all over the country, it was confined to ports, trade centres and trade routes and a few places accidentally infected, the death rate for the whole country was therefore very much less than this figure. If we take it that only one-fifth of the population were exposed to plague the death rate would only be a little over 2 per 1,000 per annum. Again if we accept the figure of 70,000 for the deaths in the last visitation of plague to London, add 30,000 for deaths in other places, which is a liberal allowance, and take this as the total of deaths for 25 years the annual death rate for the estimated population is under 1 per 1,000. Mr. Bell believes, however, that the deaths in London alone numbered 110,000, which is the not unusual proportion of 25 % of the population. But even if we estimate the deaths throughout the country at 200,000 the plague only killed proportionately about as many people in the 17th century as tuberculosis does now. Of course such a death rate is not immaterial, but the death dealing properties of the plague were exaggerated by its localization in time and place. Its chief importance was that it greatly added to the unhealthiness of the towns and cities already terribly unhealthy from other causes. It must also have seriously hampered the development of industry and commerce, since cities were practically in a state of siege during an outbreak. Graunt says that copies of the Bills of Mortality were bought in Plague time " so that the Rich might judge of the necessity of their removal and Tradesmen might conjecture what doings they were like to have in their respective dealings ". During the Plague of London the entry of English ships and manufactures was forbidden at most Continental ports.[27] Further, had the plague not been extinguished its incidence would have been very different in the 18th and 19th centuries from what it was in the 17th. From the method of infection the bubonic plague is only likely to be carried between commercial centres. In the isolated economic life of the 17th century many places were normally cut off from commercial intercourse and occasional fairs and markets could be easily adjourned in plague times. It would have been very different in the new order of things with developed commerce, industry and transport, the plague death rate of London might easily have become that of the whole country.[28]

Indeed it is difficult to believe that the modern territorial division of labour could have fully developed if subject to the serious interruptions of the plague. The disappearance of plague was both directly and indirectly one cause among many of the material advance in the 18th century. Moreover, its abolition not only removed a nightmare of horror from the life of Europe but encouraged the hope of a successful warfare against other epidemic disease. Rightly or wrongly it was believed that plague had been banished by the conscious effort of man and it was hoped that this victory might be followed by others no less startling. The methods employed against other diseases were not, however, slavishly imitative but adapted in the light of experience to the problems at issue.

CHAPTER XIV

SMALLPOX IN THE 18TH CENTURY

IT was natural that the idea of prevention should be early directed towards the most virulent disease with which 18th century Europe was afflicted.

Smallpox is a highly contagious disease yet strangely enough the fact was not recognised until modern times; indeed the Arabian physicians believed that it was due to a poison naturally incident to birth. Sydenham (1624–1689), who introduced a cool regimen which much lessened the death rate among smallpox patients, did not realize that the disease was contagious. The explanation seems to be that an attack of smallpox, in the vast majority of cases, confers a life immunity from the disease; further, it was endemic, so that most persons were attacked in early childhood and therefore a very large proportion of the adult population was immune from infection. Before the 19th century smallpox was essentially a scourge of infancy and early childhood, moreover an endemic scourge, though no doubt mysteriously altering in frequency and severity as do measles and scarlet fever at the present day. The introduction of vaccination conferred immunity on a considerable proportion of the child population, but for some years the necessity for re-vaccination was not realized; therefore from time to time during the 19th century epidemics of smallpox occurred which mainly affected the non-protected adult population, hence the idea that smallpox is an epidemic disease mainly affecting adults. This, however, is the artificial result of vaccination and the preventive method which preceded it.[1] It must be repeated, for the fact is of supreme importance from the standpoint of population, that smallpox is naturally endemic in Europe and that children and infants are extremely susceptible to it. The ravages of the disease among the infant population before the 19th century are attested by all authorities. One writer calls smallpox "the poor man's friend who happens to be burdened with a large family ".[2] A Dr. Watt [3] says, " taking an average of several years I found that more than half of the human species died before they were ten years of age and that of this half more than a third part died of Small Pox so that nearly one fifth of all that were born alive perished by this dreadful malady." [4] Haygarth of Chester made the same estimate, as did also an anonymous writer for Leeds in 1791. This writer believed that in Liverpool this proportion was exceeded.[5]

In Warrington in the year 1773 the total number of deaths was 473 of which 211 died of smallpox, all the victims being under the age of nine; of these 211 no fewer than 133 were under 2 years of age. These figures are almost certainly for a year of exceptional mortality but they suggest that practically all the adult population had suffered from the disease in childhood.

Haygarth in his survey of Chester in 1778 ascertained that only 1 in 14 inhabitants of Chester had not had smallpox. He calculated that 1 in 20 persons were incapable of infection. In the Chester epidemic of 1777 out of 136 who died only seven had reached the age of seven.

In 1774 the deaths in Chester were 546 of which 334 were under 10 years of age and of these latter 202 died of smallpox.[6] According to the Carlisle Tables there were between the years 1779 and 1787 (inclusive) 238 deaths from smallpox out of a total population of 8,177. Of the victims 225 were under five years of age, the total living under 5 being 1,096 and the total deaths for the period of those under five being 709. These figures confirm the estimates of the mortality from smallpox quoted above, yet according to Heysham the smallpox had been considerably checked during this period.

Sir Gilbert Blane writing in 1819 says, " though the term plague carries a sound of greater horror and dismay, we should probably be greatly within the truth in asserting, that smallpox has destroyed a hundred for every one that has perished by the plague." He goes on to say that it is true that the last visit of the plague in London accounted for 70,000 victims but the recorded deaths from smallpox since that time were 300,000 and a like number of survivers have been afflicted with blindness, deformity, scrofula or broken constitutions. He quotes a statement in the Report of the Hospital for Indigent Blind that " two-thirds of those who apply for relief have lost their sight by the small pox ".[7] Farr says, smallpox was "one of the most prolific causes of blindness in England. Of the 1,456 pupils received into the Liverpool School for the Blind between 1791–1860 no less than 250 are said to have been blinded by smallpox."

During the 18th century a determined effort was made to fight smallpox. The practice of inoculation was introduced from Constantinople by Lady Mary Wortley Montague about 1720. This practice is said to have been common in China from early times and a rude form of it known as " buying the small-pox " is also said to have been an ancient custom in many parts of Europe.[8] For, though the doctors did not know it to be infectious, the common people had observed that the disease could be conveyed from one person to another and that it was apt to be less fatal when sought after than when awaited. Probably the practice in Europe amounted to little more than exposing to infection by touch and mothers probably resorted to it from a desire " to get it over " in the same way that ignorant persons, even to-day, expose children to the infection of measles and scarlet fever.

Inoculation generally produced only a mild form of smallpox but occasionally it produced ordinary smallpox which sometimes proved fatal. The patient, however, was always infectious and the infected persons developed true smallpox, not the mild form to which inoculation normally gave rise. This was a grave disadvantage, moreover the early inoculators through over zeal made a very deep incision with very unpleasant and sometimes fatal results. Therefore, though inoculation when introduced in 1720 was tried successfully, first on condemned criminals and then on members of the Royal Family, a common course for new remedies, after a brief popularity the custom languished. About 20 years after it was revived again, a better technique was worked out and an attempt made to isolate inoculated patients. Inoculation became common among the well-to-do, and efforts began to be made to spread it among the mass of the people. The Middlesex County Hospital was founded in 1746 on its present site as a hospital for smallpox and inoculation. One of the reasons for its foundation was that smallpox patients were not admitted to the general hospitals, moreover patients were to be admitted at all times and without letters of recommendation. The patients in the two parts of the Hospital (inoculation and natural smallpox) were kept strictly separate. The Hospital was not altogether a success, it followed the ordinary hospital rule of the time of excluding children under 7 years of age and thus excluded the majority of smallpox patients and precluded the greatest usefulness of inoculation. For inoculation of adults the necessary three or four weeks' residence at the hospital was a strong deterrent.[9] The subscribers to the Hospital were accused of keeping it for the use of their servants.[10] Though this was doubtless true it was not the whole truth. Most native Londoners must have passed through the fires of smallpox before they reached 7 years of age, the adult victims would have been mainly immigrants from isolated country places and a large proportion of these would have been servants. After all, what was a wealthy house-holder to do with some underling who fell ill of smallpox? The patient's fellow servants would not be willing to nurse him and the ordinary hospitals would not admit him; the smallpox hospital must have been a boon to a humane master. No doubt the inoculation patients were also largely immigrant servants who were compelled by their masters to endure the irksome, though necessary, confinement. The size of the Metropolis made it very difficult to adopt inoculation successfully among the mass of the people; in smaller places the plan was to have a general inoculation from time to time and every endeavour was made to inoculate everyone who had not either had the smallpox or been inoculated previously, the problem of infection being thus avoided. A general inoculation was usually held during a smallpox scare when it was easier to persuade the mass of the people to submit themselves or their children to the ordeal, for it must be remembered that a very large porportion of the inoculated would have been young children. Many hospitals and dispensaries and most maternity institutions performed free inoculation. In Carlisle in 1785 there was a free general inoculation which was announced by the Town Crier and there are numerous records of general inoculations at various places between 1780 and 1800, several at Carlisle, also at Chester, Leeds, Liverpool and many smaller places. A most determined effort to fight smallpox was made at Chester by Haygarth. He was impressed by the success of quarantine and pest houses in the case of plague and thought that the same methods could be applied to other diseases.[11] The difficulty in the case of smallpox was the tender age of most of the patients which seemed to make hospital treatment impossible and, as Haygarth said, even had the mothers consented to part with their infants " no one could be so inhuman as to propose it ". Thus do ideas of humanity vary in different periods; an age which welcomed factory employment for children was shocked at the inhumanity of children's hospitals, not altogether unreasonably. The sufferings of many a mother parted from her sick child or of many a nervous sick child parted from its mother, though not recorded in any Government report might, if adequately described, be not unmoving. The plea that the removal was for the ultimate benefit of the child and of the community and that most children did not suffer were the very arguments raised in favour of factory employment. In all ages men close their eyes to that which it is uncomfortable to contemplate.

Haygarth, therefore, drew up a scheme for isolating the smallpox patient in his own home. A Small-Pox Society was founded at Chester in 1778, rewards were paid to informers who gave information as to the existence of the illness. The inspector of the society then visited the infected house, gave precise instructions as to the rules to be followed in order to prevent the spread of infection. A reward was paid to those who followed the rules and a further reward in cases where it was proved that no one had been infected by the patient. Those whose social position precluded their acceptance of a money reward but who carried out the Society's instructions, were gratified by having their names published in a roll of honour in the Society's Reports. The Society also strenuously advocated inoculation.[12]

A controversy as fierce as that which later raged round vaccination raged round inoculation and upon much the same grounds, though with a good deal more to be said upon the side of the opposition. Inoculation was attacked for its danger, since a certain proportion of persons died as a result of it, because it spread smallpox to other persons, because of the danger of conveying the infection of other diseases, particularly venereal diseases. It was attacked on religious grounds, as an impious interference with the beneficent plans of the Almighty and in fact upon every conceivable pretext, reasonable or unreasonable. Its defenders, among whom numbered most of the progressive and eminent of the medical profession, replied that the death rate from inoculation was very small, especially with proper methods, and the danger of conveying other diseases, again if proper precautions were taken, was remote. As to infection, inoculated patients should be isolated, but in any case the smallpox infection was so diffused that practically everyone was exposed to it.

An interesting account of inoculation, particularly as practised at the London Small-Pox Hospital, was presented to the Royal Commissioners of Health of the Kingdom of Sweden by a Dr. David Schultz, who studied the question in London for about a year and had evidently been sent to England by the Swedish authorities for that purpose. He pronounced strongly in favour of inoculation and his report, the English translation of which was published in 1758, gives an interesting account of the technique of inoculation as then practised. It was laid down that persons should only be inoculated when in good health and preferably when smallpox was not epidemical. The difficulty was that many persons only presented themselves for inoculation after they had actually been exposed to infection and deaths due to this infection were ascribed to inoculation. To avoid this the physicians at the London Small-Pox Hospital enforced a period of residence before inoculation. The patients at this hospital wore proper hospital dresses and " their own are fumigated with brimstone according to Dr. Hale's advice, in a chest constructed for that purpose ". Patients were inoculated 20 or 30 at a time, doubtless to facilitate isolation. The actual process of inoculation consisted of passing a cotton thread through a pustule, the thread was then dried by the fire and kept in a wooden box. A healthy person was chosen from whom to take the matter, usually a child, " to avoid venereal taint ". The incision for inoculation was made with a lancet either on the arm or leg but bad sores often resulted from a leg incision or from a too deep one. "Nowadays a superficial incision with the lancet on the arm " Schultz says was considered correct " and the least sign of blood is a sufficient mark that the incision is deep enough ", the infected thread was then laid on the wound, bound to it and left at least two days or until infection appeared.[13] These details are quoted to show firstly the detailed study which had been devoted to perfecting inoculation—as a modern medical writer says, it " had well nigh attained the status of a modern preventive injection ",[14] and secondly how vaccination was the offspring of inoculation. The fame of Jenner is sufficiently established to be able to bear that due honour should be paid to his predecessors. Jenner's work was built upon a two-fold prepared basis, first the fact that immunity from smallpox could be obtained by an artificially conveyed infection and secondly the technique of conveying that infection. His work consisted in allying this two-fold knowledge with the popular " superstitition " that a person who had had " Cowpock " would not catch " smallpox ". Like most discoverers in the scientific sphere Jenner's work consisted in recognising a relation between facts which had appeared unrelated and in proving that relationship by a long series of experiments.

Vaccination was a very much safer and easier process than inoculation and its adoption was therefore widespread, but it had to fight severe opposition from the first, especially among Jenner's own countrymen. All the arguments against inoculation were used against vaccination, while from the opposite side it was assailed by inoculators who did not believe in the new process. It was soon proved to be a less certain preventive than inoculation, it was more likely not " to take ".

For highly susceptible persons it was not always a complete protection and in any case it did not confer the life immunity which inoculation as a rule gave. It was some years before the necessity of re-vaccination was recognised and the many cases of adults being infected by smallpox after infant vaccination were a great blow to popular faith. The medical profession soon pronounced in favour of vaccination though for some years doctors continued to inoculate at the request of patients. Inoculation continued for many years in country districts and the two methods existed side by side. The doctors, however, became more and more adverse to inoculation but when they refused to inoculate their patients simply resorted to amateur inoculators who had the additional attraction of cheapness.

A writer on the subject describes the position of affairs in the district of Chichester as late as 1822. The last general inoculation took place in the Chichester district in 1806 but during an epidemic in 1812 considerable numbers were inoculated in some parts of the district. Vaccination was mainly confined to the children of the upper and middle classes. In 1821 a small epidemic is said to have been turned into a bad one by some women inoculating their own children; there were over 100 cases and a panic ensued with a demand for inoculation. This demand the surgeons of Chichester refused except in some 50 cases, with the result that the population flocked to the amateurs, especially to a farmer named Pearce of Boshum. This man was quite a celebrity, at a charge of 2s. 6d. he inoculated over 1,000 persons in this one epidemic; he had inherited his lancet from his father, who, Pearce boasted, had inoculated over 10,000 persons of whom not one had died. Pearce, or his father, had by observation arrived at the conclusion " that the small pox matter, by uninterrupted transmission from one body to another by inoculation, becomes eventually . . . *as weak as water* ; and that the resulting disease is always proportioned to the particular strength of the virus : and he accounts for the great mildness of the late epidemic in this manner—the first case of the disease having originated from a stock of effete virus ". No doubt the absence of mortality was due to acting upon this theory but the medical writer's only comment was that Pearce was quite uninstructed and his ideas of smallpox, " are mixed up with falsehood and fallacy." This writer would have been very crushing to any dairymaid who had talked nonsense to *him* about cowpock preventing smallpox.

Pearce had three rivals, a knife grinder, a fishmonger and a whitesmith, who travelled over the country and between them inoculated over 1,000 persons. In view of this extra professional rivalry many surgeons relented and inoculated their patients.[15] It is clear why it ultimately became necessary to prohibit inoculation. Medical opinion favoured vaccination but was often forced to yield to popular demand, otherwise their patients would have resorted to amateurs, which was not only a monetary loss to the doctors but a source of additional danger to the community. Inoculation by a skilled surgeon with proper precautions as to isolation was one thing, inoculation by a fishmonger with no such precautions was another. As medical opinion became more and more adverse to inoculation the danger from amateurs became greater and inoculation was made a felony in 1840. Vaccination was made compulsory in 1853.

Opinions differed as to whether the death rate from smallpox increased or decreased during the 18th century. One writer says, " the fatality of smallpox has been lessened by the cool regimen, inoculation and regulation ".[16] But Robertson (1827) held that smallpox was gradually on the increase during the 18th century and was only effectively checked by the introduction of vaccination. It seems probable that the realization of the highly contagious nature of the illness and imperfect attempts at quarantine tended to make the disease more epidemic in character; such epidemics naturally attracted more attention than a fairly steady annual incidence. The more successful treatment and the fact that the age of attack was often postponed probably raised the proportion of recoveries.

Great controversy also arose as to whether inoculation increased or decreased the death rate from smallpox. The truth seems to be that in small centres of population, where it was possible to inoculate at the same time all those who had not had smallpox, the method was successful. For instance, according to Howlett, in the parish of Great Chart near Ashford in Kent, burials between the years 1688–1708 were 192 ; of these almost a hundred had died of smallpox, whereas from 1760–1780 only 4 or 5 died of that disorder. This diminution was ascribed to inoculation : " no register can, as yet, properly inform us of the thousands that have been preserved by this salutary practice for these 20 years past all over the kingdom. As they have been chiefly infants and *young people* they are *ordinarily* too young to die, and scarce yet old enough to marry ; but they are latent in society, and will greatly swell *both* registers in due time ".[17]

Blane, however, held that inoculation increased the deaths from smallpox even in rural areas, but he, like Robertson quoted above, was writing at a time of acute controversy between the supporters of inoculation and those of vaccination. In large centres of population where it was not possible to inoculate every unprotected person and where often no proper measures were taken to isolate the inoculated persons these became centres of infection and caused severe epidemics of the illness. But without inoculation such epidemics would have undoubtedly occurred though not necessarily at the same period, also there is a good deal of evidence that inoculation was only resorted to in times of epidemics.

It is true that the London Bills of Mortality show an increased mortality from smallpox after 1770 and that contemporaries ascribed this to inoculation. But on general grounds this increase seems incredible. All the evidence points to the incidence of smallpox being at a maximum previous to 1770 in all centres of population. According to the Bills the mortality in London was lower than in provincial centres where reliable records were kept. This is extremely unlikely.[18] The probability is that the mortality from smallpox was grossly underestimated in the London Bills but that after 1770 there was a nearer approach to accuracy. Lettson estimated that the deaths from smallpox in London were more than double those shown in the Bills of Mortality, he also said that since the Society for General Inoculation had been established in

SMALLPOX IN THE 18TH CENTURY

London in 1775 not one patient had died nor was there any proof that the natural smallpox had been aggravated by it.[19]

Heysham records in detail the efforts made at Carlisle to deal with smallpox by inoculation and the degree of their success. In 1779 there were 300 cases and 90 deaths (86 of these victims were under 5) and during the same period several hundreds were inoculated in the neighbourhood of Carlisle without one resultant death. In 1781 again there were 19 deaths from the disease and great numbers of inoculations in the town and the neighbouring villages. In 1782 there were 30 deaths and in the autumn of 1783 the disease was again prevalent and of so fatal a kind that the monthly committee of the dispensary recommended a general inoculation which accordingly took place in November. Great numbers availed themselves of this and Carlisle was totally freed from smallpox in two months and there were only 19 deaths.

In 1783 Heysham says, " the number of persons affected with the natural smallpox in Whitehaven, within the last six months, has been almost incredible, and it is a melancholy truth, that scarcely one in three survived." In 1785 the disease was introduced into Carlisle by vagrants. Again there was a free general inoculation, which was announced by the Town Crier. There were 91 inoculations at the expense of the dispensary and rather more by the general practitioners. There were no deaths among the inoculated but there were 39 among the natural cases and all the victims were under five. In 1787 the disease was again very prevalent and again there was an inoculation. There were 30 deaths from the disease, 28 under five and all under 10.[20]

It is doubtful whether inoculation on balance increased or decreased the death rate from smallpox in large centres, but in small centres and rural districts it most probably decreased it. The introduction of vaccination [21] (1798) and the widespread dissemination of the practice enormously reduced the death rate not only in this country but throughout the civilized world.

Heysham said in 1813, " Since 1800 when the practice of vaccination was introduced into Carlisle, I have reason to believe that not one person has died of smallpox." In 1814 the disease was introduced by a vagrant, there were 12 or 14 cases and 2 deaths but by a recourse to vaccination the disease was soon checked.[20] As has been seen, these happy results were not general or permanent owing to inefficient vaccination, to ignorance of the necessity of periodic re-vaccination and, most of all, to prejudice against the practice. Nevertheless the results of vaccination upon the death rate were sufficiently astounding, as the figures in the appendix show.

The Carlisle figures, which seem absolutely reliable, show an average annual death rate of 3·64 per 1,000 at a period when the disease, according to most contemporary authorities, had been checked. The figure for the Liberties of London 1771–80 was 5 per 1,000.[22] Smallpox was endemic in all towns but the case was different in the country where isolated places might escape infection for a number of years, though when the disease did arrive they suffered severely. It is not safe, therefore, to apply the town death rate to the whole country though it would apply to villages near towns or situated on lines of communication. We have fairly reliable figures for Sweden which show an annual average death rate from smallpox in that country for the period 1774–1798 of 2 per 1,000. A large proportion of the population of Sweden lived in isolated villages and the incidence of the disease must almost certainly have been higher in England. A guess of an annual death rate of 2·5 to 3 per 1,000 perhaps would not be far from the truth. There is much evidence, however, that this rate was considerably higher prior to the last quarter of the 18th century. In estimating the importance of smallpox from the point of view of population it must never be forgotten that its victims were mainly under 5 years old. According to the Carlisle figures the death rate from smallpox of those under 5 was 28 per 1,000, a figure equal to the total death rate for this age period for the years 1876–1885. For the years 1906–1915 the *total* death rate for this age period was only 16 per 1,000. Napoleon showed a true appreciation of values when, in reply to a request for the release of some English prisoners presented in the name of Jenner, he answered, " I can refuse nothing to this man."

CHAPTER XV

THE ANTI-TYPHUS CAMPAIGN AND THE FEVER HOSPITAL MOVEMENT

Typhus. (*Synonyms :—Contagious, Spotted, Camp, Gaol, Hospital Ship, Nervous and Putrid Fever.*) Another definite campaign was the one waged against typhus. Typhus is an acute fever and though the parasite which causes it has not yet been discovered, the carrier has been proved to be the human body louse. Until the 19th century the diagnosis of typhus was confused with that of typhoid and of relapsing or recurrent fever.[1] The distinction between typhus and typhoid after a long series of researches, beginning in the early 18th century, was at last firmly established by Still in 1837. Relapsing or recurrent fever was only established as a separate disease in 1843; before that date it was believed to be a mild form of typhus; a so-called mild form of typhus fever, probably relapsing fever was very prevalent in England during the epidemic of 1826-7 and also in the '40's. Since both diseases are carried by lice they are likely to occur together and from the point of view of preventive medicine their distinction was not of great importance. The case mortality of relapsing fever is from 4 to 14%, that of typhus from 10 to 50%. Unlike most epidemic disease typhus flourishes especially in the temperate zone since the virus does not develop in the louse in high temperatures. Epidemics are favoured by any circumstance favourable to the breeding of lice.[2]

Probably much of the so-called plague of the Middle Ages was typhus. It appears to have been endemic in most centres of population in the 18th century and most probably had been so during previous centuries. It seems probable that under-fed persons have less resistance against this disease. The pestilence which follows famine is generally typhus, though this may not be entirely due to the under-fed conditions of the victims of famine but to the tendency of famine-stricken

populations to crowd together at places where there is hope
of obtaining food, or sometimes it seems, owing to blind herd
instinct. Typhus was naturally liable to appear wherever
verminous persons lived in close contact. It notoriously accompanied war and was found so frequently in camps, hospitals
prisons and ships that it was known as camp, hospital, gaol
and ship fever respectively.

While no doubt typhus was endemic in the slums of London
and other English towns in the 18th century it was generally
considered that the gaols were the great breeding places in this
country. Pringle said, " jails have often been the cause of
malignant fevers ".[3] Its presence in the gaols, particularly
in Newgate, brought an additional aspect of terror to the grim
and sordid Law Courts. In vain sweet herbs were spread
to form a barrier between accusers and accused for more than
once typhus passed the capital sentence upon the judge himself
In 1750 at the Spring Session at the Old Bailey the Court was
infected and four out of 6 Judges, 3 or 4 counsel, an under-sheriff
and several jurymen and others were killed to the number of
about 40 persons of rank sufficiently high for their death to be
noted.[4]

The gaols were also constantly infecting the army and fleet
since these forces were largely recruited from among minor
offenders. Lind showed Howard at Haslar a number of sailors
ill of gaol fever contracted from a man discharged from a London
prison. Lind in his Essay on the Health of Seamen says, "The
source of infection to our armies and fleets are undoubtedly
the jails; we can often trace the importers of it directly from
them. It often proves fatal in impressing men on the hasty
equipment of a fleet." The first English fleet sent in the war
to America lost by typhus above 2,000 men. "The seeds of
infection were carried from the guard ships to our squadrons
and the mortality, thence occasioned, was greater than by any
other diseases or means of death put together."[3] In 178
The Admiralty introduced " slop ships " on which newly raised
men were inspected, cleaned and supplied with new clothing
before being distributed; this plan much decreased typhus
in the fleet.

The appalling condition of the English gaols was first revealed by Howard who began his investigations in 1773. At a time when all administration in all countries was, judged by modern standards, inefficient and corrupt, the English prison administration stood out for laxity and corruption. The causes lay partly in the extreme decentralization of prison administration; partly in the fact that, from historical causes, the prison administration was largely independent of the magistrates and partly from the conception of prisons as places of detention provided by the gaoler for his own convenience.[5] That is to say, the prisons had no public funds upon which to draw, they had to be self supporting. Though this conception was being gradually modified and by the end of the 18th century certain grants for food were made to poor prisoners, there were no funds for general administrative purposes. It is not surprising that the sanitary condition of the gaols was horrible even according to the standards of the time. Though Howard found much to criticize in the Continental gaols, especially the survival in many places of torture, which was unknown in England, yet the sanitary conditions on the whole were better and in particular he found no gaol fever anywhere abroad. No doubt the centralized administration prevailing over most of the Continent prevented the extraordinary laxity which existed in the English gaols. But one cannot feel that Howard's evidence as to typhus is quite convincing. In England he seems to have viewed every gaol that he wished upon his own authority as a magistrate and a gentleman. The prison authorities were in a peculiarly independent position and did not much care whether his report was favourable or otherwise. As to fever, the gaolers looked upon it as natural to prisons and as Howard himself states, often asserted that it existed when it did not, in order to prevent the entry of prying magistrates. Howard's position on the Continent was very different. He entered the State prisons as the authorized visitor of the authorities, he was known as a prison reformer who considered gaol fever a sign of mismanagement, his report would be read by authority and an unfavourable one might well lead to the dismissal of the gaolers. Perhaps it is not surprising that he never found a case of gaol fever, though it is difficult to believe that none ever occurred in Continental prisons. Typhus certainly existed in the Continental cities [6] and it is mentioned as one of the prevalent diseases in the Paris Hospice de la Maternité in 1808.[7]. It has to be remembered that climatic conditions were more favourable to typhus in the British Isles than in many parts of the Continent, where the hot summers were a natural check to the disease. Howard, however, was no doubt right in attaching importance to one difference between English and foreign prison administration when he says, " May not one great cause of the unhealthiness of our prisoners be, the want of proper bedding, which obliges them to lie in their clothes?" In many foreign prisons bedding was provided, often also a change of linen and there were sometimes rules about changing linen. At Gratz " the guards see that the *men take off their clothes* at night ".[8]

In this connection it is fair to remember that at this period the use of bed and body linen was more common on the Continent than in this country. Coarse linen was not much used in England, fine linen was only possible for the well to do. The predominant use of woollen garments and bed coverings among the mass of the people did not tend to personal cleanliness. Both Smollett and Arthur Young comment on the common use of table linen in France, even among the poor, owing to its cheapness and this must have applied to body linen as well. Arthur Young says, "The expence of linen in England is enormous, from its fineness. . . . In point of cleanliness, I think the merit of the two nations is divided ; the French are cleaner in their persons, and the English in their houses ; I speak of the mass of the people, and not of the individuals of considerable fortune." [9] Blane states that body linen was not common in this country until the 18th century. The introduction of machinery in the cotton manufacture and the consequent enormous cheapening of the product led to a widespread change of habit among the mass of the people. Francis Place writing in 1822 says that the English people are cleaner in their persons and their dwellings than formerly, particularly the women, " partly from the success of the cotton manufactures, which has enabled them to discard the woollen clothes which were universally worn by them, which lasted for years, and were seldom, if ever washed."[10] Heysham says that for the ten years 1778–88 the average annual deaths from typhus in Carlisle were 13 while for the ten years ending 1814 it scarcely amounted to *one*. Discussing the reason for this decrease he says, "On this subject I cannot satisfy my own mind . . . The people in general certainly now pay more attention to cleanliness, and, upon the whole, live better than they did".[11] A sister-in-law of Sismondi's writing in 1837, referring to the latter's views says, "He has such an intemperate horror of the cotton manufacture that he could not bear my saying that it had added to the comfort of our poor in giving them sheets in their beds which in my youth few of them knew".[12] Sismondi was not the only person to adopt this attitude; the boon conferred on the mass of the people by a material for clothing and bedding which could be easily washed and cheaply renewed has been curiously overlooked, even by the defenders of machinery. Apart from general comfort and healthiness the new material must have, in particular, greatly reduced the incidence of typhus, since the body louse breeds in clothing, needs a certain amount of continuous warmth and is fairly easily destroyed by soap and water. It is moreover quite destroyed by boiling, and cotton materials can be boiled while woollens are spoiled by boiling.

But typhus was also reduced by the conscious effort of the authorities and of the medical profession. Howard's work had an appreciable effect upon the health of prisoners. He gave evidence before the House of Commons in 1774 for which he received the thanks of the House, and in the same year Mr. Popham, member for Taunton, introduced a Bill for preventing the gaol distemper. (14 Geo. III c. 59.) In his second tour Howard found that the gaol fever, though not eradicated, was much diminished. "Many gaolers" . . . (were) "more mindful . . . for the sake, not only of their prisoners, but of themselves and their own families."[13] The efforts of the Admiralty to prevent typhus infection in the fleet have already been mentioned and about this time the far more difficult task of eradicating it among the civilian population was definitely attempted.

Pringle [14] first recognised typhus under its various names as being one and the same disease but it was Lind who first laid down correct rules for its prevention. His directions have quite a modern ring. In his Essay on the Health of Seamen, 1757, he advocates the destruction of the clothing of the infected person, the washing of his body and all utensils with vinegar, the fumigation of infected parts of the vessel and the destruction of rats, mice and beetles by sulphur fumigation. In 1758 he was appointed physician to the Naval Hospital at Haslar and began to apply his methods to the hospital treatment of the disease. Lind discovered that typhus " contagion will not pass to the distance of many feet through the air ; but is communicated by close approach to the sick, or by *fomites*, i.e. substances imbued with the contagion ".[15] This was a revolutionary discovery in hospital practice, for typhus had been such a scourge in hospitals that fever patients had been rigorously excluded, these unfortunate persons being left to perish either in their homes or in workhouses, spreading infection broadcast. Edward Percival writing in 1819 stated that infectious diseases (which term at that time was practically synonymous with fevers) were excluded by the Charters of almost every County and City Infirmary in the kingdom. He went on to state, however, that the letter of the law had been ignored in many institutions since the precautions worked out by Lind at Haslar had made the establishment of fever wards possible without risk to the other patients. According to him Lind's methods were copied at Dumfries Hospital in 1776 and at the Edinburgh Infirmary in 1777, but other authorities speak of Haygarth of Chester as the first to apply the new régime to civilian practice. The probability is that the methods were only applied at Dumfries and Edinburgh in order to deal with cases which occurred in the hospital and to prevent the spread of the disease within its walls, but that it was Haygarth of Chester who first opened fever wards for the specific reception of fever patients and who inaugurated a general campaign against typhus.

A description of his work is best given in his own words which are to be found in a letter to Howard published in the

THE FEVER HOSPITAL MOVEMENT

Appendix to the latter's work upon Lazarettos. He says, "The propagation of infectious diseases has been an object of my particular attention for near a dozen years. There appears to be no doubt that the plague spreads by the same laws as many other distempers common in this part of Europe; namely, the smallpox, measles, chincough, scarlet fever, etc. I have long thought, that perfect purification . . . might be performed with great ease and certainty." In the fever wards at Chester " the chief aim of our regulations is not merely to preserve the lives of the infected patients. The principal purpose and benefit of the establishment is to prevent any infectious fever from spreading through poor families, and through the town. It effectually suppressed the febrile contagion which alarmed Chester, in 1784. A plan of this kind has been an object of my anxious wish and attention, ever since the year 1774, when we were visited by a like epidemick. The success of our small-pox society in checking the progress of the variolous contagion, in closely adjoining houses, encouraged and enabled me to propose a plan, which, by easy rules, might prevent the communication of infectious fevers from one ward of the infirmary to another ". The proposal for the establishment of fever wards in Chester Infirmary was first made by Haygarth in 1775 and the wards were actually opened in 1783.[16] Though the wards were " situated within 13 yards of some other wards of the building, yet during a space of above 12 years, the contagion of fever was never known to extend itself from thence ".[15] This experiment attracted considerable attention and was taken up by progressive doctors in other towns.

In 1792 special rooms were set aside in Manchester Infirmary for the accommodation of the fever cases which occurred in the hospital. Before that time, Ferriar relates, it was found necessary when fever began in the hospital to dismiss almost all the patients, " a measure productive of much inconvenience, and general alarm." The fever wards proved effectual in preventing this necessity but Ferriar had set his heart upon a much more ambitious scheme. About 1792 there was an abortive attempt to form a " committee for regulating the police [17] of the towns of Manchester and Salford " but " private interests prevailed over those of the public, and nothing effectual was done ". In 1795, however, an infectious fever broke out at Ashton-under-Lyne which was supposed to have originated in two cotton works. A committee was formed and a subscription raised to relieve sufferers and an attempt was made to provide a house for the sick, but their prejudices prevented removal from their homes. The Surgeon, Mr. Ogden, traced the origin to a young woman from Manchester. As a result of his report a Board of Health was formed in Manchester and Ferriar was requested to draw up a plan. He says, " a very numerous and very respectable meeting " (was held) " of the friends of the poor ; among whom were several proprietors of large cotton mills, who were desirous to use every means for preserving the health of the persons employed by them ". Ferriar addressed the meeting, describing the horrible condition of the common lodging houses and cellar dwellings and the lack of provision for the sick. He earnestly advocated the establishment of fever-wards, stating that though the cotton mills were not the original source of fevers, yet fevers were spread by them owing to night work, to the lack of cleanliness both of premises and work people and to the employment of convalescents and want of ventilation. Ferriar expressed the belief that " The remonstrances of so respectable a body, as a committee of this nature, may also be expected to have a proper influence, when they call the attention of the proprietors of manufactories, to practices evidently destructive of health and life ".

The Board of Health decided to found a House of Recovery, which name was chosen instead of that of Fever-ward in order not to alarm the patients. The necessary funds were raised by public subscription, four small houses were taken at an expense of £200 and the institution was opened in 1796. It followed the best rules as to cleansing of infected clothing, the provision of special hospital clothing, etc. and that these rules were adequately carried out is shown by Dr. Ferriar's affirmation " that so far from any contagion having been disseminated from the House of Recovery, which was erected at

THE FEVER HOSPITAL MOVEMENT

Manchester in a crowded and much infected part of the town, the district immediately surrounding that establishment was the first cleared of the fever".[15] The Manchester House of Recovery was not merely a fever hospital, it was an institution for the prevention of fever. Rewards were paid to informers who gave notice of cases of fever and also to heads of families who followed the rules for the prevention of infection. In this the promoters were probably copying the Chester Small Pox Society. Patients were removed to the House in a special sedan chair with linen covers, the infected premises were whitewashed and cleansed and new bed clothes supplied when it was necessary to destroy the old. Ferriar says that severe cases were favoured for admission, " the physicians have regarded the public good more than their own immediate reputation; and have preferred the solid benefit of preventing the wide diffusion of contagion, to an ostentatious list of cures."[20] Bernard, of the Society for Bettering the Condition of the Poor which wholeheartedly supported the movement, says in 1797 that many former opponents had become active friends and that similar establishments were proposed at Chester, Stockport and other places. He comments, " It is peculiarly in the prevention of disease and contagion, that the benefits return with increase upon the benefactor, and that the merciful receive mercy."[18] Bernard visited the House in 1798 and found it clean, airy and comfortable with iron bedsteads without curtains and with straw mattresses which were frequently renewed. The institution was then serving a radius of two miles and fevers had been greatly reduced. Ferriar said that one of the chief benefits of the House of Recovery, was that the owners of cotton mills were induced to pay a more scrupulous attention to the health of their work people and that their buildings were in general kept cleaner and better ventilated, and that " in most of the large cotton mills, the persons employed are not exposed to more numerous causes of disease, than any other class of labourers, excepting in the process of *mule spinning*" where the rooms were much over-heated. Ferriar adds, " a salutary impression has been made on the minds of the poor, respecting the utility of cleanness in their houses." In 1789

Ferriar had said that many cotton mills were dirty and unventilated.

As illustrating the kind of work which the authorities of the House of Recovery undertook an episode related by Ferriar is enlightening. Not long after the opening of the institution Ferriar was asked by the proprietor of a large cotton mill just outside Manchester to enquire into an outbreak of fever at his mill. Ferriar inspected the factory but could find nothing wrong with the arrangements, but on going into the village found several dirty families from Manchester " who had contrived to make even new houses offensive " and had overcrowded them with lodgers. Ferriar had the patients removed to the House of Recovery, recommended that overcrowding should be stopped and the incurably dirty families dismissed. He adds that the measures were adopted and were successful.

The accommodation at the House of Recovery soon proved insufficient and a subscription of £5,000 was raised to erect a new building " upon a large and commodious scale "; [19] it had accommodation for over 100 patients and was divided into 21 wards and had separate wards for scarlet fever. The new building was opened in 1805 and Ferriar says, " Since it has been in the power of the Physicians to admit every case of fever, as it occurs we have felt ourselves completely masters of the disease. Epidemic typhus is now unknown to us, while it has been raging in some of the neighbouring towns . . . and the destructive epidemic of scarlet fever, which was actually introduced into the town during 1805, from Liverpool, has been completely suppressed." [20]

At the time of the first establishment of the House of Recovery in Manchester Dr. Currie of Liverpool, the friendly rival of Percival in well doing, was still engaged in his battle for the establishment of a similar institution at Liverpool. In 1797 he wrote to Percival, " I rejoice in the final establishment of your House of Recovery; which in its consequence will, I trust, prove a national benefit. Yet, when I consider by what irrefragable as well as by what important considerations it was supported, how vehemently it was opposed, and, if I mistake not, how narrowly it escaped being overthrown . . . my satisfaction is mingled with wonder and sorrow.... Here, no progress has been made in enlarging our house of reception for fevers, and the institution remains in the same state as before." [21] In 1787 typhus had appeared in the Liverpool Infirmary. Currie says that discipline had been relaxed, the weather had been intensely cold so that ventilation and cleanliness had been neglected, consequently the contagion spread rapidly. However, two wards were fitted up for patients, one for each sex, and these wards were afterwards occupied by such cases of fever as presented themselves. This arrangement continued for five years but the wards were small and underground and in every respect inconvenient, they held at most eight beds and were properly adapted to six beds only but " they admitted of cleanliness and ventilation ". The admission of fever cases to the Infirmary (which was contrary to the rules) was objected to by some subscribers but " the want of an asylum for this disease elsewhere overcame these objections". In 1793 a contagious fever prevailed in the workhouse and two spacious wards of 18 beds each were fitted up in that building by the Parish Committee and an arrangement made by which cases of fever were admitted there instead of to the Infirmary and the admission of fever cases to the Infirmary ceased. " The wards for fever at the work-house, have secured that immense hospital, often containing 1,200 persons, from the spreading of fever, to which, previous to their establishment, it was perpetually liable ", for the contagion never spread from the wards. The wards " have relieved the Infirmary from the necessity of admitting those miserable wretches, who, under the influence of fever (perhaps caught on ship-board) and refused admittance into private lodgings, were brought up to that hospital, where, if not received, they might have perished in the streets ".[22]

But the wards were not large enough to serve as a General Hospital of Recovery and the formalities necessary for the admission of the poor from their own homes also prevented their use for that purpose and in any case Currie considered the provision hopelessly inadequate. In 1796 he brought forward and carried at an open vestry meeting a proposal for the erection of a House of Recovery ; but there was great and organized opposition and the plan had to be dropped. Currie, however, did not lose heart, his plan had been " unanimously received by the gentlemen of the faculty " and the success of the Manchester experiment must have been encouraging. Five years later there were new rectors and new churchwardens who were persuaded to " go heartily into the business "; at a great open vestry meeting of about 2,000 persons held in 1801 the proposal to erect a House of Recovery to be supported entirely out of the parish rates, was carried unanimously. Currie comments that by making the institution rate-supported, " we give it a solid foundation, and have no trouble with annual subscriptions for its support." Apparently some ratepayers thought there was another side to the question but " the honest democracy would listen to no suggestions of prudence ", as to delay till peace when the price of building would fall, etc., and treated with utter contempt the suggestion that it would raise the poor rates 6d. in the £.[23] No doubt the honest democracy was right but it is easy to be contemptuous of prudence when other people's money is in question. The institution was opened in 1806; but though the plan for it was furnished by Ferriar a writer of 1810 criticizes the building as being too high and narrow. At that date not only typhus but scarlet fever, smallpox, measles and whooping cough were treated there but, " many of the infected poor obstinately refuse to be removed from their own miserable dwellings."[23] Perhaps part of this prejudice was due to the connection of the institution with the Poor Law. However, Dr. Duncan, who gave evidence at the enquiry of 1833, considered that the institution had done much to improve the health of the town. He said that, " previously to the erection of that hospital, cases of typhus fever formed one-fourth of the whole diseases of the poor, whilst now they do not exceed one-tenth or one-twelfth."[24]

Though the Liverpool House of Recovery was the only one of the early fever hospitals to be entirely supported out of the rates, the voluntary principle was everywhere found difficult to apply to these institutions. The ordinary hospitals depended upon a system of patronage, patients were only admitted by Subscribers' Letters, though exceptions were sometimes made in cases of urgency. This system appealed to a natural love of patronage, it afforded a cheap and easy method of provision for sick servants, pensioners and protégées and, from a more legitimate point of view, gave subscribers a safeguard against abuse of power by hospital officials. This system, however, was quite inapplicable to Fever Hospitals, since the whole idea of these institutions was to remove the patient to hospital *at once* without any delaying formalities and irrespective of whether he had a well-to-do patron or not. As fever patients were excluded from the ordinary hospitals the support of poor fever patients, either in their own homes or in the workhouse, devolved upon the parish. An outbreak of fever, by laying aside many breadwinners, meant a great addition to the rates [25] and enlightened poor law authorities therefore supported the new methods. In this connection it must be remembered that the magistrates still had considerable power in Poor Law affairs and that they were more likely to be susceptible to new ideas than the overseers. An account of an outbreak of typhus in Hull in 1801 is enlightening in this connection. The victims of the outbreak applied for relief at the workhouse and the workhouse surgeon reported the matter to the magistrates who ordered immediate relief. The relief measures included repaving the street, repairing the drains and supplying a proper descent to carry off foul water. The ceilings, walls and closets of the infected houses were lime-washed and the clothing, furniture and floors washed with soap and water. The doors and windows were set open three or four times a day. One wonders what the assisted persons thought of these drastic measures, since it is stated that they habitually lived in comfortable dirt with their windows shut and " all crevices blocked up ". However, they were doubtless placated by the coals and nourishing food and by the sheets, blankets, rugs and body linen which were sent from the workhouse. Nurses were also engaged to look after the sick ; four nurses and two superintendents took the fever but recovered, but the workhouse surgeon, who had acted so promptly, died from it. It is stated that the efforts were successful, the fever was subdued in about two months and that, while out of the 17 persons attacked before the relief measures started 9 died, of the 70 afterwards attended none died. The entire cost of the relief measures was £200. In 1803 fever again prevailed, a Board of Health was set up and fever wards established in an attic of the workhouse.[26]

It is stated in the account of the Society for Bettering the Condition of the Poor that this effort was largely due to the activities of two brothers and a sister named Horner. Thus, in different parts of the country, zealous individuals attained their ends by different means, in Liverpool by persuading a noisy public meeting (but perhaps it was more important that rectors and churchwardens had previously been converted), in Hull by persuading the Bench of Magistrates, in Manchester through the activities of a little group of doctors and of the more wealthy and enlightened cotton merchants and manufacturers. If subscriptions seemed easier to raise in Manchester than elsewhere, it must be remembered that the cotton manufacturers had a direct monetary interest in stamping out fever from the factories.

The London House of Recovery was founded in 1801 in Gray's Inn Lane, it was directly modelled upon the Manchester Institution even to a special sedan chair, which caused a riot upon its first public appearance. Like its Manchester prototype, the institution cleansed and purified houses, clothing and furniture. Lime washing was sometimes objected to by landlords or occupiers, but it was applied wherever permission was given and all fever houses were cleansed and fumigated. Fever was found to be endemic in Saffron Hill, the lower parts of Westminster and in the narrower courts of the eastern borders of the City. The committee offered to whitewash and cleanse these parts and were soon afterwards able to give a certificate of health. Before the establishment of the London House of Recovery the annual deaths from fever in the Metropolis were over 3,000, afterwards they fell to about 2,000 and in 1806 to 1,354. The mortality had been 1 in 4 but in the House of Recovery it was from 1 in 11 to 1 in 18.[27] Bateman said, however, in 1815 that the exemption of the metropolis from fever could not be wholly ascribed to the efforts of the fever hospital.[28] It was partly due, no doubt, to a natural lull in the disease and

Bateman's opinion was justified by a severe outbreak in 1818. Nevertheless the activities of the institution must have greatly reduced its incidence; for instance, Bateman writing in 1818 describes how the medical officers and inspectors of the House of Recovery stamped out various outbreaks by the methods of cleansing and fumigation. He specifically mentions an outbreak in an overcrowded workhouse in Ratcliffe Highway in 1812 and describes in detail the fumigation and limewashing of a court in Cock Hill. He adds that there were several cases of the disease being arrested even among the Irish labourers of Saffron Hill and Cow Cross Street, " crowded together with all their native habits of filth and indolence," and that " the cases in which it has been stopped in single families . . . are innumerable ".[15]

But in spite of this good work the financial support of the Fever Hospital was not as good as had been hoped, it had no attraction of patronage or places for dependants. In 1804 through the instrumentality of Addington, Lord Sidmouth, a Parliamentary grant of £3,000 was obtained upon the implied condition of adequate subscriptions in the future. With this grant a building in Pancras Road, originally built for a smallpox inoculation hospital, was acquired and upon Sidmouth's suggestion scarlet fever wards were added; paying wards were also provided. If the general public were apathetic the poor law administrators realized the value of the institution. St. Pancras Parish gave a donation of £50 and an annual subscription of 20 guineas, St. Clement Danes gave twenty guineas, while other parishes paid two guineas for each parishioner treated.[27] This generosity is less surprising if we remember that typhus had been a scourge in workhouses as well as in prisons and hospitals. The account of the outbreak in the Workhouse in Ratcliffe Highway illustrates this. The workhouse was overcrowded at the time, it contained 208 persons instead of the 150 for which it was intended—typhus was introduced and spread rapidly into every ward except one and several persons died, including the Matron. At last a distracted churchwarden wrote to the doctor in charge of the House of Recovery, asking for assistance. Upon this all the patients were removed to Gray's Inn Lane, the doctor and the inspector of the House of Recovery visited the workhouse and gave detailed directions as to its cleaning and fumigation. Their efforts were successful, the disease being almost at once subdued.[15]

The Fever Hospital movement was not confined to London, Liverpool, and Manchester. Leeds erected a House of Recovery by a public subscription of £3,000 in 1802, and Stockport erected one about the same date. Newcastle-upon-Tyne and Sheffield had anti-fever campaigns which are recorded and no doubt there were many unrecorded ones. It cannot be doubted that the result of this forgotten public health campaign was an enormous reduction in the incidence of typhus. This disease is fairly easily combated by correct methods, as was proved in Serbia during the War, the methods then employed being essentially the same as those laid down by Lind. In 1819 Percival writes, " through extensive districts in England typhous fever is almost wholly unknown; and many eminent physicians in towns of some magnitude " have expressed doubts of its contagious qualities " as could arise only from the want of opportunities to observe the disease ".[29] It must be remembered that typhoid (or enteric) was not at this time distinguished from typhus and it was probably the observation of typhoid which led to this opinion.

Unfortunately typhus remained endemic in the Irish towns and cities and the migrant Irish labourers were a source of re-infection in this country. In this connection Bateman says, " In some crowded cities, indeed, in which poverty and want prevail more extensively and continuously among the lowest classes of the people than in London, as in Dublin, Cork, and some of the populous towns of the sister kingdom, contagious fever is generally prevalent and in seasons of distress rages to an extent unknown in this metropolis." Percival said that in Liverpool the fever was traced to the Irish quarter. " Typhus is now epidemic in various parts of England . . . this principle of propagation is fed by continual supplies from the sister kingdom." He adds, " In many places . . . the fever has been distinctly traced to Irish labourers; who come over in companies, especially in harvest time, in quest of employment. The

THE FEVER HOSPITAL MOVEMENT

passengers and the sailors in the Irish vessels have, in many instances, sickened on the voyage, and been landed in a state of high fever".[29] Farr writing in 1837 says, " The poor Irish, we strongly suspect, are keeping up, if they be not introducing, the fevers of their wretched country in the heart of the British cities."[30] It is possible, therefore, that but for this source of re-infection the extinction of typhus in this country might have been ante-dated by 50 years and that this ardent public health campaign, instead of being defeated and forgotten, might have been crowned with victory and honour.

CHAPTER XVI

MALARIA—GENERAL SUMMARY

By the beginning of the 19th century, the general advance in society and in particular the efforts of the medical profession, had resulted in some approach to modern health conditions as contrasted with medieval ones. Plague, leprosy, and scurvy were extinct; rickets, smallpox and typhus were scotched, with a definite hope of ultimate elimination.

It is impossible to make any exact numerical statement as to the changed incidence of different diseases since the cause of death was not recorded for the country as a whole until 1836. The sole sources of information before that date are, therefore, the London Bills and the Carlisle Tables. The method of compilation of the London Bills, their obscure and archaic nomenclature, and the fact that the classification was changed from time to time make any detailed comparison impossible. For instance, scarlet fever was at first confused with measles, it was joined with fever in 1731 and made a separate item in 1831. It is possible, however, to compare groups of diseases. Such a comparison was made by Farr for the Liberties of London, the population of which had altered little during the 200 years preceeding 1835.[1] Comparing the two periods 1771–8 and 1801–10:

Total Death Rate.	Diseases of Childhood and early Infancy ex. Fevers.	Small Pox.	Fever.	Consumption.	Dropsy
1771–80 50	16·8	5	6·2	11	2·2
1801–10 29·2	7·9	2	2·6	7	1·3

CARLISLE TABLES

Total Death Rate.	Small Pox.	Fever.	Consumption
25	3·6	4·5	3·3

This table brings out clearly that the main fall was in the diseases of infancy and early childhood,[2] probably at least 14 out of a total reduction of 19 per 1000. Whatever form these diseases may have taken, it may be safely assumed that their cause lay in bad nurture. Conversely their reduction was due to better nurture, i.e., better feeding, healthier dwellings, less drunkenness and immorality among parents, also better medical attention and advice. The reduction of smallpox was directly due to the efforts of the medical profession. This reduction mainly affected the death rate under 5, though in London there would have been more deaths among adults than elsewhere owing to the large immigration from rural districts. Among fevers, probably the most fatal were scarlet fever and typhus. The former, which mainly affected children, in 1831 accounted for one third of the total deaths from fever. Typhus is most fatal in early adult and middle life. Farr pointed out that between 1771 and 1835 fever declined in nearly the same ratio as smallpox. The reduction of fevers was mainly due to the anti-fever campaign though there were other favourable factors.

According to the Carlisle Tables one-third of those dying of consumption were under twenty years of age. The reduction of consumption [3] and dropsy Farr considered to be mainly due to the reduction of fever and dysentery, since consumption and diseases of the kidneys and heart are common after effects of fevers, including under this term enteric and smallpox. Some credit, however, must be given to better food, more sanitary dwellings, and greater temperance. Thus the reduced death rate appears to have been mainly due to a reduction of fevers and of the diseases of infancy, including smallpox. Contemporary authorities believed that there was also great reduction of dysentery (probably enteric), particularly in London. This is quite probable in view of the various improvements in town economy. Francis Place believed that there was also a great reduction in venereal disease, due to greater sobriety and the improvement of morals. The Wesleyan and Evangelical movements, which laid great stress on chastity, must have been favourable factors in this direction. Another disease that afflicted our ancestors, which is now practically extinct in this country, had been considerably reduced. That disease was malaria. Though probably its direct effect on the death rate was small, its indirect effect must have been great.

MALARIA (Synonyms: ague, paludism, marsh, remittent, intermittent, climatic, jungle, coast fever).

This disease can be caused by three different parasites. The *Plasmodium vivax* which produces tertian fevers, a mild form of malaria which seldom causes death. The *Plasmodium malariae* which produces quartan fevers, this form seldom causes death directly but it sometimes leaves morbid symptoms which ultimately do so. Both these parasites live mainly in the circulating blood and generate there, their toxins therefore produce general symptoms. The third parasite *Lavarania malariae* produces a subtertian fever, it sporulates as a rule in the spleen but it may sporulate in other organs, for instance the brain, intestines, heart or pancreas, it then produces the severe form of malaria known as Malignant Malaria. *Laverania malariae* also causes a chronic form of the disease which may be accompanied by serious lesions of various organs. Malaria, especially the malignant type, often leaves bad after-effects, it may cause mental trouble to the point of insanity and anæmia is a frequent consequence. Children suffer severely and attacks often leave them in a condition resembling that of rickets their general development is interfered with and in severe cases the onset of puberty is prevented. The miserable physique of the natives of malarious districts is notorious, though the death rate from actual malaria is always lower among the resident population than among immigrants. The residents acquire sometimes an apparent, sometimes a real immunity, but their children suffer from the disease and many die, while the survivors remain under-developed in different degrees. Hard work and under-nourishment make the individual more susceptible to malaria. All three forms of malaria are carried by the female of the anopheline variety of mosquito. In temperate zone these insects generally hibernate in the winter but occasionally emerge and bite on a warm day. In the spring they become active and breed rapidly. Still water is necessary for the existence of the larvae and pupae. The parasites of malaria also require warmth for their development and a high temperature favours the development of the disease. The *Laverania malariae* requires a greater degree of warmth than other forms, hence the variety of disease caused by this parasite rarely appears in the temperate zone except in the summer or autumn.[4]

England possesses three species of anopheline mosquito but only one of these (*Maculipennis* Meigen) has been proved to be a carrier of malaria under normal conditions. The mild form of malaria was common in certain marshy districts in this country until the middle of the 19th century and sporadic cases still occur from time to time. Owing to the usual difficulties of diagnosis and nomenclature it is very difficult to state anything definite about the incidence of malaria before the second half of the 18th century. The term ague simply means " acute " and was originally very loosely used. It has been suggested that the epidemical agues of the 17th century were either influenza, typhus or enteric. Medical writers, however, seldom used the term ague but referred to " autumnal intermittents ", or some similar nomenclature. By the last quarter of the 18th century malaria was a well recognised disease. Its marked characteristics of high incidence in late summer and early autumn, its association with stagnant water, the relative immunity of natives, its yielding to quinine were all well known. That is not, of course, to say that mistakes were not made in cases of difficult diagnosis or by ignorant practitioners in ordinary cases. But by the end of the 18th century a well qualified doctor would not be likely to mistake an epidemic of malaria for another disease or vice versa. The medical writers of the 18th century believed that malaria had formerly been much more prevalent in England, and particularly in London, than it was in their day. They also believed that a severe form had occasionally appeared. For instance Short (in 1780) in his list of mortalities and epidemics mentions for 1556–58 " agues and Remittents, which consumed much People in *England*, especially grave Men ". He also says, " Agues whereof one of 40 of the whole that died of Fevers, died ; now scarce 1 of 1100 that die of fevers die of this : This Distemper

... has sometimes raged like a Plague. In 1664 they disappeared, and scarce came on the stage before '78; but from 1720 to '29, they and Remittents afflicted the whole Nation grievously; and now as to their Severity, especially theirMortality, they are extinct, but as they decrease, other Fevers increase." Short also quotes an anonymous author as saying "Where are now our ... great mortalities by agues?" [5]

Burnett in his history of the Reformation says that in the last year of Queen Mary's reign " intermitting fevers were so universal and contagious that they raged like a plague ".[6] Bateman says, " Both Sydenham and Morton have left us ample evidence of the frequent occurrence of remittent fevers, which the latter affirms to have been extremely destructive for several years before the great plague, viz. from the year 1658 to 1664. He states, that Oliver Cromwell died of this fever in 1658; and that his own father, who was himself an experienced physician, also died of it; and his whole family, including himself, were infected." [6]

Sydenham has written of the year 1661, " the autumnal intermittents, which during the last few years, had been gaining ground, broke out afresh, the beginning of July. They gathered strength daily: by the month of August they were doing fearful mischief. In many places the mortality was excessive, and whole families fell victims ... Few were attacked during October. The colds of winter wholly dispelled them."

"The constitution" of the year 1678 " was so favourable to intermittent fevers, that they might again take the name of epidemics. Since the year 1664 they had nearly been banished from London, so that for 13 years they had attacked only a few patients sporadically, or else had been brought up from the country places ... at the beginning of autumn they were pre-eminently prevalent." [7]

It is possible that the 18th century writers placed too much faith in the powers of diagnosis of their predecessors, and Short's remark as to other fevers increasing is significant in this connection.

Malaria, however, was still endemic in certain districts in England until the middle of the 19th century and the causes of its final extinction are by no means clear. The disease was associated with stagnant water and there is ample evidence that the draining of the marshes led to a reduction of its incidence. When it was discovered that the mosquito was the carrier of malaria, historians at once jumped to the conclusion that here was the missing link in the chain of causation. Unfortunately for this theory the mosquito *maculipennis* has been found in every rural district in this country where search has been made for it and in many parts of this country its prevalence is greater than in malarious districts in the Tropics. Neither is there any correlation between the number of mosquitoes in an area and the recorded outbreaks of malaria.[8] Yet the correlation between the draining of marshes and the reduction of malaria is historically established by numerous references. Short pointed out the importance of improvements " for Health and Profit, as by draining of marshy Grounds, such as the *Isle of Ely* . . . all the circumjacent Country is hereby made more healthy as well as useful ". Before the draining he states the Births were to Burials as 61 to 70, after they were as 60 to 54.[5] The cutting of canals and the canalizing and embanking of rivers often drained the surrounding land and sometimes led to a reduction of the disease. A medical writer on the Stourport district in 1814 says, " Since the introduction of canals and the drainage of bogs, this disease " (intermittent fever) " is never met with here ; 40 years ago it was so prevalent, that the farmers could scarcely get their business done for want of hands." [9] Of course not all the unhealthiness of marshy districts was due to malaria. In low-lying, boggy districts drinking water is more likely to be contaminated and rheumatic and bronchial affections are generally more common.

There were other factors besides draining which tended to reduce malaria. An important one was the better and more frequent use of cinchona bark and its active principles. This drug was a native South American remedy, its native name was quina-quina and it was known to the Spaniards in America as early as 1600. In 1638 the Countess of Chinchon, wife of the Viceroy of Peru, was dangerously ill and was cured by cinchona bark. On returning to Spain she brought back a quantity of the bark with her and its scientific name, *Cinchona*, is due to a mistaken rendering of the lady's name. In 1670 another large consignment was sent to Rome by some Jesuit missionaries and was distributed throughout Europe by the efforts of Cardinal de Lugo, hence the popular name of Cardinal's or Jesuit's bark. About this time the drug received a great advertisement through the Dauphin of France being cured by it, while in England its use was strongly advocated by Sydenham.[4] At first, naturally, it was believed that chinchona would cure all fevers and mistakes were also made in the quantity administered. But by the second half of the 18th century both the limitations and the correct use of the drug had been fairly well learnt. It was available for the poor at the Hospitals and Dispensaries and even the humble apothecary could prescribe it. The alkaloid quinine was not extracted from cinchona until 1820 [10] and was not in use until 1840, and even then was very expensive, and it was not until about 1880 that this preparation was cheap enough to be generally available. Colonel James considers that the free use of quinine proper may have been an important factor in the final extinction of malaria, but even the less effective cinchona bark was of considerable value. The importance of quinine is that it not only reduces the severity of the disease in the person attacked but also so much weakens the parasite that a malarious person saturated with quinine is unlikely to be a new source of infection.[4] It has recently been pointed out by a medical writer that in this country the malarial parasite soon loses its virulence, unless there is a frequent transfer to a new human host. Therefore there is a normal check to the disease during the hibernation in winter. *Maculipennis*, however, is easily domesticated, provided that the right kind of accommodation is available. The mosquito enjoys an absence of draughts, a warm temperature, relative darkness and dark cracks and corners in which to hide during the day, it also requires food at night. An ideal home for a mosquito is the raftered roof of a warm building, with no intervening ceiling to shut it off from its food. The mosquito has no apparent preference between the blood of different animals, cows, pigs, and human beings suit it equally well.

Given the above conditions, the mosquito need never hibernate and she will only leave her home to deposit her eggs in the nearest available stagnant water. In modern times the mosquito finds her ideal home in old fashioned stables, cow sheds and pig-styes, but it has been pointed out that in former times she would have found it in the habitations of man. Here were found the darkness, undisturbed dirt, little ventilation and raftered, unceilinged roofs which she loved. A mosquito which visits a modern house with its inhospitable ceilings and its light and airy rooms soon leaves again. The importance of this change is that the chances of a mosquito biting a malarious person are enormously reduced. Also, hibernation under modern conditions is more common among mosquitoes and therefore this check is more active. It has also been suggested that natural conditions in this country are in some way inimical to the survival of malaria parasites. That is, that without re-infection, the disease in this country either dies out or assumes a very attenuated form. If this is true, the reduction of malaria in this country may have been largely due to a reduction at the old source of infection. Pringle describes a form of remittent fever as endemic in the Low Countries, especially in Zeeland, and malignant malaria still raged there in the early 19th century. During the unfortunate Walcheren Expedition of 1809, out of a total complement of 1,738 officers and 37,481 men, 60 officers and 3,891 men died of disease and in 1810 there were still 11,513 on the sick list. When Blane, who was sent out by the Government to report, arrived at Walcheren he found between nine and ten thousand sick and pronounced the disease to be " the endemic fever of marshy countries ", though there were a few cases of typhus. The writer of this account says that " the natives are annually liable to a similar calamity " and that one third of the French army in Flanders was annually cut off by this endemic. A petition was presented to Napoleon upon the great mortality of the French troops at Flushing and he is reported to have answered, " L'homme meurt partout." [11]

Therefore, the improved housing, the use of quinine and the reduction of foreign infection were all factors favourable to the reduction of malaria. Nevertheless, the correlation between the draining of marshes and its reduction is too well established historically to be summarily dismissed. Perhaps dampness is necessary to the well being of the malaria parasite. But in our present state of knowledge a factor remains unknown.

It is interesting to note that a recent account of the Public Health of Baltimore (Maryland, U.S.A.) points out that almost complete extinction of malaria followed from the covering in of open drains and the draining of marshes in the vicinity of the city, coupled with an increased use of quinine. There was also a cessation of regular trading communications with malarious regions. These measures were effective before the anti-mosquito campaign. The death rate from malaria was inappreciable by 1899 though the anti-mosquito campaign was only initiated in 1910.[12] In Holland, also, the draining of marshes destroyed malaria.

It is of course impossible to make even the vaguest quantitative statement as to the number of deaths due to malaria in this country, especially as the mild form does not kill directly but only renders its victims more susceptible to other diseases. Lind, writing in 1809 [13] said that agues occurred in England in low woody and marshy places, that they were seldom mortal to natives but impair the constitution and to strangers they were often fatal. Blane [14] writing in 1812 called attention to the greater mortality in the districts where ague occurred, though whether the higher death rate was due directly or indirectly to malaria is not clear. At Boston (in the fen country) the mortality was 1 in 27 (37 per 1,000), while at Stamford in the upland it was only 1 in 50 (20 per 1,000). Short in 1750 had written that, " Low Habitations especally on stiff Clay, rotten Earth or near a Level with the Sea, great Rivers, Marshes, Lakes or putrid standing Waters . . . Such are the Fens in *Lincolnshire*, the Isle of *Ely*, some Places in *Holderness* of *Yorkshire*, Iles of Lancashire, Washes of *Norfolk*, Hundred of *Essex*, etc. ", in these places the burials came near to or were even greater than the christenings, this was due to intermittents and putrid fevers and other diseases. He adds, " Though the Burials in such Places may exceed the Births, yet the Difference between Weddings and Burials, is far from being so wide as might be expected. Then it is evident, that the great Numbers dying in Infancy, are supplied by fresh In-comers, who settle and marry there; and that the Endemics of the Place are more fatal to them than the Natives ".[5]

In regard to London, many modern writers are sceptical as to whether the disease ever existed in that city, but the 18th century belief as to its former prevalence cannot be summarily dismissed. It may be noted that the conditions up to the middle of the 18th century were favourable. London was in constant communication with the Low Countries, both in peace and war and, so long as the city was unpaved and the marshes in its close proximity were undrained, there was no lack of breeding places for the mosquito. The housing conditions in the 17th century were also favourable to the disease. The re-building after the Great Fire and the gradual modernization of the houses which survived that catastrophe, would have been favourable to its reduction or extinction. Also, Westminster was paved in 1762 and the City in 1766, " Fleet ditch was then first covered in and the streets paved with large stones ",[15] and the marshes near London were drained about the same time. To this cause Lind ascribed the extinction of acute malaria in the Metropolis. A writer in 1781 said, " Very few die now of Ague in London." He added that " towns in general are less harassed with this disease than country places ".[16] Pringle had noted the same thing in the Low Countries. Incidentally this seems to prove that these writers were not confusing malaria with typhus or enteric. By the beginning of the 19th century it was generally believed that all forms of malaria were extinct in London, the cases which occurred being among immigrants from Ireland or the marshy districts of England. To the present writer it seems that the balance of evidence is in favour of mild malaria having existed in London up to the middle of the 18th century, at which time it died out owing to the above mentioned improvements. It is impossible to express an opinion as to whether the epidemics of the 17th century were visitations of acute malaria or not. But apart from these very doubtful visitations, it is unlikely that the direct death rate from malaria was ever appreciable in London.

Even mild malaria, however, impairs the constitution and therefore malaria, if it existed, would have been indirectly responsible for part of the high death rate, particularly that of children.

In many marshy districts of this country the existence of mild malaria is an established fact. It died out in the middle of the 19th century, for reasons which are by no means clear and the discussion of which are outside the province of this book. There is a considerable amount of evidence, however, that even by the beginning of the 19th century the incidence of this disease had been much reduced, and though the direct effect upon the death rate was probably unimportant, the indirect effect in certain districts can have been by no means negligible. Its former incidence must also have led to much ill-health and general debility.

There is a popular idea that though the death rate may have been higher in early times yet the population was healthier. This belief has been justified first, by the belief that the predominant medieval diseases killed more quickly than the predominant modern ones and secondly, that epidemic disease killed off the weakly members of the community, especially weakly children. As Farr put it, " where the conditions of existence are unfavourable, and a great proportion of the people are weak, sickly, and doomed to untimely death, a sudden epidemic cuts short their agonies, and purifies the race : it is an amputation of members already gangrened, and falling off by inches; at the same time, however, it carries off a great number of the healthy. If those who had cholera in Paris had been seized by consumption, they would have endured 73,600 years of sickness instead of 158,118 days : the living in the epidemics of the middle ages could not have watched the sick if their diseases had been protracted. In this sense only, epidemics can be looked upon as merciful visitations of Providence, for moderating evils self-inflicted on mankind." [17] The last point is rather obscure, certainly if an epidemic disease with the death rate of plague caused an illness which lasted as long as consumption, the sick could not be nursed and it may be added, the human race could not survive. The reason why tuberculosis kills so slowly arises from the nature of the infection and of the protective organisms which the human body has developed to deal with it. That is to say, a large proportion of those invaded by the bacillus do not contract the disease and those that do contract it continue to put up a good fight against it. In epidemic diseases the battle is short and sharp both for the community and the individual. If, however, Farr meant that owing to plague, etc., there was a less proportionate amount of tuberculosis among the surviving population it is more than doubtful if this idea is correct. In the first place there does not seem to be any good reason to believe that infectious diseases are beneficially selective, many types of fevers seem to attack and kill the strong and healthy as readily as the weak. But even if the death rate among the attacked is slightly selective, the adverse effect upon the survivors more than compensates for this. Not only is the survivor generally weakened and sometimes permanently disabled, as in the blindness which often resulted from smallpox, but he is left more liable to other diseases, for instance smallpox and dysentery leave a liability to consumption. There is a popular idea that a severe fever is purifying and invigorating to the individual as to the community, a survival of the old idea that the body is naturally full of evil humours, which are better if they " come out ". Doubtless some people do seem better in health after an attack of an infectious illness, but that is probably the result of convalescence rather than of the illness. During convalescence many people enjoy proper conditions as to ventilation, clothing, diet and rest for the only time in their lives. But this is a modern development, it is doubtful if it was true of convalescence in earlier periods.

The losses of an army in battle are not measured alone by the number of killed, but also by the temporarily and the permanently maimed.[18] So it is in the fight against disease, the reduction of the number of deaths from smallpox, typhus, and malaria meant not only a larger population but a more effective one. Apart from the reduction of the number of persons actually ill from these diseases at any given time, there was also a reduction of other specific illness and of general debility and ill health. A high death rate is a clear indication of a high sickness rate.

In spite of its imperfections for the measurement of details, the value of the crude death rate remains unimpaired for the measurement of broad changes in a large population.[19] The infantile death rate has also been held to be a reliable test of social conditions, in spite of the fact that in modern times there is not necessarily a close association between the general and the infant mortality.

Though many factors in modern life are adverse to health, it is undoubted that at the present day there is a less proportion of serious illness and disablement than in previous ages. The legend of our healthy, vigorous ancestors has as little truth in it as the legend of the healthy savage.

CHAPTER XVII

THE PERIOD 1815-1848 [1]

THOUGH the statistical material for England and Wales was growing both in quantity and quality throughout the 19th century, up to 1875 no very exact conclusions can be based upon it. The mere fact that the statistics were becoming more reliable every decade introduced a new possibility of error when they were used for comparative purposes. After 1815 the population continued to grow at a rapid rate, but the rate of growth was already established and there does not appear to have been any outstanding alteration in the birth or death rates. Once the death rate has fallen below the birth rate to any considerable degree, a population will continue to grow without any further alteration of the rates or even in spite of a degree of adverse change. As a well known writer has expressed it, the increasing number of parents can be compared to compound interest, the *rate of interest* remains the same yet the amount of interest increases year by year.

Up to 1846 the Irish immigration was believed to have roughly balanced the emigration from Great Britain to other parts of the world, after 1846 there was a net loss of population by emigration. The increase of population was, therefore, a natural one.

The registered births for the average of 5 years ending 1830 were 1 in 29 (34 per 1000). Taking the deficiency at as least 21% (this is the lowest estimate) the actual birth rate was at least 36 per 1000.[2] In 1851-61 the registered births had risen to 34 per 1000. Part of this rise was certainly due to better registration but there was also a rise in the registered marriages from 7·8 to 8·4 per 1000.[3] There is no data for anything but a crude rate and this rise may perhaps be accounted for by a change in the age composition of the population. The standardized birth rate, which is not available before 1851, shows a slight rise between 1851–76, but this apparent rise is most probably simply a result of better registration due to a stiffening of the law.[4] If we assume that the registered births were approximately accurate for 1871–75 (35·5 per 1000) and that the deficiency was correctly calculated for 1830, then there was no appreciable alteration in the birth rate between 1830–75, but the possibility of a slight rise cannot be excluded.

The death rate probably fell progressively from the middle of the 18th century until about 1815, then rose slightly until about 1830, from which date it is fairly well established that it remained practically stationary until 1870. Farr said, "It appears probable, however, that the rate of mortality had been reduced to a *minimum* in 1815, and that it increased somewhat in the interval between that and 1830." He ascribed the rise mainly to the distress following the war but thought that the Irish immigration might also have had some influence. To those familiar with the period 1815–25 it would not be surprising if the death rate had risen very considerably instead of only slightly. The period was one of intense economic dislocation, of depression in agriculture, still the main industry of the country, of widespread unemployment and of political unrest. The country was weighed down with a heavy burden of taxation, a burden which pressed unduly upon the poor and the productive classes generally. Currency difficulties and the cessation of the war demand for agricultural products and for iron and woollen manufactures had led to a disastrous fall of prices and to stagnation of trade. The continent was exhausted and offered but a poor market for our goods, and another lucrative market, that of South America, was dislocated by revolution and civil war. Though the fifteen years after peace was broken up into alternating periods of depressions and booms, the underlying feature of the period was one of stagnation of trade and industry. The revenue was stationary, the imports and exports were the same and so was the mercantile marine. The mass of the people had to submit to lower wages, in many cases after fierce but futile resistance, while, though general prices fell, the price of bread remained relatively high. The aftermath of war, as always, was poverty, disillusionment and discontent. The towns also continued to grow in size and this was an adverse factor from the point of view of the death rate.

Under these circumstances it is rather surprising that the estimated rise in the death rate was only from 1 in 55 (18 per 1000) to 1 in 51 (19·6 per 1000),[5] there were, however, important counteracting factors which are sufficient explanation. In the first place the lavish Poor Law, however ill advised the method of its administration, did prevent any large number of deaths from actual starvation. Also the potato, the use of which had rapidly extended, was a cheap supplementary food which to some extent compensated for low wages, though to the mass of the people bread was still the staff of life. Secondly there was the cessation of the war drain upon the manhood of the population and of deaths from wounds and disease contracted on foreign service. The men discharged from the army and navy in the year 1816 numbered over 200,000, though a proportion of these were foreigners. Lastly, and probably most important, vaccination was becoming increasingly effective, while the effects of the saving of infant life during the preceding 35 years was showing itself in an age composition that was favourable from the point of view of mortality.

The rise in the death rate between 1815–30 is more than explained by the after war conditions but from 1830 onwards there was recovery in the economic life of the nation, slow at first but unmistakable. The period of 1852–70 was one of unexampled progress in industry and commerce and resultant prosperity in which all classes, except the agricultural labourer, shared. Real wages rose rapidly yet the death rate remained stationary from about 1825 until about 1874. There were, however, in this period several factors adverse to public health. The most important was the rapid growth of towns, the period 1831–41 was that of the most rapid concentration of population in this country and the growth was rapid throughout the whole period under discussion.[6] Even at the present day the country is more healthy than the towns and the difference was far greater seventy or a hundred years ago. In the period 1813–30 the death rate in London was 28 per 1000 while for the whole country it was 21 per 1000 and for the rural county of Wilts, it was 17·5 per 1000. This is the crude death rate, a standardized death rate (i.e. one making allowance for the difference of age composition) would be even more favourable to the rural areas. The death rate under 5 was 36 per 1000 in Wilts, and 83 per 1000 in London.[2] Unfortunately the administrative areas of towns, for which the census returns are made, often bear no very exact relation to their actual area and therefore it is not possible to make any exact statistical statements as to the growth of towns. It has been estimated that the urban population was about one third of the total in 1831 and about one half in 1851.[7] In view of this increase of the urban population Farr stated that a stationary death rate argued improvement rather than retrogression in town conditions. There is a good deal to be said for this contention, especially in view of the fact that the growth of towns was not the only adverse factor.

In the first place there was a large Irish immigration, especially into Liverpool and Manchester. Farr was very strongly of the opinion that the Irish not only had a high death rate, but tended to lower the standard of life of their neighbours and stated that the Irish quarter in a town was generally a hot-bed of fever. Every writer of the times is agreed upon the filth and squalor in which the immigrant Irish lived. They even kept pigs and poultry in their wretched one room tenements, as they had been accustomed to do in their home cabins; but in a town slum these conditions were not mitigated by health-giving breezes from the Atlantic. To the Englishman of the mid 19th century the Irishman was what the Eastern European is to the North American of to-day. To the working class he was a rival with a lower standard of life, to the employer he represented cheap labour, to the more thoughtful social reformer and administrator he was an additional problem. It was to the benefit of both countries when the stream of Irish emigration was diverted to America.

In 1831 there was an invasion into England of very much more serious import, from the point of view of public health, than that of the poor Irish, for in that year the cholera reached this country. Asiatic cholera is an acute specific endemic or epidemic disease caused by the *vibrio cholerae* which was discovered by Koch in 1883. The cholera infection may pass from man to man by contact, by the contamination of fields and rubbish heaps by infected fæces, or it may be carried by flies. But it is chiefly carried by the infection of drinking water since the *vibrio* can live and multiply in water. Cholera infection always travels by lines of human communication, rivers, roads, railways and shipping routes. It is said that underfeeding and worry cause greater susceptibility to the disease, also anything which causes diarrhoea and therefore weakens the intestines, such as eating unripe fruit.[8] There has been a good deal of discussion as to whether the 1830 epidemic was the first visitation of true cholera in Europe ; the question is complicated, as is the history of most other diseases, by early confusion in diagnosis and nomenclature. In the past the term cholera was used to cover a group of clinically similar illnesses which are, as a matter of fact, caused by germs closely allied to the *vibrio cholerae*. It seems established that true cholera is endemic in Lower Bengal and from time to time becomes epidemic in India. Epidemic cholera was accurately described by European travellers to India from the 16th century onwards; no fewer than 64 independent authorities between 1503 and 1817 mention cholera in India and ten of these refer to epidemic outbursts. At the end of the 18th century English troops were several times attacked by the disease. It seems difficult to believe that the disease never spread to Europe and the rest of the world before the 19th century, but there is no record of any such panendemic in historic times. Sydenham, it is true, gives an account of an epidemic occurring between 1679 and 1682 in London, the symptoms of which closely resembled cholera but a contemporary of Sydenham's refers to the fact that, though the disease reigned cruelly in London, it did not extend beyond three miles outside of the city. If this statement is true the disease could not have been Asiatic cholera, it may have been one of the allied diseases or an acute form of malaria which in bad seasons often results in symptoms closely resembling cholera. As to why cholera suddenly became panendemic, this is unexplainable in our present state of knowledge. Though a rapid and widespread diffusion of the disease was doubtless aided by the development of transport, it was independent of this development, since one of the first lines of invasion to reach Europe did so by the immemorial trade route over Central Asia to Russia.

The great panendemic seems to have originated in a particularly virulent outbreak in 1817 at Jessore, where 10,000 perished in a few weeks. By 1818 the disease had spread over the greater part of India, it then travelled westward as far as the Levant, also via Persia to the borders of Russia and eastward to Burma, Siam, Further India and China ; but by 1823 it had gradually disappeared. It is noteworthy that the Chinese believed the disease to be a new one. In 1826 there was a fresh outbreak in Bengal which spread over India and reached Persia by 1829 and by that route reached Orenburg in August of that year. The following year, in spite of stringent quarantine regulations, it reached Kharkov, Moscow and Novgorod. In 1831 it was carried to Warsaw by the Russian troops who were then fighting the Poles. By another route the disease had reached Arabia in 1828 and in 1831 it raged with virulence among the pilgrims at Mecca. It was computed that nearly half the pilgrims fell victims to it and the disease returned with the survivors to Asia Minor, Turkey and Egypt. From Turkey it spread to Bulgaria and Galicia. In the meantime the northern wing had spread to Finland and Sweden and by the autumn of 1831 the disease had reached Berlin, Vienna and Bohemia, but it did not penetrate to Western Germany in that year. In October of 1831 the disease first appeared in England, at Sunderland, supposedly introduced from Hamburg. The total deaths in England between November 1831 and April 1832 were 4,621. France remained free until 1832, but in March of that year cholera broke out in Paris, within a week the mortality reached 500 a day and in 18 days the deaths numbered 7,000. In 1832 the disease spread to Ireland and there was a renewed outbreak in England, but according to one estimate the total cases only numbered 14,796, of whom 5,432 died.[9] Owing to the lack of proper registration of deaths it is, however, impossible to state the number of deaths from cholera with any exactitude. According to Farr the deaths numbered 31,376 between 1831–33 in certain districts in which fairly accurate records were kept and which possessed an aggregate population of something under 5½ millions, while in Ireland for the same period they are said to have numbered 21,171.

In June 1832 there was an outbreak in Quebec and from there the disease spread to New York and so over the whole of the U.S.A. Spain had a most vigorous quarantine law, the evasion of which was punishable with death, but though she escaped until 1833, the quarantine line was passed in that year. From Spain the disease spread to the Spanish West Indies. Its virulence was terrible in Havana and also in Mexico.

Cholera died down in Europe in 1834 but there was a renewed epidemic in 1836–37, which may or may not have been due to re-infection from Asia through the terrible epidemic which raged in Bombay during 1832–34. However, Europe remained free from cholera from 1839–46 but there was another epidemic of great virulence in 1848–53. During the first epidemic very strenuous efforts were made by all European governments to stop its spread by quarantine measures but, disheartened by the apparent total failure of these measures, only very faint exertions were made by the authorities to stay the second visitation. Some Russian doctors believed that this relaxation resulted in a much higher death rate in the second epidemic. They pointed out that during the first epidemic when there were sanitary cordons throughout Russia, only 336 towns were attacked and only 100,000 deaths occurred, while during the second epidemic 471 towns were attacked and there were a million deaths. Other medical authorities believed, however, that the virulence of the disease was greater in the second epidemic. The deaths in England during the year 1849 were 53,293.

Cholera completely baffled the medical profession. So mysterious seemed its method of propagation that some authorities even doubted its infectious character and there was a long controversy upon this subject. The *Lancet* pronounced in favour of contagion, but that the method was unknown.

In 1848–49 a Dr. Snow promulgated the view that cholera was spread by a poison contained in the evacuations of infected persons and by the subsequent contamination of drinking water and was awarded a prize by the Institut de France for an essay on this thesis.   In 1849 a Dr. Budd of Bristol put forward the theory that the disease was due to a living organism, of the nature of a fungus, which multiplied in the intestinal canal and was spread by the contamination of drinking water. He recommended that all discharges from infected persons should at once be treated with a strong disinfectant. The College of Physicians considered these views to be untenable since they ran counter to the accepted view of the nature of contagion. Budd, however, despite the College of Physicians, stopped an outbreak of cholera at some barracks near Bristol by his repudiated method.[10]   Dr. Snow also showed by an investigation in South London that there was a close correlation between cholera and contaminated water supply and this was confirmed by Farr's statistical studies.   From this time reform in methods of water supply commenced.[11]

Though it seems highly probable that the defective system of water drainage in use in London and some other English towns, favoured the spread of the disease, the cholera epidemics cannot justly be ascribed to the condition of the English towns. The disease came from the East and spread over the whole world, devastating communities of every race and every type of civilization and economic life with commendable impartiality. Further, if the English doctors and administrators failed to check the disease they at least were not more stupid than those of other countries and it was in England that the correct method of combating cholera was discovered and developed. Some writers consider cholera to have been a blessing in disguise since the hygienic measures instituted in combating it led to the prevention of other maladies which were more destructive than cholera, " though their ravages were more insidious and common place." [12]   Cholera, like plague, was a sensational disease and it aroused the petty parochialism of the mid 19th century as effectively as plague had aroused the corrupt bureaucracy of the 18th century.

Thus there were several factors adverse to public health during the period under discussion and there is some force in Farr's contention that these adverse factors must have been balanced by improvements in other directions. The 1848 reformers, however, believed that the conditions which they found were so bad that worse could not be imagined and that these conditions must represent a new and terrible problem. There is no reason to suppose that their descriptions were untrue or even exaggerated but they were perhaps partial and showed a lack of perspective that is understandable. Francis Place was strongly of the opinion that things had improved rather than worsened up to 1834; he held that the descriptions of the reformers applied only to the lowest sections of the population, whereas in earlier periods they would have applied to all. He said, " I know Dr. Kay, and I believe what he says is correct; but he gives the matter as it now stands, knowing nothing of former times; his picture is a very deplorable one. I am assured that my view of it is correct by many Manchester operatives whom I have seen; they inform me that his narration relates almost wholly to the state of the Irish, but that the condition of a vast number of the people was nearly as bad some years ago, as he describes the worst position of them now to be. Any writer or inquirer will be misled unless he has the means of comparing the present with former times." [13] Place added that he had observed the working class for nearly half a century and was positive that their habits and condition showed a great improvement.

Only a detailed study of the period could give a correct judgment as between improvement and retrogression, but there are some matters of general knowledge which make some degree of retrogression not improbable. The towns were growing at an astonishing rate and problems of mere size began to intrude themselves. The idea of town planning, except of central business streets, or of the regulation of building, had scarcely arisen. But, in any case, it is doubtful if any regulation could have been enforced since the constant influx of people had to be housed and housed as cheaply as possible and the enforcement of building byelaws, by raising the rents, would have increased the over-crowding. The population was also constantly outgrowing existing institutions such as schools and hospitals, and in the difficult times following the war it was not always easy to keep up current revenue, still less to expand it. The supporters of the hospitals had been mainly landowners and wealthy merchants, both these classes suffered severely in the after war depression and charitable subscriptions suffered accordingly. Some large centres tended to be inadequately served with hospitals and dispensaries that had been amply served only a generation previously.

It also seems probable that the growth of democracy was not at first at all favourable to sanitary reform.[14] The magistrates, whether neighbouring gentry or wealthy merchants, were on the whole enlightened, open to new scientific ideas, amenable to persuasion by doctors and others. They had the power, too, of carrying things through in a high handed and sometimes illegal manner. The magistrates after 1815 became the subject of scathing attack, not only for their faults but also for their virtues. Any reform which meant the imposition of a rate was especially the subject of abuse. The gentry tended to retire sulkily from public service or to perform the minimum duties in a perfunctory manner. A new spirit was abroad which was incompatible with the old order. On the whole the poor had trusted their old rulers who had often stood between them and their immediate oppressors and had exerted themselves to give food and money in bad times. Moreover, the poor under the old regime, except when seized with the madness of riot, were docile and generally inclined to obey the commands of the gentry, and to be suitably grateful for help in sickness. It is astonishing the things which the early typhus fighters were able to do without any legal status ; their social prestige appears to have carried them through, not only with patients but generally with landlords also. The men to whom power was passing had not the habit of ruling and the workers were losing the habit of being ruled. Sanitary reform cost money, the problem was getting too big for private charity apart from the fact that the charitable public was able or willing to give less. Any increase in public expenditure, central or local, was extremely difficult in a time of financial stringency, when the taxable capacity of the country was strained to the uttermost. The cry was " Economy and Reform ". Economy meant, not wise expenditure but the sweeping away of financial and political abuse and the ruthless cutting down of expenditure wherever possible. The Reform was destructive rather than constructive and, though the sweeping away of a mass of currupt and inefficient political paraphernalia was a necessary prelude to later achievements, the good effects were ultimate and not immediate.

Political power, especially in Local Government, was passing into the hands of the lower middle class or petite bourgeoisie; small shop-keepers and small manufacturers, a class with many virtues, thrifty, hard working, clean living but notoriously lacking in large views or sympathetic imagination. The honest among them tended to avoid local affairs except to vote against any increase of the rates, the dishonest found in local government an illicit source of income. The petite bourgeoisie have little sympathy with the working class, from which they are so often barely removed in economic circumstances, and little belief in new fangled ideas. Their numbers can never have been so *relatively* great in England as during the period from 1815 to 1870, owing to the small scale of much industry and nearly all retail trade. From 1832 to 1868, owing to the nature of the franchise, their political powers were also great, though never fully exerted. The growth of large scale industry and trading on the one hand and the political enfranchisement and economic organization of large bodies of highly skilled workers on the other, made this power short lived, except in some small areas of local government. It is, perhaps, due to the fact that our petite bourgeoisie are relatively small in numbers and politically unimportant and are without the support of a peasantry, that in this country class feeling lacks the extreme bitterness often found elsewhere.

There was also, perhaps, a natural ebb in the tide of public health reform. The hospitals and dispensaries missed the zeal of their first founders, medical science tended to fall into a rut after a period of achievement; enthusiasm found that the anticipated results were not always forthcoming and so tended to wane. The best minds in the medical profession, like those in other spheres, were much occupied with administrative abuses and with the building up of a reasonable professional organization. In the same way, though the pioneers of 1848 began their preliminary work about 1839, little was achieved for the next twenty years, since here also the aim was mainly in the direction of administrative reform which, judging by vital statistics, bore little immediate fruit. It was not until the last quarter of the 19th century that the new era of achievement set in, an era of cheap and plentiful food brought from every quarter of the globe and of astonishing advance in medicine and public hygiene.

It is curious that, though the second and third quarter of the 19th century was a period of considerable economic and social change, it was yet comparatively stable from the point of view of vital statistics. The increasing prosperity and some amelioration in water supply and drainage, etc., were sufficient to counteract the serious adverse factors of the increasing urbanization and the advent of cholera. During this period the growth of population was rapid; the rate of growth, however, was not new but already established and the reasons for that growth must be sought in the preceding period. History looks before and after. For the historian the main interest of the sanitary endeavours of the mid 19th century is the fruit which they bore after 1875. In the same way the main importance of the events described in this study lies in the subsequent cumulative growth of population, which growth, moreover, was predominantly urban. Many factors went to the making of the great urban communities which for good or ill emerged in the 19th century, but these communities could not have arisen had the death rate, and in particular the town death rate, remained at its 17th century level. Civilization could only become urban when a natural increase was possible in the towns and, filthy and abominable as were many quarters of the early 19th century English towns, yet those towns produced more human life than they destroyed.

Some degree of civic polity, lost in the dark ages, had been recovered, great cities had ceased to be merely the graves of mankind, they had become cradles; that fact was fraught with far reaching consequences which are still only very imperfectly apprehended and the importance of which can hardly be estimated.

CHAPTER XVIII

Conclusion

"Like every new force, industrialism has to many the aspect of a monster. When it has familiarised itself this uncouth appearance will seem no more horrible than that of the locomotive. It is the old and haggard things like war and tyranny, disease and squalor, that will seem more and more repulsive as the world moves on. As the snorts and hisses of the first locomotives soon subsided into the 'puff-puff' beloved by every child, so will the awkward and ferocious gestures of infant industrialism become the ordered rhythm of the great forces moving the whole world's machinery."

The Railway Centenary.
RANDALL DAVIES.

THIS study has only dealt with England and Wales but the advance in medicine was European, neither were the improvements in agriculture and in towns confined to this country. Bateman speaks of "the gradual and happy amelioration of the health of the metropolis, which has been synchronous with the changes of the circumstances above described"[1] and this not only here, but in every large town in Europe ".[2] Another writer says, "In almost every civilized country of Europe . . . every succeeding ten years produce a smaller annual proportion of deaths."[3] The disorders on the Continent due to the wars were, however, a strong counteracting influence there, though some contemporary writers hold that the centralized governments and bureaucracies had achieved more than we had. But allowance must always be made for the English habit of self depreciation both in comparison with other countries and other periods.[4] Such statistics as are available seem to show that while improvement had taken place on the Continent it was to a less extent than in Great Britain.[5] Farr in McCulloch's

"British Empire" states, "There cannot, in fact, be a question that the value of life, in England and Wales, regularly increased from 1740 or 1750 down to 1815; and there are good grounds for thinking that it then exceeded its value in any other country, with the exception of Scotland." Bisset Hawkins writing in 1829 declares roundly that "the mortality of Great Britain, its cities and its hospitals, is greatly inferior to that of any other country in Europe" [7]; and adds, "this superior value of life in Great Britain is not confined to any particular districts, or classes of individuals. To whatever point we turn our view, the advantage is still the same: the man of affluence, the pauper patient of the hospital, the sailor and the soldier on active service, the prisoner of war, the inmate of a gaol, all enjoy a better tenure of existence from this country than from any other of which we have been able to consult the records." He also says that, "It is indisputable, that the average proportion of deaths in England and her cities is less than that of any other country of Europe. And it may be added, that the powers of body and of mind are preserved to a late period in higher perfection here than in other countries . . . An analagous condition of health and vigour may be also observed in our animals and in our vegetation; and if it should be replied, that this excellence is owing to the care bestowed on their culture, the answer applies equally to the human being, on whom more attention is here bestowed, and who is really an object of greater value here than elsewhere." [3]

This latter opinion was general among educated persons who had travelled on the Continent. Lowe in 1822 writing as to the abuses of the Poor Law refers to the reluctance "of many benevolent minds to reduce our allowances to the poor", especially those who were familiar with conditions on the Continent and had there "witnessed the habitual privations of even the sober and industrious among the lower orders who have families".[7]

Many contemporary authorities could also be quoted who voiced the opinion that conditions in England of the "industrial revolution" compared favourably, not only with those then prevailing in more backward countries, but with those that had prevailed in earlier periods at home. For instance, Howlett writing in 1781 when the fact of an increased population was still questioned, was almost lyrical: " Our commerce during " the last 50 or 100 years " has been extending itself into every quarter of the globe; our manufacturers have been multiplying and improving to an astonishing degree; our agriculture has been daily receiving additional extent and additional perfection; dreary marshes and barren wastes have been gradually transformed into rich pastures, meadows, and cornfields; small hamlets have grown into considerable villages, and villages have swelled into large and populous towns. Nor have we, mean time, suffered those public calamities, which, in former ages, frequently spread such dreadful devastation among the human species. Neither famine nor pestilence have repeated, in the present century, their periodical visits, which heretofore used to sweep such multitudes to the grave, and desolate both town and country. . . . the arts of medicine and surgery have made no inconsiderable advances . . . to alleviate the miseries of life and not uncommonly prolong its duration." [8]

Blane writing in 1813 when the fact of the increase was well established says, " the counteraction of typhus by means of cleanliness and ventilation; of the small pox by vaccination in our times; and of agues in the country by the draining of marshes, and in towns by the construction of sewers, and the cleansing of the streets in the 17th and 18th centuries, are undeniable proofs of the power of human art in preventing and extinguishing diseases." [9] While Roberton, who was not unduly optimistic, wrote in 1827, " Reverting to a period as yet little more than a century removed, we find many fatal diseases prevailed then, depending chiefly on circumstances in the condition and habits of the people, the state of the soil, and want of medical knowledge, which now are unknown, or so modified as to excite comparatively little attention. Such were the plague, the milliary fever, rickets, dysentery, spotted and intermittent fevers; and it is our own disgrace if we cannot add small pox. Within the last 70 years, the habits of the lower classes especially, have been rapidly improving; and as there can be no question that the moral more than the physical condition of human beings, influences the rate of mortality, we may hope for yet greater improvement in the healthiness and comfort of our population." [10]

This improvement was largely achieved during the rigours of a hard fought war and during the still more difficult years of trade depression and poverty which followed it. To some extent, however, the improvement was not in spite of the war but because of it. As a writer in 1818 said, " The free and unsophisticated practice of English Medical Officers in the Army and Navy, during the late war, has done much to elevate the rank of their art, heretofore abused by mysteries, formalities, and mercenary intrigues." [11] There is much to put on the debit side of war, but on the credit side must be placed its stimulus to the art of medicine.

There is no necessary contradiction between the reiterated statements as to improvement and the equally reiterated description of the terrible surroundings amid which numbers were still living. In comparing the conditions in different periods a good deal of confusion is caused by vague terms such as " the mass of the people ", " the lower orders ", " the poor ".[12] In reading contemporary descriptions it is often difficult to tell to what sections or to how many of the people a particular statement applied. Herein lies the source of much error. If a perfectly true and unexaggerated description of a modern slum were to be given and the reader left to infer that the bulk of the working classes were living under such conditions, the present death rate would be incredible. Improvements in health conditions, as a rule, have begun with the rich and have spread gradually to poorer and poorer sections of the population. In some matters of health a modern slum dweller is better off than a 17th century prince ; he is probably so in regard to water supply and is certainly so in regard to medical attention. In the 18th century fairly reasonable health conditions became available for the well-to-do and for the higher ranks of the workers and, in some directions, there was amelioration even for the very poor.

In comparing the early 19th century with previous periods it has also to be remembered that it was during this period that

CONCLUSION

the mass of the people first became in some degree articulate. We know nothing, or hardly anything, of what the peasant thought of his lord, or the medieval porter of the rich merchant. A few words here and there, handed down in a ballad or a legend alone hint at forgotten discontents. What did the peasants say, when the lord feasted in the midst of Famine? What did the people of London say when their rulers fled from the plague and left them to their misery? Their bitter comments died with them. Not so the complaints of the Industrial Revolution, they survive in innumerable newspapers and pamphlets. Not only were these produced by the workers themselves but by hosts of sympathisers among the well-to-do and literature began to be full of the wrongs of the people. This was partly the result of democracy. The best way to right a wrong was no longer to present a petition to a king or noble but to produce a popular novel exposing the wrong. Moreover, the growing power of man over nature made people feel that much of the evil was preventable and, if preventable, why not prevented? Previous ages had stood helpless in the face of disease and famine and had tried to forget them. Art had been one of the principal means to this end, its main function had been to provide beauty in a world full of very ugly things while much Victorian art was essentially didactic and moral. It must not, however, be assumed that the writers of previous ages could not have found plenty of misery to describe and wrongs to inveigh against had they wished to do so. Some of the less agreeable features of low life are, indeed, described with great vividness by certain 18th century novelists. These descriptions, however, are only incidental and, of course, the novels themselves are less familiar than those of the Victorians. The numerous commissions and committees of enquiry were a further expression of the awakening of the public conscience. Again it must not be assumed that fit subjects for such enquiries did not exist in previous ages.

Our period was one of economic and social transition, though of less rapid transition than has often been imagined. Man being a social animal is necessarily bound by custom, routine and habit. He tends to dislike change in itself and since, in

CONCLUSION

this imperfect world even beneficent change is apt to bring with it new difficulties, the evil side of the change is likely to be stressed more than the good. Man develops an extraordinary moral resistance against accustomed ills so that new evils really cause more acute suffering simply because they are new. Hence the universal tendency to deprecate the present, to regret the " good old times ", which were yet not as good as still earlier times, which in their turn were but a dim reflection of the lost Golden Age. It is not claimed, therefore, that the new conditions did not cause suffering ; subjectively they may have caused more suffering than the earlier conditions. It is not even claimed that in some directions and for some individuals, material conditions were not worsened. But it is claimed that, on balance, material conditions improved enormously for the people as a whole between 1760 and 1815. To hold this opinion, it is not necessary to give the lie to a single one of the descriptions upon which advocates of the theory of deterioration base their case. According to early 20th century standards, the conditions at the beginning of the 19th century were appalling. But what will the 21st century say of ours ? If, however, the historians of that epoch are just they will admit that, " bad as were the conditions at the beginning of the 20th century, especially after the Great War, they were a marked improvement over those of a hundred years previously, the lowered death rate in itself proves this." The statement remains true if for 19th century is written 20th. Advancing civilization led, between the years 1750 and 1825, to a reduction of the death rate from about 35 per 1000 to about 20 per 1000 in England as a whole and in London from about 50 per 1000 to about 29 per 1000.

Chaotic as some aspects of industrial life may have been in the early 19th century, yet civilization was passing from the primitive to the complex. With that passing came a diminution of the evils associated with primitive civilization. The growth of commerce and the improvement of transport had made the food supply more plentiful, more varied and, above all, more certain. The effect of the changes in commerce and transport upon agriculture was partly direct, since the food supply could obviously be drawn from a wider area, but these

R

changes also led indirectly to a revolution in agricultural technique. So that Famine, which had destroyed untold millions in previous ages, had been abolished in England in our period; deaths from diseases caused by improper diet had also been reduced to negligible proportions.

We can talk lightly of Famine, it is so remote from the experience of even the poorest of us. The bald facts, as related in old chronicles or in the pages of the Indian Famine Commission, leave us cold. Literature alone can give us some dim comprehension; the vivid poetry of the Old Testament; the glimpse in Piers Plowman of he who, after meeting Famine, " looked like a lantern all his life after." But though this touches us, it is only the unrealizing response to a poet's imagination. We cannot grasp that, until modern times, our own countrymen suffered these things and that those still living in primitive conditions suffer them still. Pestilence, perhaps, we can visualize more vividly than Famine, for epidemic disease is not yet conquered. But do we really grasp what the wiping out in a few months of one-quarter of the population of a town, meant to the survivors? Do we really comprehend the general atmosphere of terror and helpless despair? Do we realize all that the total stagnation of trade meant in hopeless poverty? Nor is it true that these scourges had at least the advantage of striking all equally. The rich never died of famine, though they possibly suffered some inconvenience. The rich suffered less from pestilence than the poor, since they could leave plague stricken districts.[11] Inequality is no invention of modern times, in fact it is only modern organization that makes the hope of the abolition of gross inequality something more than a chimera.

Whatever may have been the proximate cause of the subjection of pestilence in Western Europe this subjection was undoubtedly associated with advancing civilization. It was the result of that same practical, yet adventurous, spirit, that gave us the steam engine, the railway and modern agriculture, and of which we have a further manifestation in modern medicine.

CONCLUSION

It is impossible to give even the crudest quantitative valuation to the different factors, the improvements in agriculture, in industry, in town hygiene and in medical science. But this is of little importance because, as suggested at the beginning of this study, all these movements are essentially differing aspects of one movement. They are all part of that modern world which, as an eminent economist remarked, we cannot judge rightly unless we remember its youth. Nor can we judge it rightly unless we also remember how age-long are most of the ills of mankind. We are yet on the threshhold of the door which science and freedom have opened and the study of the last two centuries, viewed in the right perspective, leads, not to a paralysing pessimism, but to an optimism illumined by the brightest hopes for the future of mankind.

APPENDIX

NOTES AND REFERENCES

(In many cases the titles are only given in these notes in an abbreviated form. For full titles readers are referred to the Bibliography.)

CHAPTER I. INTRODUCTION.

[1] Liston. Plague. British Medical Journal, 1924.
[2] This is no longer literally true, but presumably the motor car has not yet affected the life of the mass of the people.
[3] Rice, Colliver. Persian Women and their Ways. 1923.
[4] Hosie. Two Gentlemen of China. 1924.
[5] Knowles. Economic Development of the Empire. 1924.

CHAPTER II. VITAL STATISTICS.

[1] Enc. Brit. "Statistics."
[2] Hankins. Adolphe Quételet as Statistician. 1908.
[3] Finlaison. Report to Treasury on Life Annuities. 1829.
[4] Enc. Brit. " Insurance."
[5] This is the survival of a very ancient belief. See Frazer. Folklore in the Old Testament.
[6] Civil registration was introduced in the year 1836, and nominally it was made compulsory in the following year, but in fact it was not so until 1874, in which year penalties were introduced for non-compliance with the regulations.
[7] Short. Bills of Mortality. 1750.
[8] Ibid.
[9] Birch. Bills of Mortality. 1759.
[10] Edmonds. Law of Mortality in England. 1835. Lancet, Vol. I.
[11] Malthus. 1825 ed., p. 217.
[12] Birch, supra.
[13] The original tables were published at Carlisle in tract form in 1797, and had previously been inserted in Hutchinson's History of Cumberland (in 1794). They do not seem, however, to have attracted any attention until Milne's publication. Milne calculated Life Tables from and annotated the originals.

CHAPTER III. POPULATION STATISTICS, BIRTH AND DEATH RATES.

(a) POPULATION IN THE 17TH CENTURY.

The facts as to the growth of population in the 17th century are extremely obscure, but the balance of such evidence as exists seems in favour of a slow increase. It is true that some 17th century writers feared overpopulation and advocated colonization as a remedy. But in times of bad harvest and economic dislocation and consequent food shortage, unemployment and heavy poor relief, contemporaries are very apt to jump to the conclusion that the evils are due to over-population. Moreover, many of the writers were anxious for increasing colonization and therefore met the possible objection that colonization would deplete the mother country, by alleging that the latter was over-populated. Probably the rapid growth of London and its environs led many persons to suppose that the whole population was growing rapidly. Lastly, in a society which was relatively stable and inelastic, even a moderate rate of growth might be a source of embarrassment. A rate of growth which appears to us very slow might well have appeared excessive in the 17th century.

(b) THE EFFECT OF THE CIVIL WAR.

At one period it was believed and taught that the Civil War affected the prosperity of this country to a very slight degree. Modern research does not support this view. The armies withdrew a considerable proportion of the workers from production and the requisitions and heavy taxation laid a great burden upon the people. From the point of view of population, the army casualties were by no means insignificant. Apart from losses in battle, the armies suffered severely from epidemics and, in at least one case, spread these among the civil population. Large numbers of persons were also voluntarily or compulsorily expatriated owing to the Civil War. No doubt there were war profiteers of various kinds, including those who had sequestrated estates conferred upon them, or who bought such at a low price. These persons have left their monuments in the form of handsome mansions, which give an impression to posterity of general wealth in the Restoration period. But a study of the national finances tells a very different tale.

(c) MARRIAGE, BIRTH, AND DEATH RATES.

Marriage Rates are often stated per 1,000 of the total population. This is a very unreliable index for comparing different times and places owing to differences of age composition. This rate, however, is the only one available for early periods ; it is known as the *crude* marriage rate.

The number of marriages can be stated in terms of the marriageable persons, e.g. the numbers over 15 who are unmarried, widowed, or divorced.

Birth Rates may be stated as a rate per 1,000 of the total population living at all ages in the middle of the year. This is the *crude* birth rate. For many purposes it is a useful rate to ascertain, but it is obviously useless as a measure of fertility.

The corrected birth rate may be calculated from the proportion which the number of recorded births bears to the number of women living between the ages of 15–45. This eliminates the error due to the differing age and sex composition of two populations, but is no truer criterion of fertility than the crude rate.

A more accurate method is to subdivide the births into legitimate and illegitimate, stating the former per 1,000 of married women aged 15–45, and the latter per 1,000 of unmarried women aged 15–45.

For purposes of comparison of fertility at different times and places statisticians have devised an indirect method of standardizing birth rates, i.e. of making the necessary allowances for differences in the proportion of wives of 15–45 years to the total population. (For the method employed see Newsholme, Elements of Vital Statistics (1923), p. 86.)

General Death Rates. A general death rate is the number of deaths occurring among a given number, say 1,000, of the population in a given period, which period, unless otherwise stated, is taken to be a year.

The ratio between deaths and population is known as the death rate or rate of mortality. Actuaries, however, use the latter term to express the probability of dying in one year and use the term *central* death rate as synonymous with the term death rate as generally used.

This death rate, which simply expresses the proportion of deaths to each 1,000 of the population, is known as the *crude* death rate, to distinguish it from measures which are more exact for comparative purposes. The death rate for a particular area may be "standardized", i.e. its actual death rate corrected for age and sex composition by relating it to the age and sex composition of a "standardized" population. This standardization may be achieved either by a direct or by an indirect method. The former is slightly the more accurate but very laborious, and for its use detailed returns are necessary. The standardized death rate arrived at by the direct method was formerly known as the "corrected" death rate. This term is now applied to a standardized rate which has been further corrected for the deaths of non-residents. (The methods of standardization are described in detail in Newsholme, op. cit., chap. xix.)

For obvious reasons the crude death rate differs much less from the standardized death rate than does the crude birth rate from the standardized birth rate. The human being is a long time coming to maturity and often lives many years after the power of reproduction has been lost. If a population is growing by immigration the majority of the immigrants are likely to be young adults. This will raise the crude birth rate because it will raise the proportion of women of child-bearing age in the population; the emigration of young adults will have the opposite effect.

It was possibly a failure to appreciate the limitations of the crude birth rate that led to the legend of a great rise in the birth rate in the early 19th century. The high crude birth rate of the new towns was noted, it was assumed that the conditions of town life lead to greater natality and therefore, since the urban population was growing actually and proportionately, the birth rate was assumed to be rising. As a matter of fact the high birth rate in the towns was largely, if not entirely, accounted for by their age composition. (See p. 26.)

The crude death rate is also affected by the sex and age composition of the population, though to a less degree than the crude birth rate. The female sex has a superior expectation of life to the male and, in regard to age composition, the human being not only has a long immaturity, but comes into the world very helpless, and also extremely susceptible to many illnesses. The first year of life has always been and remains the most dangerous before the 7th decade. For the age group between 5 and 10 the death rate falls below the average for all ages and does not rise above it until the age group 45–50; it rises rapidly after 60, until the rate for extreme old age (to which few attain) surpasses even that of infancy. A relatively large proportion of infants and very young children will therefore in itself raise the crude death rate; the same will be true of a large proportion of old persons, while a large proportion of persons between 5 and 45 will in itself lower the total crude death rate.

It is extremely unlikely that any change in mortality due to more hygienic conditions or to an advance in medical knowledge will affect persons of all ages proportionately since the incidence of most diseases is different at different ages. The ultimate effects of a reduced death rate will depend, therefore, upon the decade of life in which the change is mainly or entirely operative. A reduced infant mortality will lead to a further reduction, after a short interval, of the crude death rate and also of the crude marriage and birth rates and, after a longer interval, to increase of these rates for the reasons already stated. A reduced mortality which mainly affects young persons just entering the healthy period will almost at once have a more than proportionately good effect on the crude death rate and will also tend to raise the crude marriage and birth rates. A reduced mortality which mainly affects the middle aged and elderly will naturally reduce the crude birth rate. The reliance which can be placed upon the crude rates as indicators of social conditions is dependent upon the size of the population and upon the amount of emigration and immigration to which it is subject. For large populations which are also little affected by migration, the crude rates, especially the death rate, are reliable indicators, though even here it is not safe to base arguments upon small variations.

[1] George. Economic Journal, Sept., 1922.
[2] See supra.
[3] An allowance was made for illegitimate births.
[4] Quételet said that, "la fécondité des mariages ne varie pas sensiblement dans un même pays et dans le cours d'un siècle."
[5] Newsholme. 1st edition, 1889.
[6] Newsholme. 2nd edition, 1923, p. 102.
[7] Italics added.
[8] McCulloch. British Empire, 1st ed. 1837.
[9] Quoted by McCulloch in note on Population in the 1863 edition of the Wealth of Nations which he edited.
[10] Finlaison. Report to Treasury on Life Annuities.
[11] McCulloch. British Empire.
[12] Mansford. Parish Registers. London Medical Repository. 1818.
[13] It is interesting to note that the estimated birth and death rates for India for 1896–1905 were 38·58 and 34·2 respectively.
[14] Edmonds. Lancet. Vol. 1.
[15] McCulloch. British Empire.
[16] See Table II.
[17] Finlaison, ibid.
[18] Lord Lonsdale said in the House of Lords in 1743 that "the excessive use of gin has hitherto been pretty much confined to London and Westminster". (Quoted by Mrs. George, Economic Journal.)
[19] The difference between the registered Christenings and Burials as shown by the Bills of Mortality for these years is 4,062; allowing for the known greater deficiency in the registration of births as compared with that of deaths, the estimate in the text seems not unreasonable.
[20] George. London Life in the XVIIIth Century. 1925.
[21] White. Observations on the Mortality at York. Trans. R. Soc., 1782.
[22] Howlett. Examination of Dr. Price's Essay. 1781.
[23] Heberden the Younger. College of Physicians. Medical Transactions, Vol. IV, 1813.

CHAPTER IV. INDIVIDUALISM AND LAISSER-FAIRE.

[1] Travels in France. Sept. 27th, 1788.
[2] Memoir of John Grey of Dilston. Quoted by Lord Ernle in English Farming Past and Present.
[3] Langford. A Century of Birmingham Life. 1868.

[4] Unwin. Samuel Oldknow and the Arkwrights. 1924. See note infra.
[5] Tammany has proved that a corrupt organization can be efficient along certain lines.
[6] Bell. Plague of London. 1924.

New Towns.

The conditions in the new towns resembled curiously those found in new countries at the present time. We find the same relentless pushfulness, a determination upon the part of the strong to " make good " at all costs and a lack of social ties which tended to an extreme individualism. If it be countered that many of the immigrants had only travelled a few miles and, in any case, only within the circuit of two small islands, we must remember how modern developments have revolutionized our ideas of distance. It was not merely that it took several days to journey from one part of England to another, but that life was extremely local in character. A man tramping a few miles from his home might easily have found his speech scarcely understood, might have gazed amazedly at an unfamiliar type of farming, and found the whole condition of life different owing to a different tradition of administration in parish affairs. Numerous small unfamiliarities, such as those of weights and measures, of superstition and social customs, would have cut him adrift from that body of inherited tradition and order which in a long settled community controls life from the cradle to the grave. In purely rural districts much of this localism survives even in the 20th century; for instance, inhabitants of West Sussex still consider those of East Sussex to be " foreigners ". Apart from changes of district, to the country dweller the new town life must have been bewildering in the extreme and again his position was not at all unlike that of the modern Eastern European settler in the U.S.A. Ignorant, illiterate, accustomed to obey in his old home, he normally accepted the conditions which he found in home and factory as part of a natural order. If unemployment or dear food drove him to despair, his sullen resentment only found expression in ill-organized strikes or futile rioting. In periods of normal employment and food prices the immigrant agricultural labourer was probably not dissatisfied ; in this again he resembled his modern prototype in the New World. Our views of life are comparative, the immigrants compare their new lot with their old one, not with some unimagined good. The erstwhile agricultural labourer coming into the town found his home in a shoddy, ill-built house without sanitary conveniences and with no water laid on. But he was not used to a well-built house, and the town accommodation, being new, was probably on the whole more comfortable and convenient than the tumble down cottage he had left. As to sanitary conveniences, he had never heard of them, and for the water, very likely his wife was thankful only to have to fetch it from a stack-pipe in the yard instead of having to pump it or to carry it a quarter or half a mile. His work in the factory or workshop was long and laborious but he had always envisaged life as consisting of long and laborious toil. It was, unlike his old work, comparatively well paid, moreover his wife and children could find paid work, too, which they had probably been unable to do in the village. The family therefore could afford better food, more meat in particular, and better clothes. The rural immigrant is not transformed at once into a good citizen, he brings with him rural ideas of hygiene which are disastrous in a town, he is readily a prey to tyranny or the tool of political corruption. It is possible to argue that a true urban democracy is impossible without a town bred population.

CHAPTER V. THE GROWTH OF COMMERCE.

[1] The sextant was not invented until 1761.
[2] In 1735.
[3] Cunningham. Industry and Commerce. 4th ed., 1905.
[4] In 1811 London still contained about ⅔ of the urban population and the northern towns had grown rapidly in the second half of the 18th century.
[5] Kalm. Visit to England. 1748. Reprinted 1892. Also others.
[6] Grant. Highland Farm. 1924.
[7] Unwin, op. cit.
[8] See note to Chapter VI.
[9] Ashton. Iron and Steel in the Industrial Revolution. 1924.
[10] Apart from coarse cotton spinning.
[11] Ashton, op. cit.
[12] Machinery only became relatively cheap with the development of the machine tool industry in the '20's.
[13] Knowles. Industrial and Commercial Revolutions. 1st ed., 1921.
[14] Ashton, op. cit.
[15] See Table X.
[16] See p. 196.
[17] Enc. Brit. " Sugar ".
[18] Pringle. Diseases of the Army. Appendix. 1752.
[19] At any rate in London and the South.

(a) INDUSTRIAL ORGANIZATION.

The idea that any considerable proportion of the population of this country ever consisted of independent craftsmen is probably fallacious. In the Middle Ages the bulk of the population were peasants in a servile condition, bound by status, not free to change their mode of life or to move from their birth place. The total town population was very small and of that population only a portion were craftsmen. Serving men, porters and petty hucksters formed a large proportion of the population, not to mention the "submerged tenth", among whom begging was the most reputable means of livelihood. Within the guilds, it is true, democracy was found, most workers normally rising to be masters ; but entrance to the guilds was generally by patrimony. By the end of the Middle Ages even guild democracy was breaking down, some guilds had developed a definitely employing class within their ranks, with subordinate organizations for the journeymen who could never hope to rise. Other guilds were exclusively composed of employers who gave out work to members of subordinate crafts. From Tudor times onwards, industry, especially the woollen industry, developed outside the corporate towns. To some extent this movement may have been fostered by craftsmen who fled from the guild restrictions, but it was largely a development of the rural peasant industry by a merchant employing class. In the districts conveniently situated for export or the London market, the clothiers gave out work on a large scale to out workers. This organization, which was definitely capitalistic, was thoroughly established in the western woollen industry by the latter part of the 17th century. The workers often had a small holding, and this may have added to their economic stability, though bad harvests and bad trade often went together. On the other hand, the double occupation did not tend to efficiency in either. In Yorkshire even as late as the middle of the 18th century, the peasant sheep farmers worked up their own raw material and sold it to agents in the local markets, but this was exceptional.

It is true that a considerable amount of industry was carried on by independent craftsmen in small towns and villages and also in London in the poorer trades. But after all, anyone who alleges that the small independent craftsman is extinct has never walked down a modern village street or down the back streets of a large town. The modern " small man " is no doubt mainly occupied with repair work, in which branch modern developments have constantly opened up new fields of small scale enterprise as others have been closed.

(b) Apprenticeship.

The assumption that apprenticeship was a democratic system is false. To be apprenticed to a good trade meant high premiums and introductions. The apprentice was generally of the same social status as his master, probably the son of a friend or relative. If the apprentice married the daughter of the house, romance probably played but a small part in this episode ; it would often be an arranged affair, especially if the master had no son to carry on the business. There is no reason to suppose that marriages between ambitious young men and the daughters of well to do trade associates ceased with apprenticeship. The marriage of Robert Owen may be cited in support of the contrary view. On the other hand, apprenticeship to poor trades or apprenticeship for labour was often little better than a form of slavery. By it the children of the poor were bound to years of drudgery, often subjected to ill-treatment and prevented from any effort to better themselves until the age of 24. Whatever apprenticeship may have been in the Middle Ages, by the 17th and 18th centuries it had degenerated into a method of preserving close corporations at the one end of the social scale and a method of social oppression at the other. If the new organization destroyed universal apprenticeship it destroyed a system which had largely outlived its usefulness. Apprenticeship survived during the greater part of the 19th century, however, as the normal and useful way of learning certain skilled handicrafts.

(c) The Factory and Health.

It is doubtful if the change to factory organization was as harmful from the point of view of health as has been supposed. Indeed it may even have been beneficial. Insanitary and overcrowded though the early factories were, yet they were probably not more so than the homes of the workers. Country workers may have possessed a rough shed at the side of the house which was used as a workshop, but the town handicraftsman and his family generally lived, worked and slept in one room. This may not have been true of the highly skilled aristocracy of labour, such as the fine muslin weavers, but it was true of the low skilled worker whose labour was earliest displaced by machinery. That the work should be carried on away from the home was an obvious advantage from the point of view of health, especially as many of the processes were unhealthy in themselves. Some woollen processes caused unhealthy dust, while cotton needed moisture, and for this reason many of the cotton weavers lived in cellars.[1] The unhealthy appearance and narrow chests of the hand loom weavers was notorious. A French doctor writing about 1815 said that the posture adopted in hand loom weaving led to a flattened thorax and that the abdomen was frequently also compressed, with results highly deleterious to health. He added that woollen weaving was peculiarly unhealthy owing to the heavy looms and to the fine particles of dust and that hand loom weavers were very likely to contract tuberculosis.[2] Francis Place described the hand loom silk weavers of Bethnal Green as " a physically degraded people ".[3]

[1] Knowles. Industrial and Commercial Revolutions.
[2] Dr. Jonas of Montjoye, quoted in review in London Medical Repository, 1815.
[3] George. London Life, p. 194.

The first factories were probably dirty and insanitary to a degree which to us would be appalling. In that they resembled the homes of the people, the hospitals, and the workhouses. The more enlightened employers, however, very soon began to try to enforce elementary cleanliness since it was obviously a good business proposition to do so. In Chapter XV the efforts of many Manchester manufacturers are recorded in some detail. The firm of Boulton and Watt, in the face of great difficulty, obtained decency and order in their factory. A notice in the factory stated, "it is for the health, interest and credit of the men, as well as the masters to keep this manufactory clean and decent ".[1] When we consider the kind of people from among whom the early factory workers were drawn, rough peasants with primitive notions of hygiene, or low class town labourers living under conditions which are not found to-day in the worst slum, we can be sure that the enforcement of decent conditions was no easy task. Many masters, no doubt, took the line of least resistance, others were too ignorant to provide, or to wish for, decent conditions. But the best factories were schools, though hard and unsympathetic as most schools of the period, in which the mass of the people learned elementary notions of cleanliness and decency, of punctuality, regularity, and relative sobriety. Every inquiry has revealed the condition of the home worker to be worse than that of the factory worker, but that condition is generally unknown and, even if known, regulation has always proved difficult and often abortive. The publicity of the factory made possible the arousing of the public conscience and the conditions of the factory made regulation possible. Of course the worker lost some independence when he left the home for the factory. Instead of working more or less at his own pace he was subject to " the tyranny of the bell " and to much other petty regulation and tyranny. The divorce of industry from the home also led to a certain break up of family life, though family life cannot have been worth much in one room in a crowded tenement house. But from the point of view of health the coming of the factory was, at any rate for the town worker, probably a change for the better.

CHAPTER VI. AGRICULTURE.

[1] Curtler. Enclosure. 1920, p. 110.
[2] Ibid., p. 138.
[3] Fitzherbert, who has been stated to have been the first writer on agriculture of any distinction after Walter of Henley (in the 13th century) had published his treatise in 1523, but he stood alone.
[4] Curtler. History of English Agriculture. 1909.
[5] " In England the wholesome custom is much in use, that nearly every district lays itself out for something particular in Rural Economy, to cultivate that which will thrive and develop there best, and leaves the rest to other places. . . . Thus their principal occupation in Hertford is *Agriculture. Hop-growing* and *Cherry-tree* cultivation in Kent, sheep farming in another place, cattle breeding in another, etc."

"They thus sell their own ware, and buy what they themselves have not, or they also exchange ware for ware." (Kalm, Visit to England, 1748, p. 205.)
[6] Curtler, op. cit., p. 148.
[7] Howlett. The Influence of Enclosure on Population. 1786.
[8] Ernle, op. cit.
[9] Weber. Growth of Cities. 1898.
[10] McCulloch. British Empire.
[11] Weber, op. cit.

[1] Lord. Capital and Steam Power. 1923.

Enclosure.

Only an extremely detailed study of the records in numerous parishes can enable anyone to have an opinion worth expressing upon this subject, for this much at least is certain, the course of events was very different in different places. In some, strict legal justice was meted out to the commoners, no less and no more and, since many cottagers proved to have no legal claim, legal justice meant receiving nothing. In other places advantage was undoubtedly taken of the ignorance of many of the participants to cheat them of their legal dues, but there are equally undoubted cases of extreme generosity to the poorer commoners. They were sometimes excused all share of the expenses of the enclosure and even those who had no legal claim were given some compensation. Of the numerical proportion between these different types of procedure the present writer does not pretend to be able to judge; but undoubtedly the procedure tended to be more regular and more considerate of the rights of the poor towards the end of the movement than it was at the beginning. The mere fact that the public opinion of the time intervened in favour of the poor commoner points to the previous existence of considerable harshness and injustice. Even if the point of view be accepted that the smaller commoners led shiftless, poverty-stricken lives it by no means follows that they appreciated the change. The old life had been free and had had many intervals of pleasant idleness, and to persons accustomed to it, a life of regular toil under supervision, even if better paid, would have had few attractions. A period of economic re-adjustment is nearly always one of hardship for individuals and however justly and carefully enclosure had been carried out the break up of ancient traditions and immemorial ways of life would have been bound to lead to suffering. Moreover the change took place rapidly mainly owing to the unhealthy stimulus of war, and to the suffering entailed by the changed economic system was added the more terrible ones of the aftermath of war. Until recent years the after effects of the war were underestimated and evils due to it were ascribed to other causes; the present generation with its own bitter knowledge is less apt to make this mistake.

It will be generally agreed that the conversion of the common fields and wastes into severalty was a necessity and in itself a desirable change, but many regret not only the methods by which the change was carried out, but also the final results of the movement. In other words, they regret that the final result was not relatively small peasant farms but large farms upon a capitalistic basis. Undoubtedly the enclosure movement hastened the extinction of the small farmer, the heavy legal expenses of enclosure and the cost of hedging were a heavy drain upon the small freeholder, while improving landlords who enclosed wanted to see their money back and had a natural bias in favour of the large farm. Enclosure, however, was not the only thing tending towards large farms, the new type of farming was easier for the big man to adopt, for it needed capital, knowledge and enterprise. Small freeholders who possessed the two latter qualities often sold their land and so obtained the first requisite, capital, and became large tenant farmers. The war and after war difficulties, in particular fluctuating prices, largely due to currency difficulties, and the burden of the Poor Law, were difficult for the small man to contend against. In fact economic forces were strongly arrayed against the small man and the enclosure movement, in itself due to those same forces, simply hastened his downfall rather than caused it. There is evidence, for instance, that his cattle were in many cases being starved on the commons before enclosure by the excessive number of beasts placed there by the large farmers. There was also the difficulty of winter feed which in the old days, when everybody slaughtered a large proportion of their beasts in the autumn, had not arisen. If the small man did not adopt the new methods he could not compete with those who did, while if he attempted to adopt them he was often forced to buy winter feed from the large farmers at excessive prices. It must also be remembered that changes in the organization of industry were destroying the by-employments both of the small farmer and the cottager and a good deal of the distress was due to this cause. It is doubtful if small holdings can ever be economic without by-employments. The experience of other countries, with soils and climates a great deal better suited to small scale farming than those of this country, suggests that without by-employments a peasant proprietary can only survive with a considerable amount of State aid, including State fostered co-operation. It is hardly reasonable to blame a government of landowners in a laisser faire and individualistic age for not artificially preserving the small farmer ; it is hardly to the point to say that had they done so untold suffering might have been saved and the history of the English countryside might have been happier. It is not given to many to see clearly the results of their actions to the third or fourth generation, their vision quite unclouded by their own interests, and it is doubtful if it has even been given to large groups as opposed to individuals. It was certainly not given to the 18th century squire, who might perhaps be forgiven for thinking that, in the circumstances of the time, the supreme and predominant object of all good citizens was to increase the national food supply. In any great social upheaval it is well-nigh impossible to draw up a balance sheet, the data are so overwhelming in number and so incommensurable in their nature. The enclosure movement was part of a greater whole ; given the other economic changes it was bound to follow, though it is arguable that the results might have been mitigated to a greater extent than they were.

A good deal of misapprehension has been caused by the use of the terms large and small farm. The terms are of course only very roughly comparative and any numerical division line is necessarily artificial. The type of farm which tended to disappear during the enclosure movement was what would now be called a small holding, something under 50 acres. But to imagine that these were replaced by great grazing ranches or huge wheat farms is erroneous. Such farms did exist but their number is easily exaggerated, they only predominated either in typical grazing areas or in the reclaimed wastes, for instance in Norfolk and the reclaimed fens of Lincoln. Only men with large capital and intelligence could farm in these difficult districts, only they could afford to pay rents which would compensate the landlord for his heavy outlay. But these farms had not been made by displacing population, they had been made out of the wilderness. The typical farm about the year 1830 seems to have been a mixed farm of anything from 80 to 500 acres with a rough average of about 150 acres. Even at this date a considerable number of " small holdings " survived, especially in some districts.[1]

CHAPTER VII. IMPROVEMENT OF TOWNS.

[1] St. Dunstan's Wardmote. Inquest Register, 1609. (Quoted by W. G. Bell in " The Great Fire of London ". 1920.)

[2] Bateman. Diseases of London. 1819.

[3] These particulars of the events in London immediately before and after the Fire are taken from Mr. W. G. Bell's invaluable work (see Note 1), to which readers are referred for further details.

[1] McCulloch. British Empire. Part III, chap. 1.

[4] Heberden (the Younger). Increase and Decrease of Diseases. 1801, p. 77.
[5] Bateman, op. cit., p. 19.
[6] Black. Observations, Medical and Political. 1781, p. 136.
[7] Hutton. A Journey to London. 1785.
[8] Chalmers. Population. 1802.
[9] The Manchester Guide. 1804.
[10] Clayton. Friendly Advice to the Poor. 1755.
[11] Henry. Manchester Literary and Philos. Society. 1786.
[12] The Manchester Guide. 1804.
[13] Liverpool. A General and Descriptive History. 1795. The writer of this book differs entirely from the usual tribe of local historians and guide book writers, from his pages dulness and sycophancy alike are absent.
[14] Liverpool. Report of the Proceedings of Court of Enquiry. 1834.
[15] Touzeau. The Rise and Progress of Liverpool. 1910.
[16] History of Liverpool. 1810.
[17] Touzeau, op. cit.
[18] Court of Enquiry (see note 14), Dr. Duncan's evidence, p. 400.
[19] History of Liverpool 1795, op. cit.
[20] Langford. A Century of Birmingham Life. 1868.
[21] New History of Bristol. 1794.
[22] Blane, quoted by Bisset Hawkins. Elements of Medical Statistics. 1829.
[23] Though it is true that the cheapest brick houses were often appallingly jerry built. See Mrs. George, London Life, p. 74. Liverpool appointed a Building Surveyor (1822) mainly owing to the scandal caused by a row of houses having been blown down in a gale. Touzeau, op. cit., p. 814. However, many of the old wooden houses had been equally insecure.
[24] Bateman. Diseases of London. 1819.
[25] Note in original text.

"This source of damp was general previously to the fire, as we are told by Evelyn, who, in continuation of the lamentation before quoted, says: 'That the building should be composed of such a congestion of misshapen and extravagant houses, that the streets should be so narrow and incommodious, in the very centre and busiest places of intercourse ; that there should be so ill and uneasie a form of paving under foot, so troublesome and malicious a disposure of the spouts and gutters, are particulars worthy of reproof and reformation ; because it is hereby rendered a labyrinth in its principal passages, and a *continual wet day after the storm is over.*'"

[26] Bateman, op. cit.,
[27] A Frenchwoman once said to the writer, "You English think of *nothing* but sanitation". Most English visitors to France would agree that our neighbours think too little of it, but would also agree that French towns surpass English ones in civic beauty ; the two facts are, perhaps, not unconnected.

CHAPTER VIII. WATER SUPPLY AND DRAINAGE.

[1] The Puritan Corporation closed all the City conduits on Sunday and it was a punishable offence to draw water on that day. (Latimer, Annals of Bristol.)
[2] The Chelsea Water Works Company, which was one of the more efficient of the London Companies, paid no dividend for 40 years and its dividend never exceeded 4%. (T. Faulkner, An Historical and Topographical Description of Chelsea, 1829.)

³ The Chelsea Company erected an atmospheric engine in 1743 and another in 1747. A Boulton and Watt engine was installed in 1778. (Ibid.)
⁴ Feltham. Picture of London. 1802.
⁵ Ibid. 1821.
⁶ Garnett. Water Supply. 1922 (from which many of the above historical details are taken).
⁷ Feltham and others.
⁸ See Chapter XVI.
⁹ Beckmann. Inventions. English Translation. 1797.
¹⁰ Smollett. Humphrey Clinker.
¹¹ I.e. in 1863. See biography of Bramah by Samuel Smiles, also article in D.N.B.
¹² Report of Meeting of City and Liberty of Westminster Sanitary Association, 1847.
¹³ New History of Bristol. 1794.
¹⁴ Feltham, op. cit.
¹⁵ The Westbourne river.
¹⁶ Quoted by Farr.

CHAPTER IX. THE 18TH CENTURY DOCTOR AND THE BRITISH PIONEERS OF PUBLIC HEALTH.

¹ Singer, C. and D. Paper at Congrès Inter. des Sc. Méd. 1913.
² Glaister. Dr. William Smellie. 1894. The fraud was exposed by Manningham.
³ Garrison. History of Medicine. 1921.
⁴ It is the opinion of a modern medical writer that the life of Louis XIV, who was a gross eater, was prolonged by the drastic bleeding and purging to which he was subjected by his medical advisers. (Doctor Deguéret, Æsculape, Sept., 1924.)
⁵ Garrison, op. cit.
⁶ D.N.B. and Works.
⁷ Creighton incorrectly ascribes this discovery to John Hunter twenty years later.
⁸ D.N.B. and Works.
⁹ See Chapter XV.
¹⁰ D.N.B. and Works. His collected works were edited by his son.
¹¹ The Life of Robert Owen by Himself.
¹² Blane. Remarks on Comparative Health of Population. 1822.
¹³ See Table.
¹⁴ D.N.B. and Works.
¹⁵ W. Currie. Memoirs of Dr. Currie. 1831. Also D.N.B. Works and other sources.
¹⁶ Blane said that " the surgeon is more regarded by us than by other nations ". He was speaking particularly of the Navy.

CHAPTER X. THE HOSPITAL AND DISPENSARY MOVEMENT.

¹ The following, communicated to me by my colleague, Mr. S. A. Peyton of the University of Reading, illustrate both the care of the parish for the sick and the advance in medical knowledge :—
Extracts from the Parochial Records of Shinfield (Berks) Overseers' Accounts.
1772. " Pd Mary Lane for Nursing and Lodging the Small Pox and Great Pox and Itch £5 18s. 6d.

1775. "Beer for children with Small Pox.
1802. "James Pither for Inoculating Cripts children 7s."
Vestry Book.

"At a Vestry held . . . in the Church on Tuesday the 2nd (Dec. 1806) . . . for the purpose of taking into consideration the inoculating the poor of the said parish—Resolved—that Mr. Golding, Surgeon, of Reading be consulted by the Churchwardens and Overseers on the subject of inoculating the poor families and that if he is of opinion that inoculation with the cow pox is sufficient preventive against the small pox that he inoculates them forthwith—should he not be of that opinion—then that he inoculates them with small pox."

[2] Account of the Establishment of the County Hospital at Winchester. 1736.
[3] Ferriar. Preface to Medical Histories and Reflections, 2nd ed. 1810.
[4] Willan. Diseases of London. 1801.
[5] See page 198.
[6] Feltham, op. cit. 1802.
[7] Lettsom. Memoirs. 1774.

LIST OF HOSPITALS AND DISPENSARIES FOUNDED BETWEEN 1700 AND 1818

General Hospitals

London.

Westminster	1720
Guy's	1724
St. George's	1733
London	1740
Middlesex	1745

Provinces.

Cambridge	1719
Bristol	1735
Hants	1736
York County	1740
Exeter	1741
Northampton	1743
Salop	1745
Liverpool	1745
Worcester	1746
Newcastle-upon-Tyne	1751
Manchester	1752
Chester	1755
Gloucestershire	1755
Birmingham	1766
Salisbury	1766
Staffs	1766
Leeds	1767
Lincoln	1769
Oxford County	1770
Norfolk and Norwich	1771
Leicester	1771
Hereford	1776
Lancaster	1781
Hull	1782
Nottingham	1782
Stroud	1790
Durham	1792
Kent	1793
Sunderland	1794
Sheffield	1797
Truro	1799
Bedford	1803
Denbigh	1807
Taunton	1809
Derbyshire Royal Infirmary	1810
Pontefract	1812
Bridgwater (Somerset)	1813
Berwick-on-Trent	1814
Bolton	1814
Peterborough	1814
Alnwick Infirmary	1815
Stoke-on-Trent	1815

London. Special Hospitals.

London Lock Hospital	1746
London Lock Hospital Rescue Home	1787
Cancer Charity of Middlesex Hospital	1792
London Fever Hospital	1802
Royal London Opthalmic Hospital (Moorfields Eye Hospital)	1804
Royal Chest Hospital	1814
Royal Ear Hospital	1816
Royal Waterloo Hospital for Women and Children	1816
Royal Westminster Opthalmic Hospital	1816

APPENDIX

Provincial. Special Hospitals.

Bath Royal Mineral	1737
Manchester Hospital for Women and Children	1790
Margate Sea Bathing	1791
Exeter West England Eye Infirmary	1808
Bristol Eye	1810
Bath Eye	1811
Manchester Eye	1815

London Dispensaries.

Infant Poor, Red Lion Sq.	1769
Royal General (Aldersgate)	1770
Westminster General	1774
London	1777
Surrey	1777
Metropolitan	1779
Finsbury	1780
Eastern	1782
Carey Street	1783
Miller (Greenwich)	1783
St. Marylebone General	1785
National Truss Society	1786
New Finsbury. Smithfield	1786
City Bevis Marks	1789
City	1789
Western	1789
Universal. Ratcliffe Highway	1792
Bloomsbury	1801
Rupture Society	1804
City of London Truss Society	1807
St. Pancras	1810
Middlesex	
Ossulston, Bloomsbury	
Royal Universal. Holborn	
James' Soho	

Provincial Dispensaries

Bristol	1775
Liverpool	1777
Newcastle-upon-Tyne	1777
Carlisle	1782
*Royal Kent	1783
Whitby	1786
*Wakefield	1787
York	1788
Horncastle	1789
*Doncaster	1792
*Stockport	1792
Birmingham General	1793
Plymouth	1798
North Shields	1802
Reading	1802
Wiveliscombe (Somerset)	1804
*Rotherham	1806
*Falmouth	1807
*Halifax	1807
Brighton	1809
*Darlington	1809
*Penzance	1809
*Warrington	1810
Bristol Eye	1812
Clifton	1812
*Newark (Notts)	1813
Hull	1814
*Swansea	1814
Morpeth	1816
*Chelmsford and Essex	1818
*Windsor	1818

* Now a general hospital.

This list is probably very incomplete, especially in regard to dispensaries. (Burdett's Hospitals' Digest; George, London Life, p. 337.)

CHAPTER XI. GENERAL HYGIENE AND MIDWIFERY.

[1] Willughby, Percivall. Observations in Midwifery. Exact date unknown but belongs to middle of 17th century. A reprint was edited by Henry Blenkinsop and published in 1863.

[2] Though apprenticeship was customary in the City of London in the 17th century. "The young midwives at London bee trained seven years first under the old midwives before they bee allowed to practice for hemselves." Ibid.

[3] Glaister, op. cit.

[4] The forceps had been a trade secret for many years in a Huguenot family of surgeons named Chamberlen. The knowledge of it became public property between 1720 and 1730.

[5] Glaister, op. cit.

[6] White, Charles. Treatise on the Management of Lying-In Women, 1777.
[7] Mémoire historique et instructif sur l'Hospice de la Maternité. 1808. The italics in the quotation are added.
[8] See page 132. The Maternité in 1808 had only recently been re-founded after its suppression during the Revolution.
[9] See Annual Report of the Chief Medical Officer of the Ministry of Health. 1922.
[10] Davis, Bunnell. Mortality among Children. 1817.
[11] See pp. 30, 210.
[12] Lettsom. Medical Memoirs. 1774.

Provincial Lying-in Charities.		Oxford	 1807
Chester	 1798	York	 1788
Exeter	 1801	Liverpool	 1796
Hull	 1802	Newcastle-upon-Tyne	. 1760

CHAPTER XII. RICKETS AND SCURVY.

[1] H,J.M.D. Scelera Aquarum. 1701.
[2] Bateman. Diseases of London. 1819.
[3] Black. Observations, medical, etc. 1781.
[4] Place said, "I remember the time when an immense number of children were bandy legged or bowed in the front . . . observing children of the poorest people . . . I find deformities very rare where they were very common. (Evidence to Select Comm. on Education, 1835 (3) VII, p. 840.
[5] For instance a 17th century accoucheur remarks of one difficult case, "this woman, in her infancy, was afflicted with rickets, which made her go waddling and cringing in her back." The same writer gives a graphic description of acute rickets in a well to do patient. He states that in 1669 he was engaged by a "worthy good loving Gentleman for his wife. She had been afflicted in her infancy with the rickets. Shee had very great swel'd ankle bones, she went waddling and her left leg was shorter than the other, and the middle of her back was much inverted, from the hips to the shoulders. She was of a very low and of a little small stature." It is not surprising to learn that the efforts to relieve this patient were unavailing. (Willughby). Op cit.
[6] See Report on the Present State of Knowledge of Accessory Food Factors (1924). Medical Research Council. This report contains a certain amount of historical material.
[7] Quoted by Bateman.
[8] Quoted by Lind on Scurvy in Appendix.
[9] Op. cit.
[10] Cabanes, Docteur. Les Vieilles Pierres de L'Hôpital Saint-Louis. Æsculape. March, 1923.
[11] Smollett. Travels through France and Italy, Letter XI, Montpelier, 1763.
[12] Pringle. Notes on Capt. Cook's Second Voyage.
[13] Tucker. Four Tracts. 1774. Quoted by Mrs. George, Econ. Journal.
[14] See Report, op. cit.
[15] Homer. The Old Englishman's Letters for the Poor of England. 1758. Quoted by Mrs. George, Econ. Journal.
[16] Blane. Observations on . . . different Diseases. Medical and Chirurgical Society's Transactions. 1813.
[17] Howard. Lazarettos. 1791.

APPENDIX

[18] Report, op. cit.
[19] Purchas. Pilgrimes.
[20] The medal was presented by proxy as Cook had already embarked upon his last voyage.
[21] Mahan. The Influence of Sea Power upon the French Revolution and Empire. Vol. I, 1892, p. 71.

CHAPTER XIII. ANTISEPTICS, SEGREGATION, LEPROSY AND PLAGUE.

[1] Simpson. A Treatise on Plague. 1905.
[2] Muratori. Quoted by Patrick Russell, see infra.
[3] The word antiseptic seems to have been first used in England by a John Pringle, who was writing about the same time as his great namesake. But the great Pringle also wrote on antiseptics, he used the term in the broad sense of anything which delayed putrification and, since he held disease and putrification to be closely allied phenomena, he held that antiseptics were great weapons against disease.
[4] See Frazer. The Golden Bough.
[5] By Fracastor.
[6] See Singer, C. and D. op. cit.
[7] A fomite is a carrier of infection. In modern times the term is applied to infected clothing, etc. In the 18th century it sometimes had this meaning but it was also applied to the hypothetical particles.
[8] Another school of thought believes that syphilis was introduced into Europe from America.
[9] Castellani and Chalmers. Manual of Tropical Medicine. 1919.
[10] Ibid.
[11] London was not reported free of Plague until 1670. The last reported case in the Bills of Mortality was in 1679. (Bell.) There is the possibility, however, that these later cases were not true plague.
[12] Simpson, op. cit.
[13] Bell. Plague of London, op. cit.
[14] For instance Farr and others.
[15] The exact date seems doubtful, 1478 and 1484 are mentioned by different authorities.
[16] Beckmann. History of Inventions transl. by Johnstone. 1797.
[17] Percival, Edward. Practical Observations, etc. 1819.
[18] Black. Observations, medical, etc., op. cit.
[19] Postlethwayt. Dictionary of Commerce. 4th ed. 1774. Article "Turkey".
[20] Howard. Lazarettos.
[21] Russell, Alexander. The Natural History of Aleppo. 1756.
[22] Russell, Patrick. A Treatise of the Plague. 1791.
[23] Black, op. cit.
[24] This is believed by some authorities to be an under-estimate.
[25] Latimer. Annals of Bristol.
[26] Graunt. Bills of Mortality. 1662.
[27] Burnet says of the plague, "It broke the trade of the Nation and swept away about an hundred thousand souls." (History of my Own Times.) It is not clear if the above estimated mortality refers to London or to the whole country; probably the latter.
[28] The incidence of the plague was probably higher in the Middle Ages when there was much movement of population owing to pilgrimages, fairs and journeys to and from manors, and when also there was an

CHAPTER XIV. SMALLPOX IN THE 18TH CENTURY.

[1] Report of Commission on Vaccination. 1896. Table 34, p. 642.
[2] Birch, Bills of Mortality. 1759.
[3] Dr. Robert Watt, "An Enquiry into relative mortality in Glasgow, 1813." Watt was a pessimist, he held that though the deaths under two years had been diminished by the reduction of mortality from smallpox this had been counter-balanced by an increase of deaths between 2 and 10, mainly owing to an increase in the amount of and virulence of measles. Watt, like so many early quasi-statistical writers, based his assumptions on the proportionate number of deaths under 10 to the total mortality, forgetting to allow for the decreased mortality. There is no reason to endorse the opinion of Dr. Woolcombe (quoted by Watt) who prophesied that vaccination would not lessen the death rate among children. " Since disease is one of the appointed checks to excessive population and the plan of Providence in the creation of human life requires the termination of the existence of one-third of its creatures before they have attained the age of two years."
[4] Daniel Bernoulli, the mathematician, writing in 1760 estimated that smallpox carried off the $\frac{1}{13}$th to $\frac{1}{14}$th part of each generation.
[5] To Inhabitants of Liverpool upon a General Inoculation. 1781.
[6] Haygarth. An Inquiry how to Prevent Smallpox. Tract. 1785.
[7] Blane. Statements of facts of Vaccination. Med. and Chir. Trans. 1819.
[8] Schultz. Inoculation report presented to Royal Commission of Health. Sweden. 1758.
[9] Plan for General Inoculation Dispensary. 1775.
[10] Gray, B. Kirkman. History of English Philanthropy. 1905.
[11] See his letter to Howard quoted on page 199.
[12] Proceedings of Small-pox Society of Chester. 1785.
[13] Schultz, op. cit.
[14] Garrison, op. cit.
[15] London Medical Repository. Vol. XVIII, 1822, p. 208.
[16] Henry. Manchester Literary and Philos. Society. 1786.
[17] Howlett. Examination of Dr. Price's Essay. 1781. Note on p. 83.
[18] See Commission on Vaccination, op. cit.
[19] Lettsom. Letter upon General Inoculation. 1778.
[20] Milne. Annuities. 1815. Appendix I.
[21] Jenner began to collect his observations in 1778. He performed his first vaccination in 1796 and published his discovery in 1798.
[22] But see p. 190.

CHAPTER XV. THE ANTI-TYPHUS CAMPAIGN AND THE FEVER-HOSPITAL MOVEMENT.

[1] It is true that Fracastor in the 15th century distinguished between typhus and typhoid, but this knowledge was lost. (C. and D. Singer, op. cit.) John Huxham of Devon (1692–1768) was one of the first modern writers to make the distinction.
[2] Castellani and Chalmers, op. cit.

[3] Howard. State of Prisons, 2nd ed. 1780.
[4] Pringle. Diseases of Army.
[5] See Webb. English Prisons under Local Government. 1922.
[6] It was a terrible scourge in Napoleon's armies. In this connection it has been described as " une ombre sur l'éclat des victoires." Æsculape, Sept. 1925.
[7] See p. 147.
[8] Howard. State of Prisons. 2nd. ed., p. 84.
[9] Young. Travels in France. Jan. 18th, 1790.
[10] Place. Principles of Population. 1822, p. 253.
[11] Milne. Annuities. Appendix 1, p. 755.
[12] Darwin, Emma. A Century of Family Letters. The letter in question was written by Emma Allen (born about 1780) to Elizabeth Wedgwood.
[13] Howard. Prisons. 3rd edition, 1784.
[14] If we omit the forgotten work of Fracastor.
[15] Bateman. Contagious Fever. 1818.
[16] Bernard. Society for Bettering the Condition of the Poor. Vol. III, p. 273.
[17] At this date the word "police" retained the wider connotation which still survives on the Continent.
[18] Bernard. Society for Bettering the Condition of the Poor. Vol. I, p. 115.
[19] Strangers' Friend Society.
[20] Ferriar. Medical Histories and Reflections. 2nd ed., 1810-13.
[21] Currie, W. Memoirs of Dr. Currie. Letter 23 ; also p. 340.
[22] Currie, James. Medical Reports. 1798.
[23] History of Liverpool. 1810.
[24] Liverpool Enquiry, op. cit., p. 470.
[25] Currie did not hesitate to use this argument; he estimated in 1797 that typhus cost the Liverpool ratepayers £2,400 per annum.
[26] Society for Bettering the Condition of the Poor. Vol. IV, p. 121.
[27] History of London House of Recovery. 1817.
[27] Bateman. Diseases of London. 1819.
[29] Percival, Edward. Practical Observations, 1819.
[30] McCulloch's British Empire. Vital Statistics.

CHAPTER XVI. MALARIA. GENERAL SUMMARY.

[1] See Table.
[2] Cf. figures of infant mortality at Lying-In Hospital, p. 145.
[3] It is possible that part of the apparent decrease was due to better diagnosis. In both periods any wasting disease would be apt to be called consumption, but the misnomers were probably greater in number in the earlier period.
[4] Castellani and Chalmers, op. cit.
[5] Short. Bills of Mortality. 1750, pp. 208, 68, 19, 69.
[6] Bateman. Diseases of London.
[7] Sydenham. Translation. 1848, Vol. I, p. 41 ; Vol. II, p. 9.
[8] James. The Disappearance of Malaria from England. League of Nations. 1925.
[9] Watson. Medical Topography of Stourport. London Medical Repository. 1814.
[10] By Pelletier and Caventon.
[11] A review article in the Edinburgh Medical and Surgical Journal. 1810, p. 338.

NOTES AND REFERENCES

[12] Howard. Public Health in Baltimore. 1924.
[13] Lind. Diseases in Hot Climates. 6th ed. 1808. Appendix.
[14] Blane. Remarks on Comparative Health of the Population. Appendix.
[15] Bateman, see p. 82.
[16] Black. Observation, Medical, etc. 1781, p. 171.
[17] Farr. McCulloch's British Empire. Vital Statistics.
[18] See Farr. Vital Statistics. 1885, p. 131.
[19] Newsholme, op. cit., 1st ed.

CHAPTER XVII. THE PERIOD 1815–48.

[1] The scope of this study was originally limited to the period 1700–1815, but it seems desirable to say a little, in a broad way, in order to link it with the well-known era of Public Health Reform which began in 1848. The writer, however, does not pretend to have made any detailed study of the period 1815–48, and the ideas put forward are quite tentative. They are for the most part based upon the conclusions of Farr, the leading authority upon vital statistics for this period.
[2] McCulloch. British Empire.
[3] McCulloch. Note on Population in Wealth of Nations, 1863 ed., p. 461.
[4] Newsholme, op. cit., 2nd ed.
[5] These are calculated from the registered deaths and are, therefore, too low. The earlier figure should probably be 20 and the later about 21·5. The average for the period 1838–61 was 22·2 (see op. cit., note 3) but this was after the advent of cholera.
[6] Weber. Growth of Cities, op. cit.
[7] Farr. McCulloch's British Empire.
[8] Castellani and Chalmers, op. cit.
[9] Macnamara. History of Asiatic Cholera. 1876.
[10] Ibid.
[11] See p. 108.
[12] Shaw. Municipal Government in Continental Europe. 1895.
[13] Evidence before Select Committee on Education. Reports and Committees. 1835 (3) VII, p. 838.
[14] See Webb. Local Government.

NOTE ON POPULATION OF IRELAND.

The population of Ireland had grown during the period 1700 to 1841 no less vigorously than that of Great Britain. The earliest estimate of the population of Ireland is that of Sir William Petty in 1672, which estimate was 1,100,000. It is usually considered tolerably reliable. In 1731 an enquiry was instituted by the House of Lords, and resulted in the estimate of 2,010,221, but this is usually considered an under-statement, a private enquirer having made an estimate of 2,309,106 in 1726. Any estimates of population in Ireland were extremely doubtful, as there were, in effect, no registers of births and deaths, the only registers that were kept being those of baptisms and burials solemnized in the Church of England which were, of course, absolutely valueless, from the point of view of estimating the population of Ireland. Such estimates as were made were based upon estimates of the number of houses, from which the number of inhabitants was deduced by taking the proportion of 6 persons to a house. During the course of the 18th century several estimates of this kind were based upon the hearth tax. In 1754 this estimate was 2·4 million, in 1777 it was 2·7 million, in 1791 4·2 million. Much reliance cannot be placed upon estimates based upon taxation returns, especially in a disaffected country like Ireland. In 1805 Newenham in his "Enquiry into the Population of Ireland" made an estimate of 5·4 million. In 1813 an incomplete census was taken from which an estimate of slightly under 6 million was made. A nominally complete census was taken in 1821 with a result of 6·8 million, but this census is usually considered to have been a failure and the result consequently unreliable. In 1831 the census gave a result of 7·8 million, but this census was vitiated by the system of paying the enumerators according to the numbers returned and is therefore usually believed to be an over-statement. The census of 1841 was carried out by the constabulary and is believed to be reliable, it gave a population of just over 8 million. Before the next census the Potato Famine had intervened and in 1851 the population was only 6½ million. The natural increase in Ireland was greater than the growth of population for there was a large emigration before 1848 both to England and Scotland and elsewhere. Besides the permanent emigrants there was a constant stream of migrant labourers whose earnings, doubtless, often made it just possible for their family to eke out a living at home.

The growth of population in England was mainly urban but in Ireland it was predominantly rural. In 1821 the estimated town population of Ireland was only 648,421, out of an estimated total of 6·8 million. Up to the middle of the 18th century Ireland was almost entirely a pastoral country. During the 17th century it had suffered severely from civil war and dissension which had checked the growth of population, but during the 18th century there was not only comparative tranquillity but also a considerable transfer from pasture to tillage . The Corn Bounty Acts, 1783–4 (passed under Grattan's Parliament) gave an enormous impetus to this movement. Free Trade in Corn with Great Britain was established in 1806, a further stimulus was given by this and by the high price of corn during the French wars.

The custom of *gavelkind*, or equal inheritance among children, prevailed in Ireland ; this led to division and sub-division of farms which the landlords failed to check. Indeed they are said to have favoured it as it gave them additional political power and further possibilities of rack renting. It is interesting to note that customs of equal inheritance in France led to a stationary population and in Ireland to a rapidly increasing one. This difference was no doubt largely due to a difference in land tenure, but the racial factor probably counted for something. The sub-division of land in Ireland was enormously encouraged by the increasing use of the potato, which by the beginning of the 19th century had become the staple food of the people. The potato is a very suitable crop for *petite culture* and subsistence can be obtained from a smaller area than by any other crop grown in Northern Europe. Arthur Young estimated that an acre of potatoes would feed double the number of individuals that could be fed by an acre of wheat. The dangers of crop failure were however very great. Writers on the subject had been pointing out for years before 1848 that the potato was unsatisfactory as a staple article of diet. Firstly it was the cheapest food available and it would be difficult for the people to turn to substitutes in the event of a shortage, secondly it did not keep from year to year nor was it easily transportable, therefore a crop failure would be particularly disastrous. They also pointed out that the potato crop if it failed, did so more completely than a corn crop. This was before the potato disease had introduced a new and terrible menace.

The growth of population in Ireland was ascribed by McCulloch (Farr ?) to the change from pasture to arable and secondly to the cultivation of the potato and the sub-division of the soil. But there were other factors. The Irish are a fertile race with the habit of early marriage, and the Irish women are successful not only in bearing children but in rearing them. The main cause for this is undoubtedly that Ireland is and has always been predominantly rural, and the rate of infant mortality is much more

unfavourably affected by town life than the general rate of mortality.
Irish towns at present show a higher infant mortality than English ones,
and probably did so in the early 19th century, but poverty and a low
sanitary standard do not necessarily lead to a high infant mortality in
rural districts though they do in urban ones.[1] Fresh air and sunshine go
a long way to counteract other bad conditions in infants and young
children. Ireland enjoys a mild climate and, whatever may be said of a
diet of milk and potatoes for adults, it is a very good one for young children.
Many Irish villages also were sufficiently isolated to escape epidemic
scourges.

The 18th century public health campaign in Great Britain was not without
its repercussion in Ireland. The three great scourges of Ireland in the
beginning of the 19th century were malaria, typhus and tuberculosis. The
second was worst in the towns though it seems also to have been endemic in
many villages. There was no Poor Law in Ireland until 1839, and it was
doubtless because of this that a certain amount of help for the sick poor was
given from public funds. By an Act of 1765 the establishment of infirmaries
was made possible by a certain amount of assistance from taxation, supple-
mented by private charity. Under this Act infirmaries were established in
every county except Waterford. In 1802 a parliamentary grant was made to
the Dublin fever hospital. In that year it was estimated that in Dublin
out of a population of 240,000 upwards of 60,000 persons received treatment in the fever hospital of the city. In 1817 another terrible visitation
of typhus led to the formation of a General Board of Health. The board
estimated that out of a population of 8 millions over one and a half million
had suffered from fever and that there had been 65,000 deaths. In 1818
an Act was passed giving additional facilities for the establishment of
fever hospitals, and help from the public funds was authorized to the
extent of not more than double the private subscriptions. Government
loans were also authorized for the creation of buildings and under this
Act fever hospitals were erected in various parts of Ireland. In 1805 an
Act was passed allowing contributions out of the public funds to dispensaries equal to the amount of private subscriptions. Under this statute
over 400 dispensaries were established, relieving half a million patients
annually. Some persons even held the view that the sick poor were better
cared for in Ireland than in England, as in England the institutions for
the relief of sickness only existed in large towns while in Ireland they were
spread over the whole face of the country, and guarded by statute.
(McCulloch. British Empire, and Note on Population, Wealth of Nations,
ed. 1863.)

CHAPTER XVIII. CONCLUSION.

[1] Bateman. Diseases of London. 1819.
[2] Widening and paving streets, etc.
[3] Bissett Hawkins. Medical Statistics. 1829.
[4] "Our medical police are behind those of every other European country." (Roberton, 1827.) Percival says much the same.
[5] Lowe thought that the increase of population in Great Britain was due to "the preservation of the lives of children by vaccination; to the better lodging, the greater cleanliness and sobriety of our lower classes." He adds that, "Similar causes prevail, though in a less degree, on the Continent : in France the increase of population, formerly so slow as hardly to yield an addition of 30 per cent. in a century, may now be

[1] Newsholme, op. cit.

computed at somewhat more than twice that proportion." He thought that the increase in Germany was about the same as that of France, but that that of Russia and the South of Europe was much less. (Lowe, Present State of England. Appendix, p. 69.)

[6] With sturdy insularity he even goes so far as to ascribe the small improvement in Vienna to " overweening paternity " and to " the excessive spirit of regulation, the dread of novelty, the restrictions imposed upon the medical profession ".

[7] Lowe, op. cit.
[8] Howlett. Examination of Dr. Price's Essay.
[9] Blane. Diseases of London. 1813. Reprinted in Dissertations, 1822.
[10] Roberton. Mortality of Children. 1827.
[11] Carlisle. Disorders of Old Age, 2nd ed., 1818, p. 92.
[12] See George, London Life, op. cit.
[13] See Bell, Plague of London, op. cit.

STATISTICAL TABLES

" La civilisation, en rendant plus douce l'existence de l'homme, est parvenue aussi à la rendre plus longue, le développement des lumières a contribué à faire assainir les demeures particulières et l'enceinte des villes, à faire disparâitre peu à peu les terrains marécageux et les causes si fréquentes d'épidémies qui désolaient nos aïeux. Les lumières, en multipliant entre les peuples les relations commerciales, ont aussi rendu moins fréquentes et moins redoutables les famines, dont les chances ont diminué d'une autre part en améliorant la culture des terres et en variant les moyens de subsistance ; les connaissances médicales et d'hygiène publique ont également trouvé des moyens précieux pour combattre la mortalité, tandis que le développment de l'industrie et les garanties que recevait la société par les institutions plus libérales contribuaient à répandre l'aisance et les moyens les plus actifs de conservation " (Quételet).

Quételet was well aware of the prejudicial effects of large towns and manufactures upon public health and was inclined to think that the decrease in mortality had been overestimated, especially in regard to England.

TABLE I
Death Rates at Various Places at Different Periods. Per 1,000.

Place.	(*circa*) 1750	1780	1800	1815	1825
England and Wales	35	28	25	20*	21·5*
France	—	34	—	—	25
Sweden	—	28·5	27	—	20
Holland	43	—	—	—	20
London	52	50	—	29	28
Manchester	40	35·5	—	—	—
Liverpool	—	—	—	33	25
Birmingham	—	—	—	33	23
Portsmouth	—	—	35·5	26	—
Paris	40	—	—	—	31
Amsterdam	—	37	—	—	41
Vienna	50	50	—	—	45
Berlin	35·5	33	37	—	29
Rome	—	43	—	—	40

* These figures are slightly higher than those given in Bisset Hawkins and others (see note, chap. xvii (5), p. 263).

Nothing can be argued from small differences in the above figures, partly owing to the looseness of the original compilations and partly for the reasons discussed on page 246.

The figures are mostly from Bisset Hawkins, though a few are from other sources. They are not strictly comparable as some are for an average of years and some for a particular year and not necessarily the exact year in the table. The original figures are in many cases only rough estimates, so that the possibility of a slightly increased inaccuracy seemed legitimate in order to gain the clarity of tabular form.

The following mortality rates are given by Bisset Hawkins for about 1825.

	Per 1,000.
Kingdom of Prussia	29
Pays de Vaud	20
Venetian Provinces	35·5
Geneva	23
Lyons, Strassburg, Barcelona	31
Nice	32
Naples (city)	35·5
Leghorn	28·5

TABLE II

Deaths. Per Cent of Living

Between ages of	6 Towns of England.* 1813–30.	Glasgow. 1821–35.	London.* 1813–30.	Sweden. 1755–75.	England* & Wales. 1813–30.	Carlisle. 1779–87.
0–5	8·63	8·10	8·27	9·01	4·98	8·23
5–10	1·03	1·24	1·08	1·42	·70	1·02
10–20	·73	·76	·60	·71	·63	·59
20–30	1·39	1·17	1·07	·92	1·02	·75
30–40	1·56	1·57	1·52	1·22	1·17	1·06
40–50	1·96	2·31	2·29	1·74	1·49	1·43
All Ages	2·95	2·83	2·84	2·89	2·12	2·50

* Corrected for deficiencies in registers.

McCulloch,
British Empire.

TABLE III
CARLISLE TABLE

Which shows the Number of Deaths by each Disease that took place in each of the under-mentioned Intervals of Age at Carlisle, during eight years, commencing with 1779, ending 1787, and excepting the year 1780.

Between ages of and	0–5	5–10	10–15	15–20	20–30	30–40	40–50	50–60	60–70	70–80	80–90	90 up	Total
Febrile Diseases													
Inflammatory Fevers	3	—	—	—	1	—	—	1	—	—	—	—	5
Nervous Fevers	2	3	1	4	3	9	15	13	7	2	—	—	59
Putrid Fevers	5	4	1	2	8	5	8	4	5	1	—	—	43
Jail Fevers	4	2	1	2	—	2	3	—	—	—	—	—	14
Mortification	—	—	—	—	—	—	—	1	—	1	1	—	3
Sore Throat	3	—	—	—	—	—	—	—	—	—	—	—	3
Stone and Gravel	—	—	—	—	1	—	1	—	6	1	—	—	9
Pleurisy	3	2	1	1	—	1	2	2	5	2	—	—	19
Rheumatism	—	—	—	—	—	—	—	1	3	2	—	—	6
Gout	—	—	—	—	—	—	1	2	—	1	—	—	4
Small Pox	225	8	2	—	3	—	—	—	—	—	—	—	238
Measles	28	2	1	—	—	—	—	—	—	—	—	—	31
Scarlet Fever	31	4	2	1	1	—	—	—	—	—	—	—	39
Thrush	63	2	—	—	—	—	—	—	—	—	—	—	65
Consumption	34	15	10	15	45	34	31	15	15	—	—	—	214
Infantile Remittents	19	8	—	—	—	—	—	—	—	—	—	—	27
Menorrhagia cochialis	—	—	—	—	—	—	3	—	—	—	—	—	3
Teething	3	—	—	—	—	—	—	—	—	—	—	—	3
Five other diseases	—	—	—	1	1	—	1	1	1	—	—	—	5
Nervous Diseases.													
Apoplexy	—	—	—	1	—	2	5	9	11	4	—	—	32
Palsy	—	—	—	—	—	—	1	5	4	3	1	—	14
Fainting	—	1	—	—	—	1	2	1	—	1	—	—	6
Indigestion	—	—	—	—	—	1	6	5	8	1	—	—	21
Convulsions	10	—	—	—	—	—	—	—	—	—	—	—	10
Epilepsy	—	—	—	1	1	1	—	1	—	—	—	—	4
Asthma	1	—	—	—	—	—	2	9	11	4	—	—	27
Chincough	18	1	—	—	—	—	—	—	—	—	—	—	19
Diarrhœa	7	1	1	1	—	1	2	2	1	2	—	—	18
Four other diseases	—	—	—	1	1	2	—	—	—	1	—	—	5
Diseases of Habit													
Weakness of Infancy	204	—	—	—	—	—	—	—	—	—	—	—	204
Decay of Age	—	—	—	—	—	—	—	—	26	90	84	26	226
Dropsy	1	1	2	3	3	5	5	7	12	7	2	1	49
Dropsy of Brain	2	2	1	—	—	—	—	—	—	—	—	—	5
Scrophula	—	2	—	—	—	—	—	1	—	—	—	—	3
Venereal	—	—	—	—	1	—	1	—	—	—	—	—	2
Jaundice	3	—	—	—	1	—	5	2	—	2	—	—	13
Local Diseases.													
Cancer	—	—	—	—	—	—	—	1	2	2	—	—	5
Difficult Delivery	—	—	—	—	4	4	1	—	—	—	—	—	9
Seven other diseases	1	—	—	1	—	1	2	1	3	—	—	—	9
Unknown	32	11	5	—	2	8	9	9	31	7	1	—	115
Accidents	7	5	2	4	3	4	2	1	1	—	—	—	29
Total	709	74	30	38	79	81	108	94	152	134	89	27	1615

TABLE IV
Rate of Mortality from Different Diseases as Shown by Carlisle Table
Per 100,000 Living (under 20 per 100,000 omitted)

Nervous Fever	90	Apoplexy		49
Putrid Fever	66	Palsy		21
Jail Fever	21	Asthma		41
Pleurisy	29	Chincough [1]		29
Small Pox	364	Diarrhœa		28
Measles	47	Weakness of Infancy		312
Scarlet Fever	60	Decay of Age		346
Thrush	99	Dropsy		75
Consumption	327	Jaundice		20
Infantile Remittent Fever	41			

TABLE V
In London
Number of annual deaths per 100,000 living

	1780.	11 years ending 1810.	Decrease by
Apoplexy	55	49	1/9
Asthma	85	89	inc. 1/21
Childbed and Miscarriage	47	32	1/3
Consumption	1120	716	1/3
Dropsy	225	131	2/5
Fevers	621	264	3/5
Measles	48	94	doubled
Small Pox	502	204	3/5

Milne. Life Annuities, vol. ii, chap. xi, xii.

TABLE VI
Deaths from Small Pox
Sweden

1779	15,000
1784	12,000
1800	12,800
1801	6,000
1822	11
1823	37

Bisset Hawkins.

London

In 6 years ending with	No. of deaths.	Annual average.
1797	10,973	1,829
1803	9,999	1,667
1809	7,094	1,182
1813	6,466	1,078

Milne, op. cit.

[1] Whooping cough.

STATISTICAL TABLES 271

TABLE VII
British Navy. Sickness, Mortality, and Desertions per 1,000 Seamen

Year.	Sent Sick to Hospital.	Deaths.	Desertions.
1779	408	26	14
1782	316	22	10
1794	250	12	7
1804	120	16	2
1813	93	7	·1

Quoted in McCulloch, British Empire, p. 566.

TABLE VIII
Mortality in Prisons

France	1 in 23	} Villermé.
France, galley slaves	1 in 49	
Netherlands	1 in 27	Quételet.
King's Bench and Fleet	1 in 50–55	Cooper.
French prisoners of war	1 in 55	

Bisset Hawkins.

TABLE IX
Maternal Mortality: Deaths per 1,000 Deliveries

	Place.	Year.	M.	Year.	M.	Year.	M.
(1)	British Lying-in	1749–58	23·8	1779–88	16·6	1799–07	4·6
(2)	Hôtel Dieu	—	—	1780	66·6	1822	33·3
(3)	Paris Maternité	—	—	—	—	1868	43·5
(2)	Berlin Lying-in	—	—	1796–06	31·2	1807–17	22·2
(2)	Stockholm Lying-in	—	—	—	—	1822	33·3
(2)	Dublin Maternity	—	—	—	—	1757–25	11
(2)	Edinburgh Maternity	—	—	—	—	1817	10
	England	1760	(4) 16·6	1781	(5) 15	—	—
(6)	Westminster Dispensary	—	—	1781	3·7	—	—
(2)	Lewes 15 yrs. private practice	—	—	—	—	1828	·8
(2)	Prussia	—	—	—	—	1817	8·8

(7) Cf. England and Wales, 1921, 3·71 per 1,000 births

(1) Report.
(2) Bisset Hawkins.
(3) Mémoire—sur l'Hospice de la Maternité.
(4) Estimate quoted by Short. Bills of Mortality.
(5) Estimate quoted by Black.
(6) Report, Westminster Dispensary. Bland.
(7) Annual Report, Ministry of Health, 1923.

TABLE X

The Growth of Towns

·000 omitted.	‡ 1377	Cir. 1700	C. '20	C. '50	Cir. 1770	Cir. 1780	Cir. 1790	‖ C 1801	C 1811	C 1821	C 1831
London	35	Es 674	—	Es 676	—	—	—	900	1050	1225	1474
Manchester*	—	—	Es 8	Es 19	* En 27	—	* En 59	81	98	134	183
Liverpool	—	Es 5	Es 12	Es 20/5	En 34	—	En 56	78	94	119	165
Birmingham	—	—	—	—	44	En 54	—	74	86	107	142
Bristol and Suburbs	9	—	—	Es 43	—	—	—	64	76	87	103
Leeds	—	—	—	—	—	—	—	53	62	84	123
Plymouth	7	—	—	—	—	—	—	43	56	61	75
Portsmouth	—	—	—	—	—	—	—	32	40	45	50
Norwich	6	En 29	—	En 36	—	—	En 40	37	37	50	61
Newcastle-on-Tyne	4	—	—	—	—	—	—	28	37	47	50

These towns were the ten largest in England and Wales in 1821.
  * Including Salford.
  ‡ Poll Tax returns, quoted by Lowe.
  Es Estimate, based on registers. Very unreliable in case of Liverpool, owing to large numbers of Roman Catholics.
  En Enumeration.
  C Census.
  ‖ Census, in some cases corrected.

Milne stated in 1815 that there were 40 towns in England with more than 10,000 inhabitants, containing a total population of 2,140,000. Excluding London, the average population was 28,500.

TABLE XI

Population of France

	Mill.	
1700	19·7	
1784	24·8	
1801	27·3	First reliable census.
1811	29·0	
1821	30·5	
1831	32·6	

STATISTICAL TABLES

There was a great difference of opinion as to the population of France, as of all countries, in the absence of statistics, in the 18th century.

"On peut cependant admettre que le total en était passé de 19 millions vers 1700 à 24½ millions vers 1790." This increase, in spite of wars and civil disorders is ascribed to " Un adoucissement général dans les mœurs, dans les rapports de maître à serviteur, une hygiène mieux comprise, les efforts quotidiens des sciences médicales ". (Histoire de la Population Française. Lucien Schöne, 1893, p. 216.)

T

BIBLIOGRAPHY

I. BOOKS AND ARTICLES

ANONYMOUS. A Plan of the General Inoculating Dispensary, in Tracts 35 (B.M. ref.). *London*, 1782.
―― Le Typhus de 1813–14 à Strasbourg, in *Aesculape*, September, 1925.
ASHTON (Thomas S.). Iron and Steel in the Industrial Revolution. *Manchester University. Economic History Series*, No. 2, 1924.

BAKER (*Sir* George), *Bart., M.D.* Medical Tracts . . . *London*, 1818. X. Observations on . . . Inoculating the Small-pox. XII. Observations on . . . intermittent Fevers.
BARTON (John). Observations on the circumstances which influence the condition of the labouring classes. *London*, 1817.
BATEMAN (Thomas), *M.D.* A succinct account of the contagious fever of this country. *London*, 1818.
―― Observations on . . . epidemic fever. 1819.
―― Reports on the diseases of London. *London*, 1819.
BECKMANN (Johann). A History of Inventions and Discoveries, translated . . . by W. Johnston. 4 vol. *London*, 1797–1814.
BELL (Walter G.) The Great Fire of London in 1666. *John Lane*: London, New York, 1920.
―― The Great Plague in London in 1665. *John Lane*: London, Dodd, Mead & Co.: New York, 1924.
BELLERS (John). An Epistle to Friends. [*London* ?], 1724.
―― An epistle to the Quarterly Meeting of London, and Middlesex. [*London*, 1718.]
―― An Essay towards the improvement of physick. *London*, 1714.
BERNARD, (T.). Editor. See below under LONDON. Society for bettering the Condition of the Poor.
BERTRAND (Jean Baptiste). Relation . . . de la Peste de Marseille. 1721.
BIRCH (John), *M.R.C.S.* A Copy of the Answer to the queries of the London College of Surgeons . . . respecting the experiment of Cow pox . . . Serious Reasons for uniformly objecting to the practice of Vaccination. *London*, 1807.
BIRCH (Thomas), *D.D.* A Collection of the Yearly Bills of Mortality from 1657 to 1758. *London*, 1759.
BLACK (William), *M.D.* An historical sketch of medicine and surgery. *London*, 1782.
―― Observations . . . on the small-pox and inoculation. *London*, 1781. 2nd ed. . . . enlarged: *London*, 1781.
BLAND (Robert), *M.D.* Some Calculations . . . from the Midwifery Reports of the Westminster General Dispensary. *London*, 1781.
BLANE (*Sir* Gilbert), *Bart., M.D.* A short account of . . . means of preserving the health of Seamen. [*London* ? 1781 ?]
―― A Statement of Facts tending to establish an Estimate . . . of Vaccination, in *Trans. Med. and Chirur. Soc.*: *London*. Vol. 10, 1819, pp. 315–38.
―― Account of a medical visitation of Walcheren and Northfleet. *London*, 1812.

BLANE (*Sir* GILBERT), *Bart.*, M.D. Observations on the Comparative Prevalence, Mortality and Treatment of Different Diseases, in *Trans. Med. and Chirur. Soc.*, vol. 4, 1813, pp. 89–141.
—— Remarks on the comparative Health and Population of England. See his " Select Dissertations " below : Dissertation 5.
—— Select Dissertations on several subjects of Medical Science. *London*, 1822. New ed. 2 vol. : *London*, 1833.
—— Warning to the British Public against the alarming approach of the Indian Cholera. [*London*, 1831.]
BLENKINSOP (H.). Editor. See below under WILLUGHBY (P.) Observations in Midwifery.
BRISTOL. The New History of Bristol. *Bristol*, 1794.
BROWNLOW STREET. An account of the rise and progress of the Lying-in Hospital . . . in Brownlow Street. *London*, 1808.
BURDETT (*Sir* Henry C.). Burdett's Hospital Annual. Edited by H. C. B. [1890, etc.]
BURNET (Gilbert), *Bishop of Salisbury*. History of my own Times. *London*, 1724–34.
BURROWS (George Man). Observations on the comparative mortality of Paris and London. *London*, 1815.
BURTON (William K.). The Water Supply of Towns. *Crosby Lockwood and Son* : *London*, 1894.

CABANES (Dr.) Les Vieilles Pierres de l'Hôpital Saint-Louis, in *Aesculape*, March, 1923.
CADOGAN (William), M.D. An essay upon Nursing. 10th ed. *London*, 1772.
CAMPBELL (Janet M.), M.D., M.S. Maternal Mortality. See under " Ministry of Health " in Section II below.
CARLISLE (*Sir* Anthony). An essay on the Disorders of Old Age. 2nd ed. *London*, 1818.
CASTELLANI (Aldo) and CHALMERS (A. J.). Manual of Tropical Medicine. 3rd ed. *Baillière & Co.* : *London*, 1919.
CHALMERS (George). An Estimate of the comparative strength of Britain . . . to which is added an essay on population by the Lord Chief Justice Hale. New ed. *London*, 1802.
CHESTER. Society for promoting general inoculation. See Haygarth (J.). An inquiry how to prevent the small-pox. 1785.
CHURCHILL (Fleetwood), M.D, Essays on the Puerperal Fever . . . Edited by F.C. *Sydenham Society* : *London*, 1849.
CITY AND LIBERTY OF WESTMINSTER SANITARY ASSOCIATION. Report of meeting, 1847.
CLAYTON (John). Friendly advice to the poor. *Manchester*, 1755.
CLUTTERBUCK (Henry), M.D. Observations on . . . Epidemic Fever. *London*, 1819.
CRESSY (Edward). An Outline of Industrial History. *Macmillan and Co.* : *London*, 1915.
CUNNINGHAM (W.), *Archdeacon of Ely*. The Growth of English Industry and Commerce. Vol. II (In Modern Times). 3rd ed. *The University Press* : *Cambridge*, 1903.
CURRIE (James), M.D. Medical Reports on the effects of water . . . as a remedy in fever. 2nd ed. *Liverpool*, 1798.
CURRIE (William W.) Memoirs of the life of J. Currie. 2 vol. *London*, 1831.
CURTLER (W. H. R.) A Short History of English Agriculture. *Clarendon Press* : *Oxford*, 1909.
—— The Enclosure and Redistribution of our Land. *Clarendon Press* : *Oxford*, 1920.

BIBLIOGRAPHY

DARWIN (Emma). Emma Darwin. A century of family letters. 1792–1896. 1915.
DAVIS (John Bunnell). A cursory inquiry into . . . causes of mortality among children. *London*, 1817.
DERHAM (William). Physico-Theology. New ed. 2 vol. *London*, 1798.
DIEMERBROECK (I. de). Several choice histories of the medicines, manner and method used in curing the plague. Translated. *London*, 1666.

EDMONDS (T. R.). The Law of Mortality in . . . England, in *Lancet*, vol. 1, 1835–6.
—— On the Diminution in the Mortality of Infants in England, in *Lancet*, vol. i, 1835–6.

FARR (William). Report on the Mortality of Cholera. 1852.
—— Vital Statistics. 1885.
—— See MCCULLOCH (J. R.). A Statistical Account of the British Empire.
FAULKNER (Thomas). An historical and topographical description of Chelsea. 2 vol. *Chelsea*, 1829.
FELTHAM (John). The Picture of London for 1802. *London*, 1802.
—— The Picture of London for 1821. *London*, 1821.
FERRIAR (John). Medical Histories and Reflections. 2nd ed. 4 vol. *London*, 1810–13.
FINLAISON (John). Report . . . on Tables of Life Annuities, in Report from the Select Committee on Life Annuities, 1829, pp. 287–305 (*Parl. Pps.*, 1829 (284) III).
FRAZER (*Sir* James G.). Folklore in the Old Testament. 3 vol. *Macmillan & Co.*: *London*, 1918.
—— The Golden Bough. 3rd ed. *Macmillan & Co.*: *London*, 1907–15.

GARNETT (William). A Little Book on Water Supply. *University Press, Cambridge*, 1922.
GARRISON (Fielding H.). An Introduction to the History of Medicine, 3rd ed. *W. B. Saunders Co.*: *Philadelphia & London*, 1921.
GEORGE (M. Dorothy). London Life in the Eighteenth Century. *Kegan Paul, Trench, Trübner & Co.*: *London*, 1925.
—— The Increase of Population in the Eighteenth Century as illustrated by London, in *Economic Journal*, 1922.
GLAISTER (John). Dr. William Smellie and his Contemporaries. *Maclehose and Sons*: *Glasgow*, 1894.
GLISSON (Francis). A Treatise of the Rickets. Translated by P. Armin. *London*, 1651.
GRANT (I. F.). Every-day Life on an old Highland Farm, 1769–1782. *Longmans & Co.*: *London*, 1924.
GRAUNT (John), F.R.S. Natural and political observations . . . on the Bills of Mortality . . . *London*, 1662. 5th ed. 1676.
GRAY (Benjamin K.). A History of English Philanthropy. *P. S. King and Son*: *London*, 1905.

H. (J.), *M.D.* Scelera Aquarum: or a supplement to Mr. Graunt on the Bills of Mortality. *London*, 1701.
HANKINS (Frank Hamilton). Adolphe Quetelet as Statistician. *New York*: *Columbia College.* Studies in History, etc., 1908, vol. 31, No. 4.
HAWKINS (Francis Bisset). Elements of Medical Statistics. *Longman*: *London*, 1829.
HAYGARTH (John), *M.D.* A letter to Dr. Percival on the prevention of Infectious Fevers. *Bath*, 1801.

HAYGARTH (John), *M.D.* An enquiry how to prevent the small-pox . . . *Chester*, 1785.
HEBERDEN (William) *the Younger*, *M.D.*, *F.R.S.* Observations on the increase and decrease of different diseases and particularly of the Plague. *London*, 1801.
—— On the Mortality of London, in *Med. Trans. Coll. Physicians in London*, 1813, vol. 4, pp. 103–18.
HENRY (Thomas), *F.R.S.* Observations on the Bills of Mortality for . . . Manchester and Salford. 1786. In *Memoirs of Manch. Lit. and Philos. Soc.*, 1790, vol. 3, pp. 159–73.
HEYSHAM (John). Carlisle Tables. See below under MILNE (Joshua). A Treatise on the Valuation of Annuities.
—— The Life of J. Heysham . . . Edited by H. Lonsdale. *London*, 1870.
HOMER (William). The Old Englishman's Letters for the Poor of Old England. *London*, 1758.
HOSIE (Dorothea), *Lady*. Two gentlemen of China. *Seeley, Service and Co.* : *London*, 1924.
HOSPICE DE LA MATERNITÉ. Mémoire historique et instructif sur l'Hospice de la Maternité. *Paris*, 1808.
HOUSE OF RECOVERY. The History of the London House of Recovery. *London*, 1817.
HOWARD (John). An Account of the principal Lazarettos in Europe. *London*, 1789. 2nd ed. 1791.
—— Nine Letters to the Lord Mayor . . . on the state of the Prisons . . . [1786].
—— The state of the Prisons in England and Wales. *Warrington*, 1777–80. 2nd ed. 1780, 3rd ed. 1784.
HOWARD (William Travis). Public Health Administration and the Natural History of Disease in Baltimore, Maryland. *Washington*, 1924.
HOWLETT (John). An Enquiry into the influence which enclosures have upon the population of England. *London*, 1786. 2nd ed. with appendix, *London*, 1786.
—— An Essay on the Population of Ireland. *London*, 1786.
—— An Examination of Dr. Price's Essay on the Population of England and Wales. *Maidstone* [1781.]
—— Uncertainty of the present Population of this Kingdom. *London*, 1781.
HUTTON (William). A Journey from Birmingham to London. *Birmingham*, 1785.
—— An History of Birmingham. 2nd and 6th ed. : *Birmingham*, 1783, 1835.

JAMES (*Col.* S. P.), *M.D.* The Disappearance of Malaria from England. Health Organization. *League of Nations*, 1925.

KALM (Pehr). Kalm's account of his visit to England in 1748. *Macmillan and Co.* : *London*, 1892.
KING (James), *Capt., R.N.* A voyage to the Pacific Ocean [by Capt. Cook], vol. iii, by J. K., 1784.
KNOWLES (L. C. A.), *Litt.D.* The Economic Development of the Overseas Empire. *George Routledge & Sons* : *London*, 1924.
—— The Industrial and Commercial Revolutions in Great Britain during the Nineteenth Century. *George Routledge & Sons* : *London*, 1921.

LANCET. Narrative of the rise, progress and ravages of the Malignant Cholera. *London*, 1832.
LANGFORD (John A.). A Century of Birmingham Life . . . 1741 to 1841. 2 vol. *London*, 1868.
LATIMER (John). The Annals of Bristol in the seventeenth century. *W. George's Sons: Bristol*, 1900; in the eighteenth century [*Frome* ?], 1893; in the nineteenth century. *Bristol*, 1887, 1902.
LETTSOM (John Coakley), *M.D.* A Letter . . . upon general inoculation. *London*, 1778.
—— Medical Memoirs of the General Dispensary in London. *London*, 1774.
LIND (James). A Treatise of the Scurvy. *Edinburgh*, 1753.
—— An Essay on Diseases incidental to Europeans in hot climates. 2nd ed. *London*, 1771. 6th ed., 1808.
—— An essay in . . . preserving the health of seamen. *London*, 1757.
—— Copy of a letter . . . on Typhus fever. *Windsor*, 1803.
LISTON (*Lieut.-Col.* W. Glen). Milroy Lectures on the Plague, in *British Medical Journal*, 1924, I.
LIVERPOOL, A general and descriptive history of . . . *Liverpool*, 1795.
—— A Report of the Proceedings of a Court of Inquiry into the existing state of the Corporation of . . . *Liverpool* [1834 ?]
—— An Address to the Inhabitants of Liverpool on . . . general Inoculation for the smallpox. *Liverpool*, 1781.
—— The History of Liverpool from the earliest authenticated period down to the present time. *Liverpool*, 1810.
—— Ladies' Charity. Eleventh, etc., reports. *Liverpool*, 1807 [–1849].
—— Society for Bettering the Condition of the Poor. First report. *Liverpool*, 1811.
—— Society for Visiting . . . the Sick Poor. First and second reports. *Liverpool*, 1816, 1820.
—— The Stranger in Liverpool. 9th ed. *Liverpool*, 1829.
LONDON. Royal College of Physicians. A further account of the Dispensaries [*London*, 1702 ?]
—— Society for bettering the Condition . . . of the Poor. Reports, 5 vol. Edited by T. Bernard (later *Sir*). *London*, 1798–1808.
—— Society for Promoting Medical Knowledge. *Medical Communications*. 2 vol. *London*, 1784–90.
LORD (John). Capital and Steam-Power, 1750–1800. *P. S. King & Son: London*, 1923.
LOWE (Joseph). The Present State of England in regard to Agriculture, Trade and Finance. *London*, 1822.

MACNAMARA (Nottidge C.). Asiatic Cholera. *Macmillan & Co.: London*, 1892.
MAHAN (Alfred Thayer). The Influence of Sea Power upon the French Revolution and Empire. 2 vol. *Sampson Low & Co.: London*, 1892.
MALTHUS (T. R.). An Essay on the Principle of Population. 9th ed. 1888.
MANCHESTER. A Description of Manchester. *Manchester*, 1783.
—— Manchester as it is. *Manchester*, 1839.
—— The Manchester Guide. *Manchester*, 1804.
—— The new Manchester Guide. *Manchester*, 1815.
—— Strangers' Friend Society. Report [1804].
MANSFORD (J. G.), *M.R.C.S.* On Parish Registers, in *London Medical Repository*, 1818. vol. X, pp. 372–9.
MASON (William Pitt). Water Supply. 4th ed. *J. Wiley & Sons: New York*, 1916.

McCulloch (J. R.) A Statistical Account of the British Empire. [Section on " Vital Statistics " by Wm. Farr.] 2 vol. *London*, 1837.
—— Adam Smith : Wealth of Nations. Edited by J. R. M. 1863.
Mead (Richard). A short discourse concerning pestilential contagion. *London*, 1720.
—— The Medical Works of R. Mead. *Edinburgh*, 1763.
Mellanby (Edward M. A.), *M.D.* Deficiency Diseases with special reference to Rickets, in *British Medical Journal*, May 24, 1924, p. 895.
Milne (Joshua). A Treatise on the valuation of Annuities, etc. [With the Carlisle Tables by John Heysham.] 2 vol. *London*, 1815.
Moore (*Sir* Norman), *Bart.* The History of St. Bartholomew's Hospital. 2 vol. C. A. Pearson : *London*, 1918.
—— The History of the Study of Medicine in the British Isles. *Clarendon Press : Oxford*, 1908.

Newsholme (*Sir* Arthur), *K.C.B.* The Elements of Vital Statistics, 1889. New ed. G. Allen & Unwin : *London*, 1923.

Owen (Robert). The Life of Robert Owen. Written by himself. *London*, 1857-58.

Percival (Edward), *M.D.* Practical observations on the treatment . . . of typhous fever. *Bath*, 1819.
Percival (Thomas), *M.D.* Observations on the State of Population in Manchester, etc. *Manchester*, 1773, etc.
—— The Works, literary, moral and medical, of T. P. 4 vol. *London*, 1807.
Picton (*Sir* James Allanson). City of Liverpool. 2 vol. *Liverpool*, 1883–86.
—— Memorials of Liverpool. 2nd ed. 2 vol. *London*, 1875.
Place (Francis). Illustrations and Proofs of the Principle of Population. *London*, 1822.
Postlethwayt (Malachy). The Universal Dictionary of Trade. Translated from the French. 1774. [See article on " Turkey ".]
Price (Richard), *D.D.* An Essay on the Population of England. *London*, 1780.
Pringle (*Sir* John), *Bart.* A discourse on . . . the health of mariners. In " A Voyage towards the South Pole " (second voyage) by James Cook. *London*, 1777.
—— Observations on the Diseases of the Army . . . with an Appendix. *London*, 1752. 7th ed. *London*, 1775.
—— Six Discourses. *London*, 1783.
Procter (Richard Wright). Memorials of Bygone Manchester. *Manchester*, 1880.
Prothero (Rowland E.), *Baron Ernle*. English Farming Past and Present. Longman & Co. : *London*, 1912.
Purchas (Samuel), *the Elder*. Purchas his Pilgrimes. *London*, 1625.

Quételet (Lambert A. J.) Recherches statistiques sur le royaume des Pays-Bas. *Bruxelles*, 1829.
—— Sur l'homme et le développement de ses facultés. *Paris*, 1835.

Rice (C. Colliver). Persian Women and their Ways. Seeley, Service and Co. : *London*, 1923.
Roberton (John) *the Elder*. Institutes of Health. *London*, 1817.
—— Medical Police. 2nd ed. 2 vol. *London*, 1812.

BIBLIOGRAPHY

ROBERTON (John) *the Elder*. Observations on the mortality and physical management of children. *London*, 1827.
RUSSELL (Alexander). The Natural History of Aleppo. *London*, 1756. 2nd ed. revised by Patrick Russell, 1794.
RUSSELL (Patrick) *M.D.*, *F.R.S.* A Treatise of the Plague. *London*, 1791.

SCHÖNE (Lucien). Histoire de la Population Française. *Paris*, 1893.
SCHULZ VON SCHULZENHEIM (David). An Account of Inoculation. Translated from the Swedish. *London*, 1758.
SCOTT (William Robert). The Constitution and Finance of English, Scottish and Irish Joint-Stock Companies to 1720. *University Press* : *Cambridge*, 1910.
SHAW (Albert). Municipal Government in Continental Europe. *Century Co.* : *New York*, 1895.
SHORT (Thomas), *M.D.* New Observations . . . on Bills of Mortality. *London*, 1750.
SIMON (*Sir* John). English Sanitary Institutions. *Smith, Elder & Co.* *London*, 1897.
SIMPSON (William J. R.). A Treatise on Plague. *University Press* : *Cambridge*, 1905.
SINGER (Charles), M.D. Greek Science and Modern Science. *University of London Press* : *London*, 1920.
—— Studies in the History and Method of Science. Edited by C. S. *Clarendon Press* : *Oxford*, 1917, etc.
SINGER (*Dr.* Charles and *Mrs.* D.). The Development of the Doctrine of Contagium Vivum, 1500–1750. In *Congrès périodique international des sciences médicales*. Sess. XVII. *London*, 1913.
SMELLIE (William). Treatise on . . . Midwifery. 3 vol. *New Sydenham Society* : *London*, 1876–78.
SMILES (Samuel). Industrial Biography. *John Murray* : *London*, 1863.
SMITH (George Munro). A History of the Bristol Royal Infirmary. *Bristol*, 1917.
SMOLLETT (Tobias George). The Expedition of Humphry Clinker. 1771.
—— Travels through France and Italy. 2 vol. *London*, 1766.
SUESSMILCH (Johann P.). Die göttliche Ordnung in den Veränderungen des menschlichen Geschlechts. *Berlin*, 1765.
SYDENHAM (Thomas). The Works of T. S. Translated . . . by R. G. Latham. *Sydenham Society* : *London*, 1848, etc.

THACKRAH (Charles T.) The Effects of the principal Arts . . . on Health and Longevity. *London*, 1831.
THROSBY (John). The History and Antiquities . . . of Nottingham. 1795.
TOUZEAU (James). The Rise and Progress of Liverpool from 1551 to 1835. 2 vol. *Liverpool Booksellers' Co.* : *Liverpool*, 1910.
TUCKER (Josiah), *Dean of Gloucester*. Four Tracts. *Gloucester*. 1774.

UNWIN (George). Samuel Oldknow and the Arkwrights. *Manchester University*. *Economic History Series*, vol. 1, 1924.

VICHY (Emile Deguéret de). La Mort du Grand Roi, in *Aesculape*, September, 1924.

WALL, (Martin), *M.D.* A letter to J. Howard, Esq. 1784.
WATSON (Kenrick). Some Account of the Medical Topography of Stourport, in *London Medical Repository*, vol. 2, 1814, pp. 459–65.

WATT (Robert), *M.D.* An inquiry into the relative mortality of the principal diseases of children. *Glasgow*, 1888.
WEBB (Sidney J.) and POTTER, afterwards WEBB (Beatrice). English Prisons under Local Government. *Longmans & Co. : London*, 1922.
—— English Local Government. *Longmans & Co. : London*, 1906, etc.
WEBER (Adna Ferrin). The Growth of Cities in the nineteenth century. New York : *Columbia College. Studies in History, etc.*, vol. II, 1899.
WHITE (Charles). A treatise on the management of pregnant and lying-in women. *London*, 1772.
WHITE (William). Observations on the Bills of Mortality at York, in *Phil. Trans. R. Soc. London*, 1782, vol. LXXII, pp. 35–43.
WILLAN (Robert), *M.D., the Younger.* Reports on the diseases in London. *London*, 1801.
WILLUGHBY (Percivall). Observations in Midwifery. Edited by Henry Blenkinsop. *Warwick*, 1863.
WINCHESTER. An Account of the Establishment of the County Hospital at Winchester . . . 1736. [*London*, 1737–38.]
WITKOWSKI (Gustave J. A.). Histoire des Accouchements. *Paris* [1887].

YOUNG (Arthur). Travels in France during the Years 1787, 1788, 1789. *London.* First published 1792 ; *Bohn's Standard Library*, 1889 ; etc.

II. GOVERNMENT PUBLICATIONS

EDUCATION, SELECT COMMITTEE ON, in England and Wales. Report, 1835, p. 838. (*Parl. Pps.* 1835 (3), VII.)

LEAGUE OF NATIONS. The Disappearance of Malaria from England. See under JAMES (*Col.* S. P.) in I above.
LIFE ANNUITIES, SELECT COMMITTEE ON. Report . . . on Tables of Life Annuities. See under Finlaison (John) in I above.

MEDICAL RESEARCH COUNCIL. Report on the Present State of Knowledge of Accessory Food Factors (Vitamins). 2nd ed., No. 38. *H.M. Stationery Office : London*, 1924.
MINISTRY OF HEALTH. Annual Report of the Chief Medical Officer of the Ministry of Health for the year 1922. *H.M. Stationery Office : London*, 1923.
—— Reports on Public Health and Medical Subjects. No. 25. " Maternal Mortality," by Janet M. Campbell, *M.D., M.S. H.M. Stationery Office : London*, 1924.

VACCINATION, ROYAL COMMISSION ON. Sixth report. 1896. p. 642. App. 5, table 34. " Deaths in Edinburgh from small-pox, 1764–83." (*Parl. Pps.* 1896. XLVII.)

III. PERIODICALS AND WORKS OF REFERENCE

AESCULAPE. Organe officiel de la Société Internationale d'Histoire de la Médecine. Paris, XIVe, 15 Rue Froidevaux.

BRITISH MEDICAL ALMANACK. *London*, 1835–39.
BRITISH MEDICAL JOURNAL, formerly Association Medical Journal. *London*, 1853, etc.

DICTIONARY OF NATIONAL BIOGRAPHY. *London*, 1885, etc.

EDINBURGH. Medical and Philosophical Commentaries. 1773–95, *London, Edinburgh*, 1773–95.
EDINBURGH MEDICAL AND SURGICAL JOURNAL. 1805–55. Continued as Edin. Med. Jnal. 1855, etc.
ENCYCLOPÆDIA BRITANNICA. 11th ed. *Cambridge*, 1910–11. See under " Insurance ", " Statistics ", " Sugar."

LANCET. *London*, 1823, etc.
LONDON. Congrès Périodique International des Sciences Médicales : *Compte-rendu*, etc., Session XVII. *London*, 1913.
LONDON. Medical and Chirurgical Society : *Transactions*.
LONDON MEDICAL REPOSITORY. *London*, 1815–28. Formerly London Medical, Surgical and Pharmaceutical Repository, 1814.
LONDON. R. College of Physicians : *Medical Transactions. London*, 1772–1820.
LONDON. Royal Society : *Philosophical Transactions*. 1665, etc.

MANCHESTER LITERARY AND PHILOSOPHICAL SOCIETY. Memoirs. *Manchester*, 1785–1802.

INDEX

Addington, Henry (Lord Sidmouth), 207
Admiralty, the 119, 120, 194
Agriculture, 6, 22, 23, 36, 47–49, 51, 52, 55, 56, 61, 63–75, 153
Ague, *see* Malaria
Alcohol, 61
Aleppo, 177
Amsterdam, 49, 267
Anderson, James, 168
Annuity Loan of 1746, 13
Anson, Lord, 159
Antiseptics, 150, 164–180
Apprenticeship, 2, 117, 251
Arabs, sugar introduced by, 60
Armstrong, Dr. George, 135
Ashton, T. S., 250

Bachstrom, J. F., 160
Baltic, the, 51, 156
Baltimore, U.S.A., 218
Bank of England, 48, 52
Baptisms, registration of, 16, 18, 31, 34
Bateman, Thomas, 88, 89, 152, 157, 206–8, 214, 236, 254, 255, 259, 262, 265
Beckmann, Johann, 256, 260
Belgium, 31
Bell, Walter G., 179, 249, 254, 260, 266
Bellers, John, 126, 127
Bengal, 227
Berlin, 267, 271
Bernard, T., 201
Bernoulli, Daniel, 261
Birch, Thomas, 17, 245, 261
Birmingham, 52, 82, 86, 88, 248, 255, 267, 272
Birth Rate, 2, 3, 6, 15–17, 19, 20, 22–35, 56, 73, 75, 78, 89, 215, 218, 223, 224, 246–248, 263
Black, Dr. William, 147, 153, 255, 259, 263, 271
Black Death, the, 65, 66, 68, 170
Bland, Robert, 147

Blane, Sir Gilbert, 28, 120, 123, 131, 153, 157, 162, 182, 190, 196, 217, 218, 238, 255, 256, 259, 261, 265, 266
Blindness, 183
Boe, Franciscus de, 115
Boerhaave, Herman, 115, 116, 118, 158
Bombay, 173
Boulton and Watt, engineers, 39, 252, 256
Bourgeoisie, political power of, 233
Bramah, Joseph, 105, 256
Breslau, 11, 12
Bricks and brick houses, 51, 53, 59, 60, 78, 79, 81, 84, 86, 88, 173
Bristol, 49, 77, 86, 97, 98, 107, 178, 230, 255, 256, 260
British Lying-in Hospital, 132, 141, 143–147, 271
Burials, registration of, 17
Burnet, Gilbert, 214, 260
Burns, Robert, 124

Cadogan, Dr. William, 148, 149
Cambridge, 117, 127, 152
Camp Fever, *see* Typhus
Canals, 38, 42, 54, 56, 60, 70, 88, 215
Capitalism, 56, 57, 61, 65, 250
Carlisle, 191, 192, 268
Carlisle Tables, the, 14, 20, 21, 28–31, 147, 182, 210, 211, 245, 269, 270
Castellani, Aldo, 260, 263
Cellar dwellings, 85
Census, 17, 20, 264
Chadwick, Sir Edwin, 26
Chalmers, G., 255; A. J., 260, 263
Chameau, 155
Charity, organization of, 44–46, 128
Charles I., 152
Chateauneuf, B. de, 24, 25, 28, 30
Chelsea, 108
Chelsea Water Company, 100, 108, 255, 256
Chester, 122, 133, 182, 185, 198, 199

INDEX

Chichester, 188
Child-birth, 5, 115
China, 5, 183, 228
Cholera, 3, 56, 108, 174, 226–30, 234, 263
Christenings, registers of, 16, 17, 33, 34
Chronometer, invention of, 49
Cinchona bark, 214, 215
City of London Lying-in Hospital, 132, 141
Civilization, primitive, 5, 6; urban, 1
Civil War, the, effects of, 246
Clarke, Dr., 149
Clayton, John, 255
Clement, Jules, 140
Climatic Fever, see Malaria
Clover, introduction of, 69
Coal industry, 53–56, 60
Coast Fever, see Malaria
Cobbett, William, 37
Cole, G. D. H., 37
College of Physicians, 230
Collingwood, Admiral Lord, 163
Commerce, 36, 47–62, 63, 90
Compass, mariners', invention of, 49
Conduits, system of, 97, 101
Constantinople, 178
Consumption, 210, 211, 221, 265, 269, 270
Contagious Fever, see Typhus
Cook, Captain, 155, 160–162, 260
Cork, 208
Corn Bounty Acts (1783–4), 69, 264
Cotton, 37, 38, 52, 56, 57, 60, 122, 130, 176, 177, 196, 197, 200, 201, 206
Coutume de Paris (1513), 104
Creighton, C., 256
Cromwell, Oliver, 214
Cunningham, W., 250
Currency, the policy of, 37
Currie, James, 85, 123–125, 202–204, 262
Curtler, W., 252
Cyprus, 172

Da Gama, Vasco, 158
Davies, Randall, 236
Davis, Bunnell, 259
Death Rate, the, 2–6, 10, 11, 13, 15–17, 19, 22–35, 59, 63, 75, 78, 81, 87, 89, 178, 179, 192, 210, 211, 215, 218, 220, 221–226, 229, 234, 239, 241, 247, 248, 263, 267
Deparcieux, A., 13,

Derham, Sir William, 11
Devon, Countess of, 98
Dispensaries, 32, 43, 45, 126–136, 150, 232, 258, 265
Dissent, 13, 16, 17, 29, 44
Dorset, 152
Drake, Sir Francis, 98
Dublin, 143, 208, 271
Dumfries Hospital, 198
Duncan, Isadora, 111; Dr., 204
Dunkirk, 176
Dutch influence on gardening, 67
Dysentery, 90, 221, 236

East India Company, 48, 61, 158
Edinburgh, 116–120, 122–124, 141, 198, 271
Edmonds, T. R., 245, 248
Egypt, 60, 110
Enclosure of lands, 65–67, 69–74, 252, 253
England, 24, 25, 192, 213, 223, 228, 250, 268
England and Wales, 24–29, 31, 223, 267, 268
Enteric, 5, 75, 104, 211, 213
Enumerations of population, 18
Emigration, 24, 223
Equitable Society, the, 13, 14
Ernle, Lord, 248, 252
Erasmus, 92
Europe, population of, 1, 6
Evangelical Movement, the, 44, 45
Evelyn, John, 255
Expectation of life, 13
Eyam, the tragedy of, 170

Factory, health in the, 251, 252; system, 57–59
Famine, 8, 9, 62, 63, 193, 238, 240
Farr, William, 14, 15, 22, 25, 27, 29, 108, 209–211, 220, 224, 226, 229, 236, 256, 263, 264
Faulkner, T., 255
Feltham, John, 256
Fen Country, the, 68, 102
Ferriar, John, 123, 199–202, 204, 257, 262
Fever Hospitals, 193–209, 261, 265
Finance, development of, 49
Finlaison, John, 13, 14, 20, 21, 23, 28, 29, 31, 245, 248
Fire of London, 78, 172, 219
Flanders, 66, 118, 217
Fleet River, the, 81
Floods, 103
Food Supply, 47, 62, 71

INDEX

Fomites, 167, 198, 260
Forceps, improvement of, 142, 258
Fracastoro, G., 111, 167, 260
France, 7, 10, 25, 28, 172, 176, 177, 228, 262, 267, 271–273
Frazer, Sir John, 260
Fumigation in infection, 164, 165, 167

Gaol Fever, see Typhus
Gaols, 194, 195
Garnett, W., 256
Garrison, Fielding, 261
Geneva, 268
Genoa, 164
George, M. D., 248, 251, 255, 259, 266
Germany, 155, 266
Glaister, J., 256, 258
Glasgow, 31, 124, 261, 268
Glisson, Francis, 152–154
Gloucester, 133
Grant, I. F., 250
Graunt, John, 10, 11, 17, 74, 75, 155, 179, 180, 260
Gray, B. Kirkman, 261
Great Britain, 29, 223, 228
Great Chart, 190
Greeks, influence of, 7, 111, 166
Grégoire, J. F. A., 142
Guild organization, 38, 43, 57
Guy, Thomas, 43, 105
Guy's Hospital, 129, 132

H., J., 152, 155
Hale, Sir M., 165, 186
Halley, Edmund, 12
Hampshire, 127
Hankins, Frank H., 245
Hardwicke's Marriage Act, 16
Harvey, William, 111
Haslar Hospital, 119, 129, 133, 162, 194
Hawkins, Bisset, 237, 255, 265, 267, 268, 270, 271; Sir Richard, 158
Haygarth, John, 122, 182, 185, 198, 261
Health, Bills of, 175, 177; Board of, 200, 206, 265; Public, 251, 265
Heberden, William, 248, 255
Henry, Thomas, 255, 261
Hentzner, P., 155
Hereford, 26, 133
Hertford, 99
Heysham, Dr. John, 14, 20, 21, 191, 197

Holland, 7, 13, 48, 69, 155, 156, 177, 218, 267
Home Office, the, 40, 121
Hosie, Lady, 245
Hospitals, 32, 43, 47, 126–136, 232, 257, 258
Hospital Ship Fever, see Typhus
Hôtel Dieu, 141, 271
Houses of Recovery, 200–204, 206–208
Howard, John, 129, 130, 133, 134, 147, 158, 165, 176, 178, 194–198, 259, 260, 262, 263
Howlett, John, 12, 34, 72, 73, 87, 190, 238, 248, 252, 261, 266
Hull, 206
Hunter, John, 256; William, 117, 143
Hutton, William, 82, 86, 255
Huxham, John, 158, 261
Hygiene, 112, 137-150

Immigration, 24, 32, 33, 223
India, 4, 5, 9, 110, 227, 228, 248
Individualism, 36–46, 65, 115, 249
Industrial revolution, the, 2, 3, 5, 6, 55, 337, 240
Industry, 37, 55
Infant mortality, 5, 30–32, 145, 151, 153, 222, 247, 264; nurture, 32, 87, 115, 139, 148
Influenza, 213,
Inoculation, 183, 185–189, 191, 257, 261
Institut de France, 121, 230
Intermittent Fever, see Malaria
Ireland, 26, 229
Irish in England, 207, 208, 219, 223, 224, 226, 231
Iron bedsteads, 144; industry, 37, 52–56, 58, 130
Italy, 7, 10, 27, 57, 164, 177

James, Colonel, 216, 262
Jenner, Edward, 121, 187, 261
Jessore, 228
Jews, 7, 137, 177
Joint Stock companies, 41, 48, 49, 99, 110
Jonas, Dr., 251
Jungle Fever, see Malaria
Justices of the Peace, 15, 40, 41, 232

Kalm, P., 250, 252
Kay, Dr., 231
Kent, 51

INDEX

Kerseboom, 13
King, Captain, 161; Gregory, 11, 22
Knowles, L. C. A., 245, 251
Koch, R., 227
Kramer, 159
Kut, 158

Laisser faire, policy of, 36–46
Lambeth Water Company, 108
La Motte, 140
Lancet, The, 30, 229, 248
Langford, J.A., 248, 255
Latimer, John, 255, 260
Lazarettos, 130, 169, 174, 176, 177
Leeds, 133, 152, 155, 208, 272
Leet River, 98
Leghorn, 176
Leicester, 132
Leprosy, 164–80
Lettsom, Dr. J. C., 150, 190, 257, 259, 261
Levant, 175–177, 228
Leyden, 115, 118, 122
Life Annuities, 12–14, 28; Insurance, 12–14, 21, 37
Lime, 165
Lincolnshire, 38, 68, 103
Lind, James, 118, 119, 121, 130, 134, 157, 160, 162, 165, 198, 208, 218, 219, 259, 263
Lister, Joseph, Lord, 112
Liston, Lieut.-Col. 245
Liverpool, 49, 54, 84, 85, 123, 124, 183, 185, 202–204, 206, 208, 226, 255, 261, 262, 267, 272
Local Government, 233
Lock Hospitals, 134
London, 5, 10, 11, 16, 17, 24, 26, 29–34, 43, 49–52, 55, 58–60, 69, 70, 74, 75, 77–80, 87, 89, 90, 94, 97, 102–105, 107, 109, 116–118, 126, 127, 131, 135, 141, 142, 152, 156, 157, 172, 173, 178, 179, 182, 190, 192, 206, 208, 214, 219, 225, 226, 240, 249, 250, 254, 256, 260, 266–268, 270, 272; Great Fire of, 78, 172, 219; Hospital, 130, 131; Rebuilding Act (1667), 79
Lord, J., 252
Lowe, Joseph, 237, 265, 266
Lying-in Charity, 143, 144, 259; Hospitals, 129, 134, 146, 150

Machinery, adoption of, 39, 56, 57
McCulloch, J. R., 27, 28, 236, 248, 252, 262–4

Macnamara, N. C., 263
Mahan, Admiral A. T., 260
Malaria, 4, 5, 43, 68, 75, 103, 104, 115, 119, 153, 166, 210–222, 262, 265
Malthus, T. R., 12, 245
Manchester, 34, 54, 83, 84, 122, 123, 127, 144, 178, 199–202, 204, 206, 226, 231, 252, 255, 261, 267, 272
Manningham, Sir Richard, 141
Manorial system, the, 63, 64, 67
Mansford, J. G., 248
Market gardening, 51, 81, 153
Marriages, in registers, 15, 16, 25, 26, 246
Marseilles, 172, 176, 178
Marshes, draining of, 68, 214, 218, 238
Marsh Fever, *see* Malaria
Mauriceau, 140
Mead, Richard, 159, 165, 175
Measles, 204, 210, 261, 269, 270
Mellanby, Dr., 151
Messina, 172, 178
Middle Ages, the, 6–8, 62, 63, 76, 94, 97, 104, 111, 164, 168, 250, 251, 260
Middlesex, 51; Hospital, 131, 141
Midwifery, 129, 137–150, 154, 258
Midwives, 139–145, 150
Migration, 19, 24, 74, 75
Milne, Joshua, 14, 20, 29, 245, 261, 262, 270, 272
Moheau, 28
Montague, Lady Mary Wortley, 183
Morice, Peter, 98
Mortality, Bills of, 10, 11, 17, 18, 21, 30, 33–35, 81, 89, 179, 180, 190, 210, 248, 260–262, 268; infant, 5, 30–32, 145, 151, 153, 222, 247, 264; maternal, 145, 147, 154, 271; table of, 10, 12, 13, 27, 268
Mosquitoes, 212–214, 216, 217, 219
Muratori, 260
Myddleton, Hugh, 98

Naples, 268
Napoleon I, 192, 217, 262
National Debt, the, 48
Navy, mortality in, 271
Necker, James, 24, 25, 28
Nelson, Lord, 163
Nervous Fever, *see* Typhus
Netherlands, 271
Newcastle-upon-Tyne, 51, 208, 272
Newenham, Sir Edward, 263

INDEX

New River, the, 99–101
Newsholme, A., 246, 248, 263, 265
Norden, John, 67
Norfolk, 38, 51, 70, 132
Northampton table, 13, 14
Northouck, J., 91
Northumberland, 38
Norway, 168
Norwich, 34, 49, 87, 272
Nottingham, 132

Old Bailey, 194
Oldknow, Samuel, 38
Owen, Robert, 122, 256
Oxford, 117, 127, 132, 152

Paludism, *see* Malaria
Paré, Ambroise, 140
Paris, 83, 104, 118, 140–142, 155, 196, 228; Maternity hospital, or Hospice de la Maternité, 146, 196, 259, 271
Parish registers, 12, 13, 15, 17, 18, 21, 33–35, 248; relief, 17
Parliamentary Commission of 1810, 100
Pasteur, Louis, 112
Patin, 155
Paving of streets, 59, 78, 81, 83
Pearce, an amateur vaccinator, 188, 189
Peel, Sir Robert, 39
Pelletier, 262
Percival, Edward, 175, 198, 202, 208, 260, 262
Persia, 5, 60, 228
Petty, Sir William, 11, 179, 263
Philanthropy, growth of, 43, 44, 46
Physicians, College of, 118
Pitt, William, 13, 14
Place, Francis, 196, 211, 231, 259, 262
Plague, 4, 17, 43, 90, 115, 164–180, 193, 199, 238, 240, 260, 266
Plymouth, 98, 133
Pommelles, 28
Poor Law, 2, 37, 41, 126, 207, 209, 225
Popham, Alexander, 197
Population, 2, 11, 19, 20, 22–35, 49, 56, 57, 63, 67, 72, 74, 78, 234, 245, 252, 256, 264
Portsmouth, 87, 267, 272
Postlethwayt, Malachy, 260
Potatoes, 68, 157, 225, 264
Potteries, the, 52
Price, Dr., 11, 13, 14, 19, 28, 72, 248, 261, 266
Pringle, Sir John, 61, 104, 118, 119, 155, 156, 161, 167, 194, 198, 217, 219, 250, 259, 260, 262
Privies, 104, 105
Prussia, 268, 271
Public Health, 15, 35, 101, 108, 111–125, 169, 170, 231
Puerperal Fever, 145, 147
Putrid Fever, *see* Typhus

Quadrant, mariners', 49
Quakers, 16
Quarantine, 165, 171, 173–178, 229
Quételet, Adolphe, 245, 248, 267, 271
Queen Charlotte's Lying-in Hospital, 142
Quinine, 213, 215

Ramsden, Jesse, 124
Rats, disease carried by, 170, 172, 173
Relapsing Fever, 5, 90, 124
Religion, in 18th century, 44
Remittent fever, *see* Malaria
Rice, Colliver, 245
Rickets, 6, 43, 151–163, 238
Rickman, John, 15–17, 20, 21
Roads, 38, 41, 54, 56
Roberton, John, 189, 190, 238, 266
Rodney, Lord, 120, 162
Roman Catholics, 16
Romans in Britain, 68, 103, 137
Rome, 110, 155, 267
Romney Marsh, 103
Root crops, 64, 69
Rouen, 176
Royal Maternity Hospital, 141
Royal Society, 112, 118, 121, 161
Russell, Alexander, 177, 260; Patrick, 177, 260
Russia, 158, 228

St. Bartholomew's Hospital, 126 131
St. George's Hospital, 132
St. Thomas's Hospital, 28, 120, 126, 129, 131
Salford, 144, 200
Scarlet fever, 202, 204, 207, 210, 211
Scavenging, street, 77, 78, 82, 84, 86, 104, 105, 110
Schöne, Lucien, 273
Schulz, David, 186, 187, 261
Scotland, 3, 51, 168, 172, 237
Scurvy, 6, 115, 119, 120, 151–163, 259
Segregation, 137, 164–180
Serfdom, 63, 65

U

INDEX

Settlement Laws, 34
Sewers and Drains, 59, 81, 91, 96–110, 230, 234, 238
Shaw, Albert, 263
Sheep-farming, 65, 66
Sheffield, 52
Short, Thomas, 28, 29, 147, 179, 213, 214, 218, 245
Shrewsbury, 133
Simon, Sir John, 121
Simpson, James, 108, 260
Singer, C.and D., 256, 260, 261
Sismondi, Sismonde de, J. L. L., 197
Smallpox, 4, 5, 21, 43, 75, 115, 150, 181–192, 199, 204, 210, 221, 238, 256, 257, 261, 269, 270
Smellie, William, 117, 142, 143, 256
Smiles, Samuel, 256
Smith, Adam, 3, 51
Smollett, Tobias, 105, 156, 196, 256, 259
Smyrna, 177
Snow, Dr., 230
Sobriety, increase of, 61
Society for Bettering the Condition of the Poor, 201, 206, 262
Somerset, 152
Spain, 60
Spalato, 178
Spirit drinking, 33, 81
Spotted fever, see Typhus
Statistics, vital, 10–21, 223, 234
Steam engine, the, 37, 53, 56, 100
Stockholm, 271
Stockport, 208
Street improvements (Birmingham), 86 (Liverpool), 84, 85 (Manchester), 83 ; paving, 59, 78, 81, 83 ; widening, 79, 82, 84–86
Sugar, 60
Sulphur fumigation, 198
Sun Life Insurance Co., 14
Suessmilch, J. P., 10, 11, 28
Sweden, 15, 27, 261, 267, 268
Sydenham, Thomas, 89, 90, 138, 146, 150, 153, 181, 214, 216, 227, 262
Syphilis, 168

Tea, introduction of, 60, 61
Thames, 99, 107
Tiverton, 98
Tontine, 12–14, 28, 31
Toulon, 172
Touzeau, J., 255
Town improvements, 42, 47, 59, 76–95
Towns, growth of, 225, 226
Trade Unions, 38, 41

Transport, 6, 49, 54, 56, 59, 62, 63, 69, 70
Tucker, Josiah, 157
Turkey Company, 120, 176
Turnips, introduction of, 68, 70, 72, 73
Tyburn, 97
Typhoid, 193
Typhus, 3, 5, 56, 115, 119, 121, 145, 147, 165, 170, 193–209, 211, 213, 261, 265

Universal Dispensary for Sick Children, the, 150
Unwin, G., 249, 250
Utilitarianism, 45

Vaccination, 29, 31, 181, 187, 188, 190–192, 225, 261, 265
Van Deventer, Hendrik, 141
Van Swieten, Geerard, 116
Venereal Disease, 5, 169, 186, 211
Venetians, 174, 175, 177
Vermuyden, Sir C., 68
Vesalius, A., 111
Vienna, 116, 267
Villeneuve, 271
Vitamins, 151, 155

Walcheren Expedition, 121, 217
Wales, William, 12, 72
War, 37, 52, 56, 58, 70, 71, 74, 239
Wargentin, P. V., 28
War Office, the, 121
Warrington, 182
Water closets, 105–108, 131 ; mains, 99, 100 ; supply, 33, 42, 59, 60, 77, 84, 86, 96–110, 230, 234, 256
Watt, James, 55 ; Dr. Robert 182, 261
Weavers, 251
Webb, S. and B., 262, 263
Weber, A. F., 75, 252
Wedgwood, Josiah, 39, 42
Wesleyan movement, 44
West Indies, 60
Westminster, 80, 82, 91, 107, 108, 127, 132, 141, 206, 219, 256, 271 ; General Dispensary, 144, 147
White, Charles, 259 ; William, 87, 248
Willughby, Percivall, 258, 259
Winchester, 127, 133, 257
Wren, Sir Christopher, 79

York, 34, 87, 133, 248
Yorkshire, 68
Young, Arthur, 37, 67, 83, 196, 262 264